TED GUP

NATION OF SECRETS

Ted Gup is an investigative reporter who has been a staff writer for *The Washington Post* and a correspondent at *Time* magazine. He is the author of *The Book of Honor* and the recipient of a George Polk Award and a Worth Bingham Prize. A professor of journalism at Case Western Reserve University, he lives in Pepper Pike, Ohio.

Also by Ted Gup

The Book of Honor

NATION OF SECRETS

·

The Threat to

DEMOCRACY

and the

AMERICAN WAY OF LIFE

·

TED GUP

Anchor Books
A Division of Random House, Inc.
New York

The Library of Congress has cataloged the Doubleday edition as follows:
Gup, Ted.
Nation of secrets : the threat to democracy and the American way of life /
by Ted Gup.—1st ed.
p. cm.
Includes bibliographical references and index.
1. Official secrets—United States.
2. Freedom of information—United States.
3. National security—United States.
I. Title.
323.44   830973—dc22
2006039443

Anchor ISBN: 978-1-4000-7978-0

Author photograph © Pollack Studios
Book design by Michael Collica

www.anchorbooks.com

For Peg

Contents

5

6

7

8

Let every man make known what kind of government
would command his respect, and that will be one step
toward obtaining it.

If you go dark, the whole world goes dark.

NATION OF SECRETS

1

Silent Encroachments

The greatest threat to liberty, warned the nation's Founding Fathers, comes not from abroad, but from within, and advances slowly, under cover of secrecy. "I believe there are more instances of the abridgement of the freedom of the people by gradual and silent encroachments of those in power than by violent and sudden usurpations," warned James Madison, a framer of the Bill of Rights.

Today his words seem prescient. What was once unthinkable—what would have been resisted as an intolerable affront to democracy and American values if it had befallen us all of a sudden—is now routine, a way of life.

As I finish the first draft of my study of secrecy, I scan the day's news. It is Thursday, February 2, 2006. There are no portentous headlines. As news days go, this one is seemingly unremarkable, which may just be the most remarkable thing about it. If nothing else, this day provides a snapshot of a nation slipping further into the shadow of secrecy, conducting its affairs beyond public scrutiny, and not just at the White House or in Congress, but across a wide swath of American life—in city councils, corporations, courts, clinics, universities. Secrecy has engulfed them all.

Today the Justice Department resisted calls from members of the Senate Judiciary Committee to turn over legal memoranda that are said to offer the legal justification for President Bush's domestic surveillance program, the one that went forward in secrecy without warrants or recourse to the courts, as required under the Foreign Intelligence Surveillance Act of 1978. The president insists that the secret surveillance within America was perfectly legal. But the legal memos said to support that claim are classified, beyond the reach even of Congress.

This day a blistering report is released that examines the government's inability to cope with Hurricane Katrina. The report cites the failure to establish a chain of command in the face of a catastrophe that claimed 1,307 lives and left thousands of Americans to fend for themselves. But the president, also on this day, refuses to turn over documents that might set forth who was responsible for the calamitous response and explain how it occurred. Emergency relief planners see it as a matter of some urgency—the next hurricane season is only months away. But providing those documents, says the White House, invoking executive privilege, would undermine the candor of advice the president receives.

This same day, at a Capitol Hill hearing on intelligence, Porter Goss, the embattled head of the CIA, rails against loose lips. "I'm stunned to the quick," he says, "when I get questions from my professional counterparts saying, 'Mr. Goss, can't you Americans keep a secret?' " He calls for an investigation into leaks and says reporters should be hauled before grand juries and made to reveal their sources. He and others are irate that Americans and the world have learned of a network of secret prisons overseas and of a sweeping surveillance program at home.

This same day, the vice chairman of the Senate Select Committee on Intelligence, Sen. John D. Rockefeller (D-W.Va.), says the new national director of intelligence, John D. Negroponte, has already failed his "first test" in addressing the vulnerabilities exposed by 9/11. But classification, says Rockefeller, forbids him from saying what that "first test" is. It's a tantalizing hint, but one that, like many this day, will leave the public largely in the dark.

On this day, it is also reported that the Patriot Act has been extended for another month. Misgivings about excessive secrecy and intrusions into citizens' civil liberties and privacy will be taken up another day.

Also reported this day is the existence of a secret team ready to collect forensic evidence left by a terrorist's nuclear explosion on U.S. soil. The *New York Times* cites "a senior military official, who insisted on anonymity because he was not authorized to disclose details of this program." Anonymity is the price of secrecy; one secret in exchange for another. "Trust him and trust us," the *Times* is saying. It is a mantra repeated throughout the day in newspapers, over the airwaves, and on the Internet.

This day, too, Congress is reported to have approved nearly $40 billion in budget cuts that are said to fall disproportionately on women on welfare, recipients of Medicaid, college students in need of student loans, and state efforts to get delinquent fathers to pay child support. "This vote," NPR reports, "will occur in the open on the House floor, but the deals were cut in secret behind closed doors." Rep. John D. Dingell (D-Mich.) fumes: "This bill is Exhibit A for special interests and lobbyists writing legislation behind closed doors at the expense of the ordinary citizen."

Also in today's news is reference to a closed-door session in which House Republicans challenged the leadership and forced back substantive reforms to the system of lobbying that gave rise to the scandalous influence of the lobbyist, now inmate, Jack Abramoff. About the only measure that survived the secret session was a prohibition on lobbyists plying their trade directly on the House floor and in the House gym.

Another story involves former House majority leader Tom DeLay, who resigned while under indictment. Finding his successor, we learn today, will be determined by secret ballot.

What has happened in Washington is mirrored in state after state as lawmakers increasingly shut the door on the public. On this day, it is reported that last year alone some 62 bills that reduced transparency in state government were signed into law.

This day, every city and shire in the land seems to be succumbing to secrecy, as public business is transacted behind drawn curtains, records are sealed, and citizens rebuffed. For those fighting for transparency, victories are few and Pyrrhic. After months of wrangling, San Diegans are given the records of legal bills incurred by six current and former members of the city council. But the documents are so heavily redacted that it is impossible to determine why legal counsel had been considered necessary.

A wait of months is nothing for those at the *Southern Illinoisan,* in Carbondale. In the town of Taylorville, population 12,000, four children had come down with a rare cancer, neuroblastoma, which strikes nine in a million children. In 1997 the paper had asked the state health department to identify the zip codes of neuroblastoma cases and the dates of diagnosis of the disease to see if there was a link between the cancer cluster and pollution from a local utility company that turned coal into a gas. The fight for those records lasted nine long years. On this day, February 2, 2006, the records were finally released.

Also on this day, in Richmond, Virginia, the *Richmond Times-Dispatch* writes of a bill that would deny citizens access to information about quasi-public hospitals that receive public money. That would include "information on medical-staff qualifications, strategic planning, fundraising, grants, contracts, and real estate proposals." If passed, all would be secret. Those who oppose the measure argue that the public has a right to know where its money goes.

On this day, the Fort Wayne newspaper takes up a loophole in Indiana's Open Door Law that allows public business to be conducted behind closed doors. The writer noted that simply by avoiding a quorum in a public meeting, and isolating four Indiana University trustees in one room and four in another, the university president had been able to fire the school's basketball coach without any public input and still claim compliance with the law—a memorable lesson in the avoidance of open governance not lost on that public university's tens of thousands of students.

And in the nation's capital, this day, it is recounted how Superior Court Judge Erik P. Christian locked the doors of a U.S. courtroom while a "guilty" verdict was read in a murder trial. A court spokesman said the judge had merely intended to exclude prospective jurors in an unrelated proceeding. But also left standing in the hallway were members of the press and even the victim's advocate assigned to the case.

Secrecy's grip on business was also in the day's news. A *New York Times* editorial was headlined "Seducing the Medical Profession." A whistle-blower alleged that Medtronic had paid millions to physicians in an effort to influence them to use that company's products. "A prominent Wisconsin surgeon received $400,000 for just eight days' consulting," the editorial noted. That nugget of information was something the surgeon's patients might have found of value in choosing whether to heed his advice.

This same day, Enron's former head of investor relations testified that in the first half of 2001, the company had "fudged its quarterly earnings," and given bogus numbers to Wall Street to prop up its stock price. To the thousands who, not long after, lost their jobs, pensions, and life savings, such secrets were bared too late.

These and scores of other such accounts of spreading secrecy made the news this February 2, 2006. But there was no public outcry or protest. It was just another day in the life of the nation.

Oh, yes, one more item from the day's news: "Sunshine Week," a national observance of the virtues of open government, was but one month off. Preparations were under way. But the weeklong event was taking on the demeanor of a resistance movement and a collective dirge, as if something precious had already disappeared before our very eyes.

•   •   •

The events of February 2, 2006, come upon the heels of more than a thousand other such days in which excessive secrecy has expanded its hold on the country. Beneath the headlines, connecting disparate scandals and tragedies that might have been contained or averted, there was secrecy. In business there was the secrecy that preceded implosions of major corporations and vast economic wreckage at Enron, WorldCom, Arthur Andersen, and Qwest, to name but a few. Stories of secret partnerships, concealed liabilities, and companies covertly plundered by their own CEOs have filled the news in recent years.

Such secrecy has engendered discord and distrust between business and consumers, Wall Street and investors, labor and management. Example: in 2003, as American Airlines struggled with mounting losses and won $1.8 billion in wage concessions from its workers, its CEO, Donald Carty, and 44 of the company's top executives secretly set up a trust fund to protect their own pensions from bankruptcy. The trust was not disclosed until *after* the unions had accepted massive benefit cuts. As if the secret trust were not inflammatory enough, a company spokesman said that union leaders had been informed of it weeks earlier but had signed a confidentiality agreement that kept them from sharing the information with the very rank-and-file workers they represented.

In hospitals and clinics, life-threatening defects in medical devices go unreported. Studies adverse to drug companies go unpublished and fatal side effects surface belatedly. "FDA Official Alleges Pressure to Suppress Vioxx Findings," one headline reads. "U.S. Not Told of 2

Deaths During Study of Heart Drug," reads another. And this one: "Antidepressant Makers Withhold Data: Info from Clinical Trials on Children Kept Secret."

Each year, in hundreds of courtrooms, secrecy allows deadly products to remain in the stream of commerce. Scores have died as a result of defective tires. The families of the injured and bereaved are written checks in exchange for their silence, as judges lend their imprimatur to secret settlements that cloak the dangers, leaving the public at large exposed to the very same perils.

States, counties, and municipalities have also increasingly embraced secrecy. In Los Angeles, the police commission reversed a quarter-century-old policy of identifying officers implicated in shootings. The decision was made in secret, behind closed doors, fueling community perceptions of official complicity in the use of excessive force. And it is not only overseas that the holding of prisoners is wrapped in secrecy. In 2005, reporters conducted a statewide audit of Kentucky's jails and found that 70 percent of the time county jailers would not provide even the names of those held, either in defiance or in ignorance of the law.

The nation's most esteemed cultural institutions are also creatures of secrecy. New York's Metropolitan Museum of Art steadfastly refused to show me acquisition records for its most celebrated Greek vase, the Euphronios Krater, whose provenance was long mired in suspicion. Only in 2006, after a much-publicized Italian investigation into the looting of antiquities, did the Met own up. "It now appears that the piece came to us in a completely different way—through machinations, lies, clandestine night digging," acknowledged the Met's director, Philippe de Montebello, as if it were the first time questions had been raised. Museums in Boston, Cleveland, Los Angeles, and elsewhere face their own questions.

Abusive secrecy has shaken the nation's faith in one institution after another. As pedophiliac priests were silently shuffled from parish to parish, free to prey upon the unsuspecting, the Catholic Church made secret payments to silence the victims and quash the scandal.

Even the press, society's most vociferous champion of transparency, has become tainted by secrecy. More and more often, journalists resort to unnamed sources. Even the American Civil Liberties Union, an outspoken proponent of transparency and unfettered speech, has attempted to silence its own board members from speaking publicly of internal policies and operations.

But nowhere is secrecy more rampant than in government. Those investigating the failure of the intelligence community to thwart the attacks of 9/11 concluded that agencies and departments had failed to share vital intelligence. Some believe that greater coordination and a less rigid grip on secrets might have uncovered and even foiled the plot. And the threat of weapons of mass destruction, the casus belli for invading Iraq, is a testament to the abuse of secrecy by those at the highest levels; the full truth of this abuse is still cloaked in classification.

Today, the most critical national policies, and not just those concerning national security, are the products of secret meetings and cloaked deliberations. Knowledge of which key energy policies were cobbled together behind the closed doors of Vice President Dick Cheney is denied the press, citizens, and Congress alike—and withholding this information is upheld by the courts. Congressional legislation routinely appears without any author's name, masking the identity of special interests and those under their sway. Deals are struck out of public sight. Example: Behind closed doors, federal lawmakers quietly inserted a provision into Medicare legislation that created a $22 billion windfall to the health insurance industry.

Presidential papers from earlier administrations are no longer subject to automatic release. Government websites are vetted and scrubbed. Environmentalists are barred from seeing routine dam and drainage maps, in the name of homeland security.

The search for hundreds of children missing after Hurricane Katrina was stymied by government's refusal to share information from its evacuee database with those searching for the children.

The once-open administration of justice is now undermined by secret courts, closed tribunals and deportation hearings, hidden prisons, covert renditions, and unnamed prisoners sequestered beyond the reach of judicial review. Between 2003 and 2005, the number of criminal cases in federal courts in which records were sealed more than doubled. In 2006, the Reporters Committee for Freedom of the Press attempted to examine 469 cases sealed in the U.S. District Court in the nation's capital. The court's electronic docket spit back this deceptive response: "No such case."

In recent years, the number of government secrets has exploded, and classification decisions have more than doubled over the decade since 1997. The government's own figures record that in 2005 the U.S. brought down the stamp of classification a staggering 14.2 million times. That's 39,000 a day, or 1,600 every hour of the night and day. Four out of five of those documents were classified "Secret" or "Top Secret." By definition, their disclosure threatens the security of the nation. And yet not one of those secrets can tell us where bin Laden is or where he may strike next.

Even those numbers fail to tell the full story. An obscure footnote in the 2005 report to the president from the government's collecting agency, the Information Security Oversight Office, notes that three key players in the nation's security apparatus—the Office of the Vice President, the president's Foreign Intelligence Advisory Board, and the Homeland Security Council—"failed to report their data" to the federal collecting agency. The vice president's office argued that it was exempt from such reporting requirements—in essence, that even the number of its secrets was a secret.

The direct cost to government (read "taxpayers") of securing secrets—the locks and vaults, the training of personnel, the background checks and clearances—exceeds $7 billion annually. Tending to those secrets and the vast infrastructure that supports them creates a classification clutter in which critically sensitive secrets can be lost or waylaid.

And these are only the official secrets. Post-9/11, public agencies and departments have created entirely new categories of information designated "sensitive but unclassified" that are beyond the purview of the public and are dramatically contributing to the sclerosis blocking information sharing at all levels of government. Many now argue that this new brand of restricted information, discretionary and amorphous, poses an even greater threat to accountability and transparency than classification itself. A March 2006 investigation by the Government Accountability Office (GAO) found at least 56 different names and categories of restricted but unclassified information, with little or no uniformity of definition—a result of the vast discretion of thousands of government officials and civilians alike to simply move unclassified information beyond the public's reach. At the National Aeronautics and Space Administration (NASA), for example, 20,000 government employees and 80,000 private contract employees have the authority to arbitrarily designate unclassified information as sensitive, thereby removing it from public scrutiny.

Today America is a nation of secrets, an increasingly furtive land where closed doors outnumber open ones and where it is no longer "the right to know" but "the need to know" that is the measure against which access is determined. There has been a sea change in the fundamental presumption of openness. It is not secrecy per se that is the root cause, but the perversion of secrecy, the rote invocation of classification, the habitual dependence by government and industry upon secrecy, the growing aversion to accountability. Abusive secrecy is based not upon rational and legitimate public interests—national defense, privacy, proprietary data—but upon raw self-interest, fear, expedience, bureaucratic jockeying for advantage, or just a lack of regard for the democratic process. America's historic experiment with openness is now in peril from, to use Madison's words, "gradual and silent encroachments."

Ironically, all this occurs as the nation extols transparency and revels in the so-called Information Age. True, Americans can retrieve a universe of information at the touch of a finger, but terabytes of data and factoids should not be mistaken for the real-time transparency upon which democracy depends. Democracy is defined by process, not product, the realization of the public's right to both observe and participate in self-governance. This virulent new strain of secrecy now threatens to subvert this right.

The object of this book is to examine the nature of this new secrecy, to explore its causes and casualties. Along the way, I intend to reveal some secrets of my own to make more visible secrecy's often unseen toll.

For nearly thirty years, I have been an investigative reporter, confronting secrecy within a broad array of public and private institutions. For a number of years I worked on the investigative staff of the *Washington Post* and, later, of *Time* magazine. I have revealed a number of secrets, but on occasion, where genuine national interests could be adversely affected, I have also remained silent. Whether this makes me an expert on secrecy I leave to others to decide. But I have spent years reporting from within various subcultures of secrecy and their tightly knit communities, reflecting upon the nature of restricted information, interviewing those in possession of secrets and those dispossessed by them.

The perils of unrestrained secrecy are anything but abstract. Like the unchecked printing of currency, the indiscriminate minting of more and more secrets creates inflation and devaluation, which discredits the entire security process and prevents vital information from reaching those most in need of it. Ultimately, it profoundly undermines the respect due true secrets—secrets that genuinely safeguard time-honored societal values and interests: national security, privacy, intellectual property rights, medical records, fair trial, diplomatic and business negotiations, journalistic enterprise. Even voting, the quintessential act of democracy and self-governance, is itself performed in secret, behind a drawn curtain. Secrecy and democracy are not irreconcilable, but the former often advances at the expense of the latter.

So if dismantling all restrictions on information is not the answer, what is?

A few years ago, Porter Goss, then chair of the House Select Committee on Intelligence, lamented that America was afflicted with a "disdain for secrecy." He is right. In the nation's capital people quip that "a secret is something you tell one person at a time." More than a few officials have been known to take classified materials home, discuss them in unsecured environments with individuals without proper clearance, and otherwise treat them with an insouciance bordering on recklessness. Why? Because they have become desensitized by the avalanche of secrets and recognize that many, if not most, are undeserving of the designation.

Goss's solution, championed by many in Congress today, is to further tighten the bulkheads of enforcement with threats of more polygraphs and more prosecutions of leakers. But that will only exacerbate the contempt in which secrets are held and continue the nation on its path of becoming a repository of perpetual secrets, a veritable sepulchre of information. What is needed, first, is to identify and protect truly legitimate secrets, that small core of highly sensitive information that is now in jeopardy of being buried by counterfeit secrets. Second, we must as a nation and as a society exercise far greater discipline and restraint in designating what does and does not enjoy the protective status of a secret. Finally, we must adopt a bona fide timetable for automatic review and declassification. Technically, such a system already exists, but it is so riddled with loopholes that individual agencies can and do effectively blunt its intent, emboldened by the knowledge that senior officials are focused on stanching the hemorrhage of leaks rather than examining the systemic abuse that is their underlying cause.

In the 1971 Pentagon Papers case (*New York Times v. United States*), Supreme Court Justice Potter Stewart wrote: "I should suppose that moral, political, and practical considerations would dictate that a very first principle of that wisdom would be an insistence upon avoiding secrecy for its own sake. For when everything is classified, then nothing is classified, and the system becomes one to be disregarded by the cynical or the careless, and to be manipulated by those intent on self-protection or self-promotion. . . . The hallmark of a truly effective internal security system would be the maximum possible disclosure, recognizing that secrecy can best be preserved only when credibility is truly maintained."

Abusive secrecy has fathered a multitude of sins, provided the enabling cover for larceny and lies, profiteering and predation, propaganda and tyranny. "Where secrecy or mystery begins, vice or roguery is not far off," wrote Samuel Johnson. These days, government representatives are eager to note that "loose lips sink ships," a reminder that in war, compromising a secret can cost lives. But sealed lips—that is, the sort of smothering and obsessive secrecy we have today—also cost lives. The legacy of secrets concerning the effects of cigarettes, asbestos, thalidomide, and a host of other deadly materials revealed too late puts the lie to the old bromide, "What you don't know can't hurt you." Secrecy has defined today's regulatory landscape and compromised Americans' safety.

- The United States Department of Agriculture has signed secrecy agreements—"memorandums of understanding," Agriculture calls them—with fourteen states that have pledged that in exchange for receiving a general notification of contaminated foods they will not disclose to their own citizens the specific supermarkets, restaurants, or outlets where the contaminated foods were sold. In 2004, the USDA refused to name the 580 groceries, restaurants, and distributors in six states that handled at least 19 tons of beef recalled after a Washington state cow tested positive for mad-cow disease. Federal food recalls are voluntary and the Faustian deal made with the food industry is notification in exchange for anonymity. A 2004 study found that only half of the contaminated meat and poultry recalled is ultimately recovered. Much of the rest is assumed to end up in America's belly.

- The federal response to fatalities caused by Firestone tire separation and Ford Explorer rollovers was to create, in 2000, the Transportation Recall Enhancement, Accountability, and Documentation Act (TREAD). But in July 2003, early-warning data regarding auto safety defects—consumer complaints, warranty claim issues, and information on child restraints and tire performance—were specifically exempted from the Freedom of Information Act. The government argued that if such knowledge were public it could put one auto manufacturer at a competitive disadvantage to another.

- The National Practitioner Data Bank maintained by the Department of Health and Human Services collects information on malpractice payments and adverse actions, loss of medical licenses and clinical privileges, and actions taken against physicians by the Drug Enforcement Agency regarding controlled substances. By 2004, the data bank contained reports on 364,296 adverse actions and malpractice payments by 215,350 medical practitioners. But the National Practitioner Data Bank is not accessible to the public, only to health care professionals. A doctor who has lost his or her privileges, has abused controlled substances, or has been sued multiple times can access the data bank, but his or her patient cannot. Defenders of this regime argue that the public's interest is best protected when those in the medical field and on review boards are kept informed.

- Often the casualties of inappropriate or excessive secrecy are the most vulnerable citizens. In Florida, a state with one of the nation's highest populations of retirees, the legislature in 2001 exempted nursing homes from public-records legislation, blocking access to adverse-incident reports as well as internal risk and quality reviews. Those accused of misdeeds may see the records, but their victims may not. An estimated 4,000 reports of injuries and problems of care were reported within the first year after passage of the exemption, but the reports were beyond the reach of those affected.

- In 2006, Congress was poised to make it a felony for law enforcement officials to share some types of information related to illegal gun trafficking. Already, Congress has made it illegal to release to the public, the press, and even in some instances to law enforcement professionals information from its Firearms Trace System database. Such secrecy has been hailed by the National Rifle Association as a major victory for gun-owner privacy, but many in law enforcement fear it makes solving shooting crimes more difficult. A 2004 study by the National Academy of Sciences concluded that it was impossible to conduct meaningful research into gun violence because of the dearth of available data. Each year, more than 30,000 Americans are killed with handguns. "It is a ghastly fact of public safety that for the past three years the most basic information about illegal gun trafficking in America has been hermetically classified as a state secret," the *New York Times* editorialized in June 2006.

•   •   •

The United States is no stranger to secrecy. From the beginning, the nation waged a chrysalis-like struggle to free itself from its own past and to insist upon greater transparency, accountability, and participation. Federalist and anti-Federalist alike fretted about secrecy. In 1788, James Madison, a Federalist, noted of the wartime Congress, "They held their consultations always under the veil of secrecy; they had the sole transaction of our affairs with foreign nations; through the whole course of the war [the Revolutionary War] they had the fate of their country more in their hands than it is to be hoped will ever be the case with our future representatives."

That same year Patrick Henry, deeply wary of the proposed Constitution, demanded, "Give us at least a plausible apology why Congress should keep their proceedings in secret. They have the power of keeping them in secret as long as they please. . . . They may carry on the most wicked and pernicious of schemes under the dark veil of secrecy. The liberties of people never were, nor ever will be, secure, when the transactions of their rulers may be concealed from them. . . . I am an advocate for divulging indiscriminately all the operations of government, though the practice of our ancestors, in some degree, justifies it. . . . To cover with the veil of secrecy the common routine of business, is an abomination in the eyes of every intelligent man, and every friend to his country."

In those early years, it was easy to lapse into what Henry called "the practice of our ancestors." The Continental Congress and the Constitutional Convention both met behind closed doors. No press, no public. The U.S. House of Representatives frequently held secret sessions until the end of the War of 1812. The Senate met in secret until 1794. Treaties and nominations considered by the U.S. Senate were weighed behind closed doors until 1929. Since then, the Senate has met in secret 53 times.

Progress in ridding our democracy of its penchant for operating in secret has come in fits and starts. Each new crisis, real or imagined, has temporarily set back the cause of open government, leaving a record of cyclical expansions and contractions. From the Alien and Sedition Acts to the Civil War, from the Red Scare of 1917 to 1920 through both world wars, Korea, McCarthyism, and the Cold War, openness in government has ebbed and flowed, with the security/secrecy mind-set often enjoying transient supremacy over that of transparency. The advent of nuclear weapons ushered in its own expansion of secrecy with its ratcheting up of the stakes and its apocalyptic dangers. The physicist Edward Teller cautioned, "Secrecy, once accepted, becomes an addiction."

Allegations of abusive secrecy, synonymous with skullduggery and usurpations of power, have also long been a staple of politics and partisan rhetoric. The Democratic Party platform in 1956 declared: "During recent years there has developed a practice on the part of Federal agencies to delay and withhold information which is needed by Congress and the general public to make important decisions affecting their lives and destinies. We believe that this trend toward secrecy in Government should be reversed and that the Federal Government should return to its basic tradition of exchanging and promoting the freest flow of information possible in those unclassified areas where secrets involving weapons development and bona fide national security are not involved. We condemn the Eisenhower Administration for the excesses practiced in this vital area and pledge the Democratic Party to reverse this tendency."

Again in 1960, the Democratic Party platform declared: "The massive wall of secrecy erected between the Executive branch and the Congress as well as the citizen must be torn down."

Incumbents such as President Dwight D. Eisenhower skillfully demonized America's adversaries, speaking contemptuously of those nations that "make a fetish of secrecy," even as our own secrecy deepened. (Americans have always defined transparency in relative terms and used it as a cudgel against their enemies, a stock response to totalitarian regimes that has sometimes blinded us to our own penchant for secrecy.)

In 1964, it was the Republicans' turn with a national political platform that charged, "This administration [President Lyndon Baines Johnson's] has adopted policies of news management and unjustifiable secrecy, in the guise of guarding the nation's security; it has shown contempt for the right of the people to know the truth."

Eight years later, when Richard Nixon was in office, the Democratic Party platform proclaimed: "Executive secrecy runs wild with unparalleled efforts to intimidate the media and suppress those who seek to put a different view before the American people."

Buffeted by intermittent crises and quadrennial politics, the nation has lurched between secrecy and openness, between periods of alarmism and relative calm. But always, in the past, the ship of state has ultimately righted itself and resumed a course favoring at least moderation, if not outright transparency. "Our great political system needs information [in order] to be self-correcting. While excesses and imbalances will inevitably exist for a time, fortunately they tend not to last. Ultimately truth prevails." Comforting words spoken in 2004. The speaker? Then secretary of defense Donald Rumsfeld.

So why, then, should we not now assume that the current wave of secrecy is but one more in a series of periodic setbacks to be endured before we resume our pursuit of openness?

Because today the nation faces an unprecedented confluence of circumstances that together conspire to create what, in the parlance of the day, may be called a "perfect storm" of secrecy, one that may neither abate nor subside, but that threatens to engulf democratic institutions and irrevocably alter the landscape of America. The complex interaction of these influences is giving rise to a climate of secrecy that is not confined to government or industry but is pervasive, insidious, and of indeterminate duration. These factors could produce a shift that, if allowed to go unchallenged, could permanently transform the way Americans live and the way they think.

Begin with 9/11. It is the most obvious influence, but one whose less obvious elements exert far-reaching influence over diverse aspects of ordinary life. The attack of 9/11 did not of itself birth this new age of secrecy. In fiscal year 1993, there were 6.4 million total classification decisions. In fiscal year 2000, the number crept up to 8 million.

The real jump, though, occurred in fiscal year 2000, when total classifications skyrocketed by 186 percent—as much as in the preceding four years—rising from 8 million to almost 23 million. Most of that increase reflected not a policy change but a technological revolution, the advent of the Internet and the growing reliance on e-mails, as opposed to phone calls, at the Department of Defense and the Central Intelligence Agency. Each e-mail that contained classified material itself became a protected document.

In contrast, the increases in classification that came with the arrival of the Bush administration in 2000 reflected a dramatic change of course, a radical shift not in technology but in policy. By 2005, four years after 9/11, the number of classification decisions had grown to 14.2 million. Declassifications, which had averaged 180 million a year under Clinton, fell under Bush to 29 million a year by 2005. (In part, the decline reflected the bulk declassifications of older documents undertaken by President Clinton, in part the dwindling resources accorded declassification efforts under Bush.) Cumulatively, the decade produced more than 100 million classified documents added to the already staggering mountain of secrets.

Even before Clinton had left office there were many in Congress intent upon derailing and reversing his declassification efforts and establishing a regime of greater control over information. For them, the Clinton years represented a permissiveness that constituted gross irresponsibility and unjustifiable risks. It was they who in the final days of the Clinton administration passed without debate and behind closed doors a measure that would have criminalized all leaks of classified information, whether properly classified or not. It stealthily appended itself to the 2001 Intelligence Authorization Act that, but for an eleventh-hour appeal by news organizations, would have been signed into law by Clinton.

To those who already wished to roll back Clinton's declassification initiatives, 9/11 demonstrated the imperative of restoring what they saw as the proper balance between security and secrecy. The tragedy of 9/11 brought them out of political exile and put declassification itself in a suspect category.

There are many factors that set 9/11 apart from its predecessor crises and none of them augur well for the return of open government. Among these is the widely held belief that the war on terror, unlike World Wars

I and II, and the Korean and Vietnam wars, is a war without end, one that will not conclude neatly with a surrender or even the assassination of bin Laden and his deputies.

As of this writing, it has been more than 1,500 days since the events of September 11, 2001. More time has elapsed since that between Pearl Harbor and the surrender of Japan, and still there is no end in sight—to the war, nor to the environment of urgency in which so many secrecy measures have passed. Indeed, the only thing that has been rationed in this strange undeclared war is information.

The prospect that such a conflict may go on interminably bolsters arguments that a less permissive, more restrictive attitude to information should also be permanent, that there should be no sunset provision in legislation expanding secrecy. The old openness is viewed as a luxury the nation can no longer afford, an artifact of less parlous times.

Add to this the argument that post 9/11, the nation has suffered no major terrorist attack on U.S. soil (as of this writing), and it buttresses the position that expanded secrecy has worked and warrants continued support. Even another attack might well be construed not as a failure of expanded secrecy but as evidence that the nation's residual laxness somehow rendered it vulnerable.

But by far the most potent argument for massively expanding secrecy—and the one most transformative of public attitudes—is the one that arises out of the sui generis nature of the terrorist threat, directed as it is against a civilian population on American soil. The domestic aspect and the targeting of civilian infrastructure has radically redefined the debate about open government and allowed secrecy to migrate well beyond the traditional confines of the intelligence and military realm to Main Street, U.S.A.

Today, everything is a potential target—nuclear power plants, refineries, power grids, bridges, skyscrapers, natural gas depots, food supplies, water reservoirs, Super Bowls and World Series, pipelines, borders and ports, pharmaceuticals, railways, toxic waste sites, airports, national landmarks, shopping malls, subways. In short, no aspect of ordinary life is seen to be exempt from the terrorists' crosshairs. More than any other single factor, this sense of ubiquitous vulnerability, that everything is considered part of the "critical infrastructure," has been the impetus for expanding the breadth and scope of secrecy.

Virtually every level of government—federal, state, and local—and all the private-sector industries that intersect with these potential targets have themselves been dragooned into the war against terror and deputized with the implicit authority to withhold previously available information.

This means that the security apparatus, historically confined to the defense-related entities, has spread across the spectrum of civilian life, and with it, a security consciousness that elevates even the most quotidian of facts—the blueprints for a bridge, the disposition of waste, the security of a refinery, the regulation of an industry—into a realm of sensitive information subject to restrictions and withholding.

As elemental facts appear to reveal potential chinks in the nation's armor, those in custody of such facts have become encumbered with new concerns and responsibilities, chief among these the concealment of information that could benefit an unseen enemy. In the aggregate, such restraints now leave the citizenry in the dark, unable to assess the risks of the landscape around them. The new opacity of regulatory processes conceals the dangers posed by defective structures, environmental hazards, and political corruption. Public exposure of vulnerabilities has always been one of the chief corrective influences on industry, which, left unmonitored, has often shown itself to be slow to fix the holes in its own fence. Still, the prevailing mind-set today can be reduced to "When in doubt, leave it out."

At the federal level, no greater testament to the spread of secrecy exists than the creation of the vast Department of Homeland Security or the recent granting of classification authority to the Department of Agriculture, the Environmental Protection Agency, and the Department of Health and Human Services.

As the influence of 9/11 swept across the land and appeals for enhanced security became a juggernaut, the safeguards and counterbalances that had long thwarted the efforts of those bent on expanding secrecy were systematically disabled or weakened. Attorney General John Ashcroft, in October 2001, radically reinterpreted the Freedom of Information Act of 1966, the crown jewel of open government, when he gave a green light to the entire federal government to resist disclosure if there was any plausible reason to do so.

Ashcroft's reinterpretation of the FOIA emboldened the entire federal bureaucracy to simply say no to journalists, scholars, historians, public interest groups, and private individuals who had come to rely on the act as an essential tool of citizenship. At the same time, the federal courts grew more and more deferential to executive power and warier of the press's willingness to unilaterally disclose information the government wished to keep secret. The press for its part became increasingly sensitized to how it was perceived and concerned that it not do anything to harm national security. The press also increasingly became the subject of investigations and subpoenas.

Nor can the press or public look to even the highest court in the land to restore balance, strike down the excesses of secrecy, and reassert the public's right to transparency in government. Supreme Court Justice Antonin Scalia has repeatedly demonstrated his own penchant for secrecy and disregard for the values of openness. On March 19, 2003, in one of the more ironic displays of contempt for openness, Scalia was honored by the City Club of Cleveland with its Citadel of Free Speech Award, even as he banned radio and television from covering the event. A year later, on April 7, 2004, while giving a speech at Presbyterian Christian High School in Hattiesburg, Mississippi, a deputy federal marshal demanded that two reporters, one from the Associated Press, the other from the *Hattiesburg American,* erase their tapes of Scalia's remarks. At the time, Scalia was speaking of the need to preserve the Constitution.

Whistle-blowers, one of the final checks on excessive secrecy, have found themselves exposed to retribution from an increasingly politicized administration and equally unsympathetic courts. Those who have dared to leak information to the press or Congress have faced bureaucratic exile, prosecution, and loss of employment. Congressional oversight was weakened in the control of Republicans, who grew reluctant to criticize the Republican administration or undermine its security programs; Democrats, chastened by repeated defeats at the polls, proved generally timid and unwilling to speak out for fear of being cast as unpatriotic and weak on national security.

Politics became a blood sport, and the trust between the two sides of the aisle, essential to maintaining oversight and the sharing of sensitive information, withered. Capitol Hill hearings became less about fact finding and more about advancing partisan interests. Congressional investigations ceased to play a major role in producing information, and once-powerful chairmen deferred to claims of executive privilege as the power to create and hold secrets was increasingly vested in the White

House. Administration briefings became less frequent and more restricted. The threat of polygraphs and investigations became a constant. When evidence surfaced of malfeasance or negligence, the response was to identify the source of the leak instead of pursuing the malefactors.

When the *Newark Star-Ledger* reported in October 2006 that Transportation Security Administration officers had managed to sneak 20 of 22 dummy bombs and guns past airport screeners at Newark Liberty International Airport, the government launched a criminal investigation—to hunt down the person who had leaked the story. When the Office of the Special Inspector General for Iraq Reconstruction reported troubling findings about the industry giant Halliburton's activities in Iraq as well as the inability to account for thousands of U.S. weapons, Republican members of Congress, in a closed-door conference, quietly slipped in a provision that closed the IG's office. In short, mechanisms that once acted as a brake on secrecy are being removed.

Still, there has always been the constraining knowledge in the back of every bureaucrat's mind that one day his or her decisions, no matter how highly classified, might be declassified and become a part of history. That prospect, remote though it may be, has exerted a salutary effect on government because it held out the possibility, if not inevitability, that one day in the future today's nefarious act of adventurism would be exposed to the light. Those who operate in secret know they might be held accountable, if not in a court of law, then at least in the court of public opinion to be convened by posterity. History is a restraint that might pull them back from reckless decisions that would blot their reputations in perpetuity. But today, even history is being purged. Dusty old records are being removed from the U.S. Archives and presidential libraries. Other records are being withheld or simply disappearing. The corrective hand of history with its distant day of reckoning is itself now manacled by secrecy.

Cumulatively such changes threaten to redefine the relationship between the governed and the government. When citizens enjoy wide access to information, they chafe for more, their demands rising on a sea of expectation that will inform their decisions and their assessments of those in power. As that access is taken away, expectation is replaced by resentment and frustration. Ultimately, it is followed by resignation, a realization that they will not have access to information they once deemed vital to their role as citizens.

When citizens and their proxies are routinely denied information, something fundamental happens; stripped of the authority that comes with being informed, they feel marginalized. Citizens are reduced to mere residents. They come before government and industry alike as supplicants, pleading for what was theirs for the asking not so long before. The resistance they once provided yields to a complacency and deference to authority, a withdrawal from the political process that may be interpreted by those wielding power as a grant of further license in pursuit of the very policies that marginalized the electorate. In the end, citizens are the final check on secrecy, but, stripped of information, they no longer possess the wherewithal, the confidence, or the courage to challenge the system. Like all who formerly challenged secrecy, they are effectively neutered, sidelined by lack of access. The less one knows, the less one is in a position to question. That goes for citizens, consumers, and Congress alike.

Such a sea change is not the product of chance. President Bush is an ardent champion of the doctrine known as "unitary executive," an expansive definition of the powers and authority of the president. He has often cited the principle as he puts his pen to so-called signing statements, which he claims exempt him from the provisions of legislation with which he disagrees but consents to sign—in essence, he is picking which laws to recognize and which to disregard. The subject may be torture, national security, even conservation. In July 2006, a bipartisan panel of the American Bar Association concluded that such signing statements were "contrary to the rule of law and our constitutional system of separation of powers." The report cited Parliament's condemnation of James II in the seventeenth century and quoted the English bill of rights: "The pretended power of suspending of laws, by regal authority, without consent of Parliament, is illegal."

Cumulatively, "unitary executive" theory provides a virtually unfettered license for government secrecy, making access to information a matter of presidential prerogative. Unitary executive theory does not merely justify expansive secrecy, it depends upon it as its principal tool, blunting congressional investigations, judicial challenges, and press inquiries. Unrestrained, the unitary executive doctrine can rapidly transform a government that is genuinely representative into one that is merely representational; that is, it preserves the outward image or shell of a functioning democracy even as secrecy gnaws away at democracy's internal safeguards, checks and balances, and vital access to information.

It does not take long for excessive secrecy to infantilize a population. It is not whether excessive secrecy makes democracies anemic or whether anemic democracies give rise to regimes of secrecy; both are true. Post-9/11, the administration deftly parlayed public fears and insecurities into support for its expanded secrecy and concomitant widening of executive authority, equating both with greater safety. This is not a new phenomenon. Benjamin Franklin warned, "Whoever trades liberty for security deserves neither." It was also a familiar strain in World War I, says Harold Relyea, a secrecy expert with the Congressional Research Service. Then, too, he says, many Americans seemed only too willing to cede their liberties. "It's a little disturbing," says Relyea. "There have been other times when people have rolled over and just stuck their legs in the air like dead beetles."

The spread of secrecy has created an entirely new paradigm as it converges with information technology. Instead of the much-heralded transparency many imagined and hoped the Information Age would bring, the nation has awakened to vast new domestic surveillance programs. Instead of a window, Americans are increasingly facing a two-way mirror, unaware they are being observed. In 2004 the number of court-authorized secret wiretaps surged 19 percent. Some 1,710 applications for wiretaps were requested and not one was denied by the courts—and these were for non-terrorist-related investigations. Under the provisions of the USA Patriot Act, some 47 secret warrants were issued between October 2001 and April 2003, meaning government investigators could enter a citizen's home and conduct a search without promptly telling the resident they had been there. Between April 2003 and January 2005, the number of such secret warrants more than doubled, to 108.

As government has become more and more opaque, the lives of ordinary citizens have become more and more transparent to government, the objects of secret data mining, monitoring, record collection, and remote scrutiny. Privacy and civil liberties have become early casualties of the new secrecy. Once, the tide of information flowed from the government to the people. Now that tide has largely been reversed. Government is less and less the consummate purveyor of information and more and more the supreme collector.

And because this new threat originated overseas but was carried out within our own borders, 9/11 became the impetus for integrating the methodologies of foreign and domestic intelligence. The firewall that had long separated the two was brought down, as controversial surveillance techniques long used abroad but anathema at home became ubiquitous. Many of those techniques would offend American sensibilities and notions of civil liberties. Today, those activities—intercepting e-mail, stealthily harvesting tens of millions of citizens' private phone records, collecting private financial records, shadowing individuals and groups regarded as potential threats—have all been cloaked in secrecy. Then, too, the corporations and private entities that become witting or unwitting participants in the network of surveillance—telecommunications companies, financial institutions, Internet providers, universities, libraries—all find themselves a part of the expanded security apparatus, with all the entanglements of secrecy. Secrecy is the principal tool used to ferret out secret enemies, and so the cycle expands.

Even before 9/11, a philosophical and political sea change was taking hold, one whose advocates championed privatization and believed that industry could take over many of the jobs government had once performed. Today the line between private corporations and government is so blurred that regulations are often written by industry representatives and responses to Freedom of Information Act requests are often delegated to private contractors. That philosophical shift put its faith in free-market forces and a laissez-faire attitude toward business. Government became suspicious of costly and nettlesome regulation and looked askance at policing industry, preferring instead to forge partnerships between business and government. Lobbyists became government regulators. Dale Moore, a former lobbyist for the cattle industry, was named chief of staff at the Department of Agriculture; Mark Rey, a vice president of the American Forest and Paper Association, was placed at the helm of the Forest Service; David Lauriski, a longtime coal industry executive and lobbyist, oversaw the Mine Safety and Health Administration—before returning to industry. The pattern repeated itself across government.

To its proponents, the shift was about priming the economic pump of America. To skeptics, it was about giving over the reins of government to big business. But the commingling of interests and objectives emboldened corporations to believe that government was more an ally and partner than disciplinarian or overseer. Accountability, regulation, and transparency atrophied.

At the helm of many federal regulatory agencies sit former lobbyists, former corporate executives, and ideological allies, individuals sympathetic to industry's interests. In this new environment, corporations and private entities of all sorts enjoy a new measure of sovereignty and the capacity to determine for themselves what they will and will not disclose to the public. In the regulatory sphere, reporting on activities and conditions affecting worker safety, environmental compliance, product liability, and other heretofore strictly regulated and monitored areas has become more a matter of discretion. The punitive sting of noncompliance is less determinative of corporate conduct and public reporting.

Ironically, America's growing culture of secrecy may itself be a byproduct of the Information Age. Along with unprecedented promise it brings unprecedented threats. The more the Internet, search engines, and data-mining democratize the potential retrieval of information, the more those in possession of sensitive materials and proprietary data feel threatened and driven to take elaborate countermeasures to safeguard that information. Entire industries have emerged to cope with perils, real and perceived.

The information superhighway poses a double threat: First, it aggregates enormous repositories of information, which create unimaginably rich targets of opportunity for mischief-makers such as hackers, foreign spies, and practitioners of industrial espionage. Second, any penetration carries with it an unprecedented threat of vast and instantaneous dissemination across borders. There is no smuggling out of documents, no issue of portability. One push of the "send" button and a document is on its way. In 1971, Daniel Ellsberg reportedly spent six weeks secretly photocopying thousands of documents—*The Pentagon Papers*—before he could offer them to the *New York Times.* When former treasury secretary Paul O'Neill left office in December 2002, he took with him a CD that held 19,000 documents.

The Information Age and the digital technologies, rife with these new vulnerabilities, have ushered in a new Security Age. In government and industry alike, the technology of access has spawned an equally robust technology of denial.

For all these profound changes, one thing remains a constant: in a system of self-governance, information is vital, as essential as water is to life. Information has much in common with water. Like water, information is democratic by nature—it wants to spread itself evenly across the land, inviting all to partake of it. And like water, it resists confinement, but can be diverted and even dammed. Secrecy arrests the natural flow of information. Like water, even vast amounts of information can be restrained. But over time, its impoundment erodes democracy and ultimately threatens it with collapse.

2

Case Study: Inescapable Secrecy

To understand the allure as well as the perils of secrecy, meet Melissa Mahle. Don't expect too many details—her lips are still sealed by an agreement she signed nearly two decades ago, but she can speak to the personal sense of isolation created by secrecy, and to the mischief and skullduggery that it invites.

Melissa Mahle entered the CIA as a covert operative in 1988. She was then in her late twenties. "At first, it was very seductive, the secrecy," she recalls, "because in many ways you are being indoctrinated—wrong word—you are being inculcated into a secret society with all the trappings—prestige, the power and the promise of being able to do something different." Fluent in Arabic, Mahle's assignments included an undercover tour of duty in the Persian Gulf, in North Africa, and two stints in the Occupied Territories. These assignments were not without challenge or risks for this blue-eyed California blonde. Along the way, she says, she received a presidential citation and laudatory evaluations, that is, until it all ended as it began, with sealed lips.

But not until she left the Agency in 2002, 14 years later, did she have time to reflect on the toll secrecy takes. "I have shed it in layers," she says, "a lifestyle that was largely defined by secrecy, and I don't think I understood the depths or the full parameters of how the culture of secrecy took over my life.

"First you sign the secrecy agreement," she recalls. "You can't talk about your job. You get further and further into it, to the point where you don't socialize outside the secrecy circle. You compartmentalize a whole portion of your life, your professional life, so that in your private life you begin to play a very odd game of losing who you are in the process of it all. . . . How you're feeling about what you're doing gets lost in the process of staying true to the requirements of your professional life. You lose the independent side of you. You get sucked into this lifestyle and you live with and eat with and argue with this very closed group of people. That's not to say you don't interact with others, but they fall into either agents you are running or potential agents you can recruit—or people you need to avoid to the best of your ability." Such isolation and studied duplicity can put terrific strain not only on one's self but on one's marriage, fueling the sense of isolation.

Because Mahle's life depended on secrecy, she remains a staunch supporter of its strictures. But she also has witnessed how it can be manipulated and exploited in ways that ill serve both the Agency and the nation's security. "The dichotomy of it is 'us-against-them,' but inside the building, it's a different game. Does that mean we use secrecy against each other? We certainly do. One of the tried-and-true tactical moves is if you are running an operation and all of a sudden someone is a critic and tries to put roadblocks up to your operation, you classify it and put it in a channel that that person doesn't have access to, and that's an abuse of classification."

Specifically, what Mahle said she saw were operatives elevating the classification level from a broad code word, that anyone with a plausible need-to-know would have access to, to a code word so restricted that it would effectively exclude all outside review and criticism. And why go to such ends?

"If you have somebody from another office or another field station who is asking a lot of hard questions and you can't answer those hard questions because your operation has something that stinks to it—and I have had it done to me—they will reclassify the operation and put it in a more classified compartment . . . and all of a sudden it goes away and you don't see it anymore. It's a very effective ploy and it's not visible to the outside. As far as anybody outside, it's still just secret. That's how internally we play the game."

Mahle says every CIA case officer has seen the misuse of secrecy. "Secrecy is power in the CIA," she says. "Power means control—control of people, control of resources, control of decision making. Some of it is gross abuse and some of it is petty abuse."

Isolation and chicanery help explain how secrecy produces bad, even corrupt, decisions. But it is the basic mind-set of a culture steeped in secrecy that may explain why the same mistakes are repeated again and again. The focus of the CIA, like that of nearly all institutions engaged in secret intelligence gathering, is on the immediacy of operations, at the expense of reflection. "Our mission is so forward-looking," says Mahle. "We don't have a lessons-learned tradition at all. I think it is part of our culture because we don't look back to lessons learned. You have to look back, but you know what, you can't. It's a secret, and you don't have a 'need-to-know.' "

From April 2001 until July 2002, Mahle was assigned to the Agency's recruitment center and helped screen candidates and subtly test them on the demands of secrecy. "You have little clues from them right away," says Mahle. "I always tell people that when I talk to them, I want them to talk to me on landlines. Someone who repeatedly calls me from a cell phone, that tells me they don't get it." At the first face-to-face meeting, recruits sign a secrecy agreement; Mahle would stress its importance. She would tell recruits that they could only speak to someone very close and someone in whom they had absolute trust. Later, when they would return for security processing, they would be asked exactly whom they spoke with. It was an early check to gauge their compatibility with a life of secrecy.

But the same secrecy intended to safeguard sensitive information and protect the nation can, taken to extremes, arrest the flow of critical information, degrade the quality of intelligence, and ultimately put the nation at greater risk. "Compartmentalization came to own the CIA in quite negative ways," says Mahle. She will not discuss specifics, but she says that "need-to-know" has been applied with a literalness and narrow-mindedness that has put the CIA at a disadvantage. She notes that case officers working against Al Qaeda in the Middle East may interpret "need-to-know" so narrowly as to exclude their Agency counterparts working on Al Qaeda issues in Africa or the Far East, thereby cutting themselves and others off from vital collaboration. Fighting a global enemy like terrorism requires information sharing and operational integration across geographic lines. A slavish adherence to compartmentalization and the "need-to-know" can create a dangerous myopia.

Ultimately Mahle herself became a victim of secrecy. In a not-too-cryptic way, she suggests that she was forced out of the Agency for violating a rule forbidding unreported contacts and relationships with foreign nationals. "I made a mistake," she says. "I admitted my mistake, I reported my mistake, and I dealt honestly with the Agency, but they couldn't accept that." Beyond that, she will say little of why she left the Agency. "I have been trying to get the Agency to tell me what I can talk about and what I can't talk about," she says, still a captive of secrecy.

Mahle authored a sobering book last year, fittingly titled *Denial and Deception*. It focused on the CIA from the Iran-*contra* scandal to 9/11. Again she ran headlong into restrictions and was forced to submit her book to exhaustive Agency vetting. Mahle says it was obvious early on that the reviewers were not just seeking to protect national security, but the CIA's image as well. One passage she says they initially deleted was a description of how the Agency had mishandled the annuity of Johnny Spann, a covert operative killed in Afghanistan. According to Mahle, despite public displays of honor for Spann, the Agency paid his widow only a single year's annuity. Agency colleagues got wind of this and were incensed; they took up a private collection using the internal e-mail system, for which they were chastised by CIA management. Eventually, Mahle says, the Agency reviewers relented and allowed her to include the incident in her book.

They did not, however, allow her to include a favorable reference to my book, *The Book of Honor*, which she had suggested ably demonstrated the cost of secrecy on the lives of covert officers killed in the line of duty. The CIA reviewers, she says, suggested such a reference obliquely confirmed the book's content. "It was absolutely ludicrous," says Mahle.

Perhaps most revealing about the vetting process, she says, was how it exposed the arbitrary and often inconsistent standards of what constitutes a secret. First her manuscript was submitted to her CIA division, the Directorate of Operations, or clandestine service. They designated those portions of the book that they considered must be deleted for reasons of classification. But when the same manuscript was circulated for review beyond the Operations Directorate, it was returned with three times more passages identified as containing classified information.

"What is a secret?" asks Mahle. "When they can't agree on what a secret is, you're not going to be able to protect secrets." It is a problem she sees writ large in the world, where information that is clearly now a part of the public domain—the rendition program, secret prisons in Europe, and more—continues to be treated as deep dark secrets by the Agency even years after they have appeared in the headlines, roiled Congress, and become the subject of lawsuits and scholarly papers.

"We are in a real crisis of what is a secret," says Mahle. "Today it doesn't have a sense of internal logic."

Ultimately her book was published with sixteen blacked-out items ranging from individual words to entire paragraphs.

In January 2006, Mahle was invited to speak before an assembly of some 200 current and former intelligence officers and academics gathered to consider ethical issues related to intelligence. As required by law, Mahle submitted a text of her intended remarks for review by the Agency. The Agency, she said, so "gutted" her talk, blacking out a fourth of the 23 pages, that she decided there was not enough material left to even bother with the presentation.

"I have learned a lot about secrecy," says Mahle. "The bottom line is that the organization needs secrecy and needs people to buy into secrecy in order to function, but there is a strong inclination to use secrecy to cover up failure and to cover up bureaucratic practices that would not withstand scrutiny in daylight."

Even today, four years after leaving the CIA, she continues to peel away the layers of secrecy that surrounded her life, a circumstance she likens to peeling an onion. She knows that, in one way or another, she will always be in the Agency's grasp.

"Secrecy," she says, "has a way of getting its arms around you all the way."

National Insecurity, Part I:
A Secrecy Born of Fear, Not Reason

Construct high fences around narrow areas.
—National Research Council's advice to the Department
of Energy, "A Review of the Department of Energy
Classification Policy and Practice," 1995

Too much secrecy can be self-defeating just as too much
talking can be dangerous.
—Allen Dulles, former director, Central Intelligence
Agency, in *The Craft of Intelligence*, 1963

On a clear April morning in 1971, a senior CIA analyst named John Seabury Thomson, a scholarly man dressed in coat and tie, was paddling his 17-foot aluminum canoe across the Potomac River on his daily commute to Agency headquarters in Langley, Virginia. When he reached the far shore and the mouth of Pulp Run, he noticed a milky white substance carried along by the tiny stream and drifting out into the river. A yellow fungus-like growth appeared in the discharge and slime covered the near bank. A committed environmentalist, Thomson decided to investigate and track the pollution back to its source.

He did not have far to look. It was his own employer, the CIA. The milky effluent clouding the shoreline, he learned, were liquefied secrets, the residue of thousands of classified documents that had been chemically reduced, then discharged into the river. For five years the slurry of secrets had gone undetected. Not one to let the matter drop, Thomson pressured the Agency for months to clean up its mess and to find another way to rid itself of its secrets. Finally, the Agency relented. In the years after, some secrets were pulped and solidified, mixed with seed and fertilizer, and spread across parts of West Virginia that had been ravaged by strip mining.

Thomson died in 1998 at the age of 77, canoeing the Potomac. His ashes were spread across its waters. But what had been an unseemly trickle of secrets back in 1971 would today be a torrent threatening to capsize him, so great has been the recent flood of new secrets.

Few have a better vantage point from which to assess the dangers of excessive secrecy than J. William Leonard, the man who oversees the government's Information Security Oversight Office, or ISOO, part of the National Archives and Records Administration. His job is to track the creation and costs of federal secrets, to decipher patterns in those numbers, and to make recommendations on how to improve the system. Leonard spent thirty years in the Pentagon, including a stint as deputy assistant secretary of defense for security and information operations. Security sensitivities are no abstraction for him. He was at the Pentagon, a mere 100 yards from where the terrorists crashed a commercial jetliner into the building on 9/11. One of his sons was a platoon leader with the First Infantry Division in Iraq. The other is with the CIA.

A consummate insider, Leonard nevertheless frets about the risks of runaway secrecy. Some of his colleagues pooh-pooh his warnings. " 'That's nice, Leonard,' " he says they tell him, " 'but don't you realize we are at war now? We don't have time for these administrative niceties.' I do recognize we are at war from my personal and professional life," Leonard answers them. "The fact that we are a nation at war is not a time to disregard basics. If ever there was a time to get it right, it is when we are at war."

He has more than once gone public with his concerns, including in an annual report to his boss, the president. In June 2003 he wrote: "When it comes to classification activity, more is not necessarily better. Much the same way the indiscriminate use of antibiotics reduces their effectiveness in combating infections, classifying too much information or for too long can reduce the effectiveness of the classification system, which, more than anything else, is dependent upon the confidence of the people touched by it."

Part of Leonard's mission is to calculate the annual number of new secrets. It is a daunting task, akin to counting grains of sand in a stiff wind. A precise inventory would be unthinkable, so he relies on sampling techniques and the good faith of some 50 federal agencies and departments. This much he knows: the number is staggering and on the rise. Just a fraction of the nation's secrets—about a billion—were declassified during the decade before 9/11.

Concerns over excessive secrecy have been brewing for decades. Fifty years ago, the eminent sociologist Edward A. Shils penned *The Torment of Secrecy* as America attempted to extricate itself from the paranoia and humiliation of the McCarthy era. He worried that the spread of secrecy he observed was imperiling democracy itself, blotting out government accountability, alienating citizens, and creating a dangerous and isolated subculture that dwelled in the shadows. In July 1970, the Defense Science Board Task Force on Secrecy, a commission set up by the Pentagon, offered this radical observation: "More might be gained than lost if our nation were to adopt—unilaterally if necessary—a policy of complete openness in all areas of information."

In 1996, Sen. Daniel Patrick Moynihan wrote a new introduction to Shils's classic, in which he observed, "There are at present some 3.2 million Americans with official clearance for Confidential, Secret, and Top Secret material. About 2.3 million are in direct federal employ, about 850,000 are federal contractors. Too many by a factor of ten."

But all that was before 9/11, before secrecy exploded.

Today, some 99 percent of government secrets are generated by the four big dogs of the national security apparatus: the Department of Defense, the State Department, the CIA, and the Justice Department. Some 4,000 government employees known as original classification authorities, or OCAs, are empowered to create new secrets. In fiscal year 2005, they designated some 262,592 new secrets. The year after 9/11, secrecy authority was conferred upon agencies well beyond the traditional orbit of security, including the Department of Agriculture, the Environmental Protection Agency, and the Department of Health and Human Services. The volume of secrets doubled over the past decade.

But that's only a tiny sliver of the story. The real action in secrecy lies in the so-called derivative classification decisions, which refers to the fact that if a secret is included in another document in whole or in part, that document must also be classified. Derivative classification is a kind of secondary market in secrets, the trafficking and commerce in secrecy. It is how secrets proliferate, like cancer cells dividing and metastasizing from one locus to the next. It is the mechanism by which information's flow can be reduced to that of sludge.

At the Pentagon, some 1,059 officials possess original classification authority, but a whopping 1.8 million officials can classify them derivatively. In 2005 the number of derivative classifications hit 14,206,778. More than 80 percent of those classifications were stamped "Secret" or "Top Secret," meaning that disclosure could cause "serious" or "exceptionally grave danger to the national security." But almost no one in government believes that anywhere near that number of secrets actually meet the critical standards to be a bona fide secret.

Even such tallies as are kept by ISOO only touch upon the vast and rapid growth in the restriction of information. For every document that bears the stamp "secret" or another formal classification, there are today, post-9/11, countless others that carry the designation "Sensitive but Unclassified" or one of scores of other similar designations: For Official Use Only, Sensitive Internal Use, In Confidence, Limited Distribution Information, Non-Public Information, Safeguards Information, Critical Infrastructure Information, Predecisional Draft. Though undeniably unclassified, this hybrid category of documents, records, memos, and correspondence is also inaccessible to the public and press. The Department of Energy alone has at least 15 different designations for documents whose contents are unclassified but off-limits to the public and press.

In 2004, the vast Department of Homeland Security (DHS) attempted to demand that all 180,000 of its employees sign a nondisclosure agreement preventing them from discussing with the press or public any information the department deemed sensitive, even if unclassified. The secrecy oath was written so broadly as to include "a virtually unlimited universe of information that is relevant to important matters of public concern," wrote the presidents of two unions protesting the proposed move. In January 2005, facing public outcry and further union opposition, DHS backed down, but not before at least one air marshal was reportedly fired, another suspended, and others resigned under pressure for allegedly disclosing too much. Such actions are a shot across the bow of all who might consider going public with grievances and security concerns.

These "Sensitive but Unclassified" materials, SBUs, as they have come to be known, pose a new threat to open government. Some 4,000 individuals possess original classification authority to create a formal secret, and though many routinely ignore the definitional strictures of the process, a definition of a formal secret does at least exist on paper. Today, in addition, hundreds of thousands—probably millions—of public employees and private contractors can and do arbitrarily and with complete immunity write "Sensitive" on a document and instantly restrict its distribution.

In recent years, agencies and departments of government have seized upon the device to cloak their activities and internal workings. Multiplied across the breadth and scope of government, the proliferation of such designations, together with the indiscriminate minting of formal secrets, has produced a stealth government that defies scrutiny and is anathema to democracy.

The literal cost of secrecy is now somewhere north of $7 billion, an amount equal to the entire budget of the Environmental Protection Agency. That number is growing. The surge in secrets, spurred in large measure by 9/11, has created bureaucratic gridlock, clogging the flow of vital information and costing the government, industry, and taxpayers billions. To process the new secrets and to accommodate the expanded security apparatus that supports them requires a vast new deployment of government workers and contractors with security clearances. In 1996, the Office of Personnel Management received 325,000 annual requests for clearances. Post-9/11, it received 1.6 million, a fivefold jump.

By May 2004, the queue of government workers and contractors left waiting for security clearances, background checks, and adjudications numbered 340,000. Were these people to form a single-file line, it would stretch 100 miles, the distance from Washington to Richmond, Virginia. The average wait pre-9/11 for private-sector employees to get clearance was 56 days. By 2004, the wait averaged more than a year for private and government employees alike. Some waited considerably longer. The highest classification clearance, "Top Secret," requires the most exhaustive checks and consequently takes the longest to process. "Top Secret" clearances are also potentially the most critical to national security.

To some in this "Information Age," the government's clearance system appears antiquated and Byzantine. "These guys are using Eisenhower-era processes," says David Wagoner, who chairs the Intelligence Committee of the Information Technology Association of America (ITAA), a trade association that includes as members such heavyweights as Microsoft, Lockheed, IBM, and Northrop. Despite laws promoting interagency reciprocity, each of the 16 agencies within the intelligence community—including the CIA, the National Security Agency, and the Defense Intelligence Agency—still insists on conducting its own clearances. Each agency still has its distinctive culture. The CIA administers a more personally invasive "lifestyle polygraph," probing areas that other agencies might find repugnant. The Department of Defense (DOD) relies on a "counterintelligence-scope polygraph," which asks questions related to espionage and professional conduct but steers clear of personal habits and behavior. "The signal boys—NSA— don't trust HUMINT [Human Intelligence]," says Relyea. "Those who get it by one technique don't trust the others." The lack of reciprocity creates a drag on the entire clearance process.

Five years after 9/11 and its harsh lesson in the critical importance of collaboration and working across bureaucratic boundaries, the massive expansion of secrecy and the culture it supports continue to bedevil the system. The DHS insists that it accepts security clearances from the DOD, but it, like others, imposes yet another filter, called a "suitability determination." Even within DHS, such "suitability determinations" can bar someone with a clearance from Customs and Border Protection from gaining access to information or employment at Immigration and Customs Enforcement.

Just how often do security-related positions go unfilled or face serious delay because of such obstacles? A May 2006 survey by the ITAA of its members found that a third of the companies' personnel—many of them providing the backbone of America's defense, IT, and counterterrorism efforts—reported having to go through another full screening process before an agency would grant them a clearance. And there remains stiff resistance within government to granting clearances to the foreign-born or those married to foreigners, a mind-set that substantially impedes the hiring of translators and regional experts crucial to the war on terrorism.

In 1996, the Clinton administration privatized the entire clearance apparatus that conducts non-intelligence-related background checks. Today, the U.S. government's Office of Personnel Management's clearance program gets no congressional funding and relies exclusively on a "pay-for-service" plan. OPM charges America's agencies and departments—the DOD, the DHS, the EPA—a per-person fee for conducting each background check. It then farms out the great majority of the fieldwork, record searches, and interviews to private for-profit companies.

The OPM charges the Pentagon, by far its largest customer, $200 per person to conduct a background investigation for a "Confidential" or "Secret" clearance. The more demanding "Top Secret" check, known as a "single-scope background investigation," or an SSBI, costs $3,150 per person. If the DOD feels the position is urgent or "mission-critical," it can, if it has the money, pay a premium of $3,655 to jump the queue and expedite the process. A few others can also avoid languishing in bureaucratic limbo, such as those seeking "Yankee White" access, a "Top Secret" clearance with special entree to the White House.

Since 2006, when the OPM took over background investigations for the DOD, relations between the two have been icy at best. The DOD and the OPM constantly feud over the bill. DOD believes it's being gouged. The OPM insists that the DOD fails to budget for its needs. In late April 2006, things got so bad that for two months the DOD suspended all requests for clearances for contractors. The DOD's clearance needs had exceeded its budget by $90 million. "They had no money to pay for it," says the OPM's associate director, Kathy Dillaman. "If you run out of milk [and have no money], can you go to the store and get it?" (But of course, this is not a pint of milk under discussion, but the potential security of the nation.)

Five years after 9/11, adjusting to the new demands of secrecy has wrought disarray, delay, and conflict. The post-9/11 clearance process, a barometer of secrecy's ravenous capacity to consume resources, has variously been described as a flood, a logjam, and a train wreck. Since January 2005, the Government Accountability Office has placed the DOD's clearance program on its "high-risk list," meaning it "needs urgent attention and transformation." The storm surge in secrets has overwhelmed little OPM. In 1996, its Federal Investigative Services Division had a staff of 775. Today investigators number about 8,000, all but 1,800 of whom are private contractors. And still OPM is falling short as it faces a projected 1.5 to 1.8 million clearance requests a year.

"Large backlogs, long wait times, and convoluted bureaucratic hierarchies have plagued this process for years, endangering national security and costing the taxpayers millions of dollars a year," said Rep. Tom Davis, a Virginia Republican who chaired the House Government Reform Committee. As for the Pentagon, Davis said in May 2006 that its clearance "system seems to be suffering a cyclic downward spiral."

As befitting an entity that services the secrecy realm, the OPM does not permit anyone but its public affairs officers and designated senior management to speak to the press, and even senior management must have a public affairs officer on hand to babysit. OPM insists that its unclassified handbook for conducting investigations, which is distributed to more than 8,000 government and private contract investigators, is not subject to the Freedom of Information Act and not available to the press. Like an ever-increasing volume of government materials, it is marked "Official Use Only," putting it beyond the eyes of ordinary citizens, scholars, and the press.

• • •

But the real cost of expanded secrecy is not to be found in the number of new clearances, or in the dollars and cents they represent. Information is valueless if not provided to those with a need to know. A government that has carte blanche to create secrets will constantly be tempted to use secrecy to smother controversy and conceal its own failings. Those who suffer are not policy makers but citizens whose very lives may depend upon getting information.

Take 24-year-old Spc. Joseph Fabozzi, of the New Jersey Army National Guard. While on home leave from Iraq in November 2003, he felt anxious speaking about the inadequacy of the body armor that was supposed to protect him and those with whom he served. Fabozzi was concerned that the outdated flak jackets he and his fellow soldiers had been issued simply did not stop the sort of bullets most commonly fired against them in Iraq.

But he feared that speaking out would get him into trouble with the brass. Before exiting Iraq, he was told to sign a nondisclosure form, in effect a promise not to speak to the media about equipment problems. Certainly the enemy knew the toll they were taking, and within the

Pentagon, it was hardly a secret that better flak jackets were in short sup-ply. But it was a fact that the DOD preferred to keep secret, recognizing its own political vulnerability in the matter.

But as is often the case with abusive secrecy, keeping one party quiet puts others at risk. A 2005 Pentagon study conducted by the Armed Forces Medical Examiner for the Marine Corps concluded, on the basis of forensic examination of torso wounds, that up to 80 percent of the Marines killed in Iraq between March 2003 and June 2005 could have survived if they had had proper body armor. By one estimate, that would have been several hundred lives saved. But that study was stamped "secret" and only came to light in January 2006, when it was published by a military advocacy group, Soldiers for the Truth. The Pentagon, refusing comment, says such information might aid the en-emy. Historically, public disclosure has often produced timely relief and new funding, even as it exposed the chinks in Pentagon planning.

That excessive secrecy can imperil those who are asked to defend the country is hardly news to those who understand the system best. The Pentagon asked the JASON Group, an independent scientific advisory panel whose members have included numerous Nobel laureates and members of the National Academy of Sciences, to examine the defense information classification system. Its report, delivered in December 2004, concluded that "users," that is, the soldiers at the front, "see an overly rigid, out-of-date, bureaucratic structure of information classifica-tion." They went on, "We must also change a culture in which the logi-cally separable roles of 'content producer' and 'content protector' has become completely entangled, and in which 'knowledge is power' is too frequently mutated to 'withheld knowledge is power. . . .'

"The current situation of out-of-date or operationally unimple-mentable rules, combined with widespread violation of those rules, is a bad place to be," the JASON Group report stated. It concluded, "The present system of classification, clearances, and access protection is bro-ken. It is giving rise to a complicated, and largely uncontrolled, set of workarounds. The perceptual gap between those who use information and those who protect it is unsupportably wide."

Excessive secrecy can prevent vital information from reaching those who need it most; it can also lead to such information inadvertently be-ing handed over to those whose right to it is questionable. Deprivation on the one hand and sloppiness on the other—these are two sides of the coin of excessive secrecy.

Former national security advisor McGeorge Bundy observed, "If you guard your toothbrushes and diamonds with equal zeal, you'll probably lose fewer toothbrushes and more diamonds." Bundy's words have proved prophetic. Three months after 9/11, the Department of Energy reported that it had accidentally released some 318 pages of sensitive documents pertaining to nuclear weapons design and assembly systems, stockpiles information, storage locations, and targeting information. Those documents were made available to the public for three years by the Department of State, Defense, and National Archives. Their content was described as the sort of material that aspiring nuclear powers and would-be bomb builders would love to get their hands on.

Five years later, in 2006, the investigative arm of Congress, the Government Accountability Office, reported that what is a secret varies not only from one department to another, but even within departments. The GAO found that the Pentagon used multiple, inconsistent, and sometimes contradictory standards. What was classified in one office was unclassified just down the hall. The problem is government-wide. In one agency, "R" means "releasable"; in another, "to be retained and kept classified." "D" can mean "declassify" on one side of the street and "deny automatic declassification" on the other. The lack of uniformity, the widely divergent standards of what constitutes a secret, and the sheer volume of government secrets together create a system vulnerable to mistakes, misjudgments, and abuse.

No case better illustrates the absurdities that secrecy can produce than that of Zacarias Moussaoui, the only co-conspirator of the 9/11 attacks to be charged and convicted. In response to Moussaoui's requests for documents needed to represent himself in court, the government unwittingly provided him with scores of highly classified documents that put at risk a number of ongoing terrorism investigations. Moussaoui does not have a security clearance and was in many ways the last person the U.S. government would have wanted to furnish with sensitive materials exposing their "sources and methods" and the status of terrorism cases.

In August 2002, the mistake was discovered and government prosecutors pleaded with a federal judge for permission to retrieve the documents. Finally, humbled federal marshals were permitted to go into Moussaoui's cell and retrieve armfuls of classified reports in his possession. Later, it occurred to them that some of these same classified files were on a computer disk still in his possession. (As if the government had not already been sufficiently embarrassed, ABC and CNN reported the slipup on the basis of a leak from the Justice Department.)

But the case was about to take an even more bizarre twist. Government lawyers argued that the families of 9/11 attack victims were not entitled to the aviation security documents that had been made available to Moussaoui's defense team, even though those documents were not even classified and pertained only to pre-9/11 security measures. Some carried a "Sensitive Security Information" (SSI) designation.

Dr. Stephen Alderman, whose son, Peter, died in the World Trade Center, scoffed at the Transportation Security Agency's position. "SSI," he said, "should have a different acronym—CYA [cover your ass]. . . . TSA's only conceivable motive is avoiding embarrassment or protecting the airlines."

In April 2006, U.S. District Court Judge Leonie Brinkema agreed, ruling for the 9/11 families and scolding the government for its obsession with secrecy. "I've always been troubled to the extent our government keeps things secret from the American people," she said. "It's amazing to me what some agencies think is secret. As a culture, we need to be careful not to be so wrapped up in secrecy that we lose track of our core values and laws."

Of course, passengers looking to complain to the TSA about screening procedures, safety lapses, or other concerns can always contact the agency's ombudsman, appointed in February 2002. "Our door is always open," it says at a TSA website for the ombudsman's office. One caveat: At a press conference announcing the appointment, the TSA's director, John W. Magaw, declined to provide the identity of the ombudsman, and a slide shown to Congress in January 2004 called "How to Contact the Ombudsman," featuring a toll-free number, was marked "sensitive security information."

Secrets are treated like the crown jewels of government, secured in vaults and guarded by phalanxes of specially trained personnel. Yet many of these secrets are only factoids whose disclosure would reveal nothing so much as the pedestrian nature of the bureaucracy that gathered them. Some may seem downright silly. In 2003, the Pentagon, in an act imbued with supreme irony, refused to release a video produced to instruct its staff on how to deal with Freedom of Information Act requests. In denying the request, it cited the FOIA's "trade secret" exemption.

On October 31, 2005, Mary Margaret Graham, deputy director of national intelligence for collection and a 27-year veteran of the CIA, was speaking in San Antonio, Texas, before a national conference, when she let slip a figure for the nation's budget for intelligence gathering—some $44 billion. For years, news organizations, scholars, and government watchdog groups had sought to get that figure, and lawsuits had been filed against the government in an effort to pry loose the number. With the exception of its 1997 and 1998 intelligence budgets, the government has steadfastly denied those requests, arguing that the numbers were highly classified and that their release would materially damage national security. Yet somehow, after Graham's stunning gaffe, the republic was intact and Graham remained in office, embarrassed but employed.

Other secrets conceal darker machinations. A decade ago, DOD's National Reconnaissance Office, one of the most furtive of government entities, was discovered to have secretly hoarded well over $1 billion, a slush fund whose existence it concealed from the public and Congress alike. More recently, on May 29, 2003, President Bush declared, "We have found the weapons of mass destruction," a statement based on two trailers found in Iraq and identified as biological labs. But just two days earlier, a secret fact-finding group dispatched to Iraq by the Pentagon had reported back to Washington that there was no connection between the two trailers and biological weapons. The contents of that report, classified and shelved (contrary to the expectations of those who had been on the mission), did not surface until April 2006 when the *Washington Post* published a story on the report.

Today, for the exhausted Pentagon and beleaguered intelligence community, it has sometimes seemed that the one secret they would least like to have exposed is how few truly valuable and actionable secrets they possess. In late 2005, the CIA unit tasked with hunting down bin Laden was quietly disbanded, another sign that the welter of secrets had not moved the nation any closer to bringing the mastermind of 9/11 to justice.

But if today's secrets are not defined by their intrinsic national security value, then what accounts for such exponential growth? Not long after my book on the CIA came out in 2000, I was contacted by a man who had recently retired from the federal government. His principal job had been to classify documents at one of the intelligence agencies. He said that in recent years he had witnessed a profound change in the attitude toward secrecy and a degradation of respect for the system. When he started his career decades earlier, classification was wielded *relatively* sparingly. It signified a clear determination that a particular document demanded special handling and attention above the din of ordinary bureaucratic business. Its disclosure, it could reasonably be argued, posed a palpable threat to the nation.

But in recent years he and others had noticed that classification was used not to highlight the underlying sensitivity of a document, but to ensure that it did not get lost in the blizzard of paperwork that routinely competes for the eyes of government officials. If a document was not marked "classified," it would be moved to the bottom of the stack, eclipsed by more urgent business, meaning documents that carried a higher security classification. He observed that a security classification, by extension, also conferred importance upon the author of the document. If the paper was ignored, so too was its author. Conversely, if the materials were accorded a high degree of protection, they would redound to their author's credit and enhance his or her authority and bureaucratic standing.

Over time, what he and others came to recognize was that secrecy had become not merely a tool of national security but a bureaucratic instrument, one that determined status, conferred power and authority, and defined the internal dynamics of government. It was all about access, who had it and who did not. Access equaled power. To be in the loop of a secret was to be among the anointed. To be left out was to be not merely sidelined but effectively exiled. Whether it was competition for scarce resources or making the case for war, control of information was everything.

That played out not only at the individual level but at the institutional level, as organizations vied for preeminence, access, and credibility, all largely on the basis of the information they possessed. Such a system rewards hoarding and views sharing as a dilution of power and, therefore, contrary to self-interest.

The wider implications of such a system are daunting. For starters, ordinary open information, that which requires no devious or clandestine means of acquisition—newspaper accounts, television and radio broadcasts, and official government reports—becomes increasingly devalued, debunked, or ignored. Such low-hanging fruit is often passed up by our intelligence personnel in favor of items that are harder to reach. The pursuit of others' secrets—a reflection of America's own fixation with secrecy—creates, if not an outright disdain for open-source materials, then at least a failure to appreciate and fully mine what is there before them and which historically has provided the daily grist for the mill of solid intelligence analysis.

Consider the CIA's failure to foresee India's nuclear test in 1998. The Hindu nationalist party, Bharatiya Janata, had openly declared that if they won power they would test a nuclear weapon. Had they been taken at their word, the intelligence community would not have been caught so flat-footed.

•　　•　　•

Today, within the national security realm, secrets have emerged not merely as discrete documents but as esteemed tokens of individual and bureaucratic initiative, risk, and enterprise—qualities that can elevate an individual, a branch, even an institution. Citing an open radio source gets one nowhere in such an environment. Getting the ear of power—be it that of the president, the national security advisor, or the director national intelligence—becomes an end unto itself.

Furthermore, there are no disincentives for classifying materials, no penalty for arbitrarily secreting information. There are, however, considerable risks attached to letting a sensitive document slip through. To those empowered to wield the stamp of secrecy, the message is unambiguous. As Harold Relyea of the Congressional Research Service puts it, "When you give a small boy a hammer, there isn't much that doesn't seem to need pounding. . . . If you are in a culture of creating secrets, you will advance accordingly."

With the proliferation of documents stamped "Confidential" or "Secret" came the compulsion to elevate the level of classification and regain the higher ground of visibility, both for the work product and for its author. In some quarters this created "bracket creep." So numerous were the documents stamped "Secret," by far the most common level of classification, that in many quarters they lost their cachet and came to be regarded with the same kind of indifference once reserved for documents classified "Confidential" or "Restricted."

The answer: Resort to "Top Secret" or the once-stratospheric "Sensitive Compartmented Information." It's not that better and more insightful intelligence is being collected, but rather that such classifications translate as "Ignore me at your peril." This change could be seen coming a long way off. In his 1985 book *Secrecy and Democracy,* former director of Central Intelligence Stansfield Turner wrote: "An intelligence document that is Top Secret, but not further restricted by a code word, is considered barely classified." Former secretary of state George P. Shultz made a similar observation: "The higher the classification of secrecy, the quicker you will report it." Since that time, code word "secrecy" has proliferated.

Harold Relyea knows the problem well. "A general once told me he only reads things that were marked 'Top Secret.' If it was less than that, it wasn't worth his time."

During J. William Leonard's thirty years at the Pentagon, including time as deputy assistant secretary of defense for security and information operations, he had a similar observation. Because of his senior rank he had access to intelligence briefings. "Frankly, this was all 'Top Secret Code Word' stuff," he told me. "I stopped going because I found them to be useless and uninformative and of dubious analytical quality. I got more out of the open sources. I would look at the classification of some of this information and also look at its usefulness and often times it was proportionately opposite. The higher the classification, the less useful it was."

For Leonard and others, excessive secrecy is not merely a nuisance but a danger. Once again Iraq comes to mind. "Excessive secrecy begets things like New Coke," Leonard says. "When you hold things so tight, when you compartmentalize especially policy recommendations and analysis, you cut down on the universe of give-and-take of the deliberative process where you can have the all-important questioning of fundamental assessments which is essential if you are going to come up with the optimal result. You may be able to deny information to an adversary but at the same time what secrecy does to us is it guarantees you will not have the optimal outcome because you are cutting yourself off."

Over time, those in possession of secrets become increasingly isolated from the wider community and evolve into a distinct culture within a culture. There is a real danger that those who possess secrets become possessed by them. As in Tolkien's *Lord of the Rings,* the bearer of the ring comes under its spell. Secrecy is rarely surrendered voluntarily and can consume even (perhaps especially) the most patriotic and loyal of Americans.

In 1992 I broke the story of a top secret government bunker long buried beneath the posh Greenbrier resort in West Virginia, where members of Congress were to go in the event of a catastrophic attack on Washington. For 30 years the massive facility had been lovingly tended by a secret cadre of government communications and security experts posing as the resort's television repair crew. Over the decades they had become increasingly cut off from the world; while the nature of threats changed dramatically, they did not keep pace, but went on with their mission, not unlike Japanese soldiers deep in remote jungles who never heard of the surrender. In time it seemed that the enemy they feared most was disclosure itself and the sundering of their secret world.

But how did secrets become the coin of the realm? Clearly, one factor is the changing nature of the threats to our national security. In an age of terrorism, where the enemy is not a sovereign state but an agile and faceless foe, there is little or no open information to draw upon—no official Al Qaeda newspaper, no production figures, no published budgets. In the Cold War days, the United States monitored the Communist giants, China and the Soviet Union, as well as their proxies, largely by covering their respective capitals and providing intelligence officers with embassy-based cover positions. Tracking terrorism is a stealthy pursuit and requires a different model.

Penetrating terrorist cells is an order of magnitude more difficult than keeping tabs on mass armies or prolific government pronouncements. Even nations that have been identified as hostile to U.S. interests, such as Iraq, Iran, and North Korea, have proved isolated and opaque, and their alleged connections with terrorists have proved elusive at best. It was inevitable that the new threats posed by 9/11 would lead to greater emphasis on covert collection and secrecy.

But the post-9/11 environment also proved what every experienced CIA case officer already knew: if secrecy can illuminate, it can also beguile. What happens when a person whispers? People draw near. They crane their necks and cup their ears. When the human voice is lowered, when there is an attempt to create a limited audience, there is a presumption that what is about to be communicated is worthier than that which is broadly distributed. (The German writer Goethe observed, "Secrecy has many advantages, for when you tell someone the purpose of any object right away, they often think there is nothing to it.") The sotto voce communication—the secret—is deemed to possess greater value and credibility. The added precautions surrounding its delivery attest to its preciousness, like the presumptions that attach to the contents of an armored car. We guard what we deem to be valuable.

That gives rise to one of the central fallacies of the post-9/11 era—that secrets are somehow truer and more reliable than their open-source counterparts. In fact, just the opposite is true. The secret is often untested against reality, coddled against the challenge of outside debate, the pull and tug of common discourse. All too often that is precisely why it is ushered into the world as a secret—to avoid that truth-forging crucible to which all broadly disseminated information is subjected. The secret is often protected not because of its high value but because of its innate fragility and inability to withstand scrutiny. It is the child who lacks an immune system that must be kept in the bubble, and not for others' protection, but his own. Think of the secrecy surrounding the intelligence that supported the argument for Iraq's alleged weapons of mass destruction. Cloaked in anonymity, unnamed sources of both the press and government avoided the sort of skepticism and probing inquiries that might have exposed their latent self-interests and cast doubt on the credibility of their statements and the very existence of WMDs.

Those in power have become adept at exploiting the irresistible cachet of secrecy. The very officials who publicly bluster and rail most about the need for tight security are often the first to compromise a secret behind closed doors to gain a reporter's favor, discredit a rival, or float an idea to see how it might be received. "Government is the only vessel that leaks from the top," noted James Reston, the late editor of the *New York Times*, decades before George W. Bush gave the order to selectively share information from an otherwise classified intelligence report to bolster the wobbly case for war with Iraq.

Rarely is anyone held to account for such leaks, and for good reason. "The people who leak information are not the mid-level people," says William McNair, a former CIA information review officer (he retired in

2003). "If you look at most of these leaks they are fuzzy on details because the people are so high up they don't even know the details."

Leaks are now part of a well-established cat-and-mouse game. Each secret to come out is another salvo between warring camps. McNair worries deeply about the consequences. "I think we are just falling off the cliff," he says, concerned that one individual bent on torpedoing an entire government policy has the power, though not the authority, to derail that policy with a single leak of classified information. That in turn encourages senior officials to engage in their own leaks to counteract or discredit the first leak. "I think leaks are just terrible," he laments. "The president signs a covert action and it's announced in the paper that afternoon."

It can also affect our relationship with allies. In September 2004, the *Guardian* newspaper reported that Homeland Security secretary Tom Ridge had to apologize for an American intelligence leak that compromised a major MI5 and police surveillance operation in Britain. Whitehall was said to be "furious" over leaks that disclosed the names of suspects and their putative targets in both the United States and Britain. Here at home, leaks to the press were said to have unraveled a yearlong covert FBI operation into a federal employee with a "Top Secret" clearance who was suspected of turning over classified information to Israel.

Often these leaks take juvenile forms. For years I worked on a book about CIA officers who were killed in the line of duty and whose identities were concealed. They could not be released, I was told, because it would compromise national security.

In the course of researching the book, a pattern emerged among current and former CIA officers: they would coyly provide clues that allowed me to quickly identify Agency fatalities, but they would never utter or write down an actual name. One former CIA counterterrorist officer let me know that the first casualty in the 1992 Somalia operation was a CIA covert operative. A check of the clips revealed that the first person to die in that operation was named Larry Freedman. The officer had provided me the name of a CIA operative without speaking it.

In another instance, an Agency official told me I should get a copy of a particular book and gave me the ISBN number as well as a partial title, *China Spy . . . ;* when I pressed him for the full title, he declined.

When I got the book I discovered that he had deleted a person's name from the subtitle. That name, Hugh Francis Redmond, it turned out, was one of the nameless stars in the CIA's Book of Honor. And why had he too not simply given me the name outright? Because he wanted to be able to pass the "black box" or polygraph test and truthfully deny that he had ever provided any names or classified information.

•   •   •

Today, more than ever, the husbanding of secrets is used not to keep information from America's enemies but rather to keep it out of the hands of Americans—the press, members of Congress, government watchdog groups, agencies with rival agendas—who threaten to question and challenge administration policies and presumptions.

Former secretary of state Colin Powell's senior advisor, Col. Lawrence B. Wilkerson, has said that the National Security Council staff stopped using e-mail for substantive discussions when they realized that their e-mails were being monitored by Vice President Dick Cheney's national security advisors and were being used against them. The rivalry reached such heights that Wilkerson has said he does not know if, as a result of such actions, a memo calling for more troops in Iraq ever made its way to the president. That, too, is wrapped in secrecy.

Under cover of secrecy, the intelligence community in particular—16 separate entities—often acts like anything but a community. Under Secretary of Defense Donald Rumsfeld, the Pentagon's internal ad hoc intelligence operations sometimes seem more competitive than collaborative with those of the CIA, and rely on secrecy not only as a security imperative but as a way to outmaneuver opponents and achieve hierarchical supremacy. Inquiries and investigations into the failure of intelligence pre-9/11 produced intragovernmental backbiting, scapegoating, and recriminations. Behind the shroud of secrecy, the FBI and CIA engaged in a bitter blame game. The legendary CIA mole hunter, James Angleton, patron saint of paranoia, would have felt right at home.

Ironically, it was 9/11, the very event some cite as justification for the new regime of secrecy, that made manifest the very real dangers of failing to share intelligence and information, a problem that had gone largely unnoticed until then. Out of the fear and confusion that followed 9/11 emerged two distinct visions of national security: one was predicated upon the notion that a nation that can control its secrets is a nation that is made more secure; the other, that a nation that cannot control its impulse for excessive secrecy is a nation made more vulnerable. The two views are by no means contradictory, but have evolved into competitors, fueled by a false dichotomy in which proponents of the former seek to discredit those who would rein in secrecy and the unchecked authority it abets.

Many within the nation's security ranks who investigated the intelligence failures that preceded 9/11 reached a common conclusion. The GAO, citing Lee Hamilton, former vice chair of the National Commission on Terrorist Attacks Upon the United States (the 9/11 Commission), noted: "The government's single greatest failure in the lead-up to the September 11, 2001, attacks was the inability of federal agencies to effectively share information about suspected terrorists and their activities." That inability or unwillingness to share within and across bureaucratic boundaries, the lack of "connectivity," was, they concluded, what most impeded America's ability to uncover and thwart the attacks, not any breach of classification or reckless transparency. The commission targeted information sharing as a top priority in the war on terrorism. So too did the 2001 USA Patriot Act, the 2002 legislation that created the Department of Homeland Security, and a half dozen subsequent presidential directives and executive orders.

As a testament to the gravity of the problem, the Intelligence Reform and Terrorism Prevention Act of 2004 established the position of program manager and the office of Information Sharing Environment, or ISE. It was placed under the Office of Director National Intelligence; its mission, to enhance connectivity, take on the culture of secrecy, and get people to talk to one another. It was a daunting task that amounted to reversing decades of information hoarding, bureaucratic turf wars, incompatible technologies, and outsized egos. ISE was tasked with finding ways of getting diverse agencies and departments to, in the parlance of kindergarten, "make nice and play well with others."

In April 2005, amid much fanfare, President Bush designated John A. Russack, a career veteran of the intelligence community, head of the effort to create the vaunted Information Sharing Environment. On November 8, 2005, Russack told Congress, "I believe there is not an issue more seminal to the security of our nation than information sharing." Members of Congress declared Russack's mission to be of paramount importance. On December 16, 2005, the president issued government-wide guidelines supporting information sharing.

But beyond repeated public pronouncements and posturing, how serious was the White House about promoting information sharing, and how much was intended simply to silence administration critics without rattling the status quo? Seven months into his job as the information sharing czar, his mandate being to cover the entire universe of U.S. government agencies and departments as well as state and local governments and also the private sector, Russack's office had but one full-time employee and two contract workers.

In January 2006, nine months after taking office, Russack announced he was resigning. He told colleagues he had never been given the authority or resources needed to tackle the task he faced. The problems were deep-rooted, the culture of secrecy dug in.

Two months earlier, a prescient Lee Hamilton had warned, "You can change the law, you can change the technology, but you still need to change the culture."

Today, indiscriminate secrecy continues largely unabated, narrow parochial interests still chafe against wider national interests, and resistance to information sharing, though marginally improved, remains dogged. In March 2006 the GAO reported, "More than 4 years after September 11, the nation still lacks the governmentwide [sic] policies and processes that Congress called for to provide a framework for guiding and integrating the myriad of ongoing efforts to improve the sharing of terrorism-related information critical to protecting our homeland."

The culture of secrecy has shown that it will not yield to rhetoric alone nor to appeals to some higher good, not so long as the old habits of hoarding information are still practiced at the highest levels and rewarded with favor and influence. The system takes its cue not from words but actions.

From the beginning, the administration had sent mixed signals when it came to information sharing. Even as the rhetoric of information sharing became fashionable post-9/11, the old uses of secrecy continued at the highest levels. At the White House and Defense Department, in the lead-up to the war in Iraq, senior policy makers cherry-picked intelligence, manipulated analysis, shunned disconfirming data, and shifted authority and influence to ad hoc intelligence units within the Pentagon. These provided career bureaucrats not with any template of new connectivity but with an all-too-familiar model of business as usual, complete with the "stovepiping" of intelligence and the deft management of secrecy to cut off doubters' and dissenters' access to decision makers.

Again and again, information sharing has run headlong into the administration's resistance to having its intelligence-gathering processes scrutinized or evaluated. The Office of the Director of National Intelligence (ODNI) is the administrative home to the ISE. But even here, the spirit of interagency collegiality faces resistance. In March 2006, the GAO, the official investigative arm of Congress, completed a sweeping examination of the status of information sharing within the federal bureaucracy and asked for ODNI's comments on its draft findings. ODNI's response was to refuse all comment, arguing that the GAO lacked the authority to inquire into, much less judge, matters related to intelligence. ODNI did not even bother to offer a legal argument in defense of its position.

And George Bush, the president who publicly champions the Information Sharing Environment, privately sets the ultimate example of information hoarding. On May 18, 2006, even one of his staunchest supporters, a fellow Republican, Rep. Peter Hoekstra (R-Mich.), chair of the House Intelligence Committee, could stay silent no longer. As first reported in the *New York Times,* Hoekstra wrote a confidential letter to the president rebuking him for hiding various intelligence programs and surveillance efforts from the committee, and wrote that cutting them out of the loop was "a direct affront to me and the members of this committee who have ardently supported efforts to collect information on our enemies." It was also, he warned, quite possibly a violation of law. "The U.S. Congress," he said, "simply should not have to play Twenty Questions to get information that it deserves under our Constitution."

•　　•　　•

Officials say that secrecy, like obscenity, may be hard to define, but they know it when they see it. But that is not always so. Even within the CIA, there is considerable dispute about what constitutes a secret. For more than 20 years, William McNair was with the Agency, much of that time as a covert operative. His last ten years at the CIA, he was the information review officer, under the deputy director of operations, the clandestine branch of the CIA. Before retiring in 2003, he earned the sobriquet Dr. No for his unflagging resistance to the declassification of information. His vision of what was a secret more than once clashed with that of those around him.

For instance, it came to his attention that the CIA's own Recruitment Center was saying things to potential recruits at job fairs and so-called flash sessions that McNair felt crossed the line. "They would talk about cover and lifestyle and mission in ways that I thought were illegal and certainly fit our definition of classified materials," he recalls. "So we had some meetings and we looked it over and the Recruitment Center agreed to tone down their presentation." Even within the Operations Directorate the standard of secrecy changed somewhat as director followed director. McNair recalls that James Pavitt, former head of the CIA's clandestine branch, sometimes dismissed his concerns as "legalistic bullshit."

Nora Slatkin, the Agency's executive director in the mid-nineties under Director John Deutch, had her own views of secrecy. Nicknamed "Tora-Tora Nora" for what some saw as her brash and assertive manner, she early on announced that she was intent on reducing the level of secrecy at the Agency. McNair recalls, "She said to me, 'There are too many secrets.' " But she underestimated the power of the CIA culture to resist change, and the secrets outlasted her.

What few relaxations of secrecy did occur during that time were soon reversed. At the CIA's annual memorial service in May 1996, an observance restricted to Agency personnel and the families of the fallen, the names of all seventy casualties inscribed in the CIA's Book of Honor were for the first time read aloud, including several dozen who had died under cover and whose names were still considered classified. Agency veterans such as the former director Dick Helms were aghast. In all subsequent years, the service reverted back to reading only the names of those who were no longer considered covert, even in death, and even then, attendees were cautioned not to discuss the service with outsiders.

Sometimes Dr. No even ran afoul of the director Central Intelligence himself. It came to his attention that CIA director John Deutch's wife, Patricia, who traveled internationally with Deutch, was writing letters to friends not only about her travels but about some of the people she and her husband were meeting.

Her letters, says McNair, included references to the heads of foreign intelligence services, including some rather unflattering characterizations of them. McNair considered such matters to be sensitive and unfit for open correspondence. Time and again, he would have to ask for such references to be deleted from the letters. "I was just writing to my friends," she would say. At the funeral of former director Dick Helms in 2002, McNair ended up sitting next to Deutch. "Did you work for me?" Deutch asked. "I used to," McNair responded, at which point Deutch's wife piped up, "John, he was the one I used to tell you about who censored all my letters."

It was the rare time indeed when McNair was cast as an advocate of openness and information sharing, but on at least one occasion he was convinced that secrecy must yield to a higher purpose. That was during the trial of Libyan suspects for the downing of Pan Am flight 103 over Lockerbie, Scotland, in December 1988. That bombing killed 270 people. (One of those was Matthew Gannon, a covert CIA operative who is still a nameless star in the CIA's Book of Honor at headquarters.) The dilemma facing the CIA was whether to share highly sensitive classified information with prosecutors or risk having the suspects walk.

McNair says he faced stiff opposition from the CIA brass but convinced them to share a massive amount of materials, exposing an asset and standing ready, if need be, to expose four or five CIA officers. For several nights McNair and the Scottish lord advocate prosecuting the case, Colin Boyd, stayed up until three in the morning at a protected site going over classified CIA documents. "I showed him, a foreign national without a clearance, documents that 95 percent of Americans with a 'Top Secret' security clearance could never be able to see," recalls McNair. But the gambit paid off, he says. On January 31, 2001, after a 12-year investigation and an $80 million trial, the former Libyan intelligence agent Abdel Basset Ali al-Megrahi was convicted of murder.

• • •

There is concern that if and when there is another terrorist attack on American soil, secrecy may well prove an impediment to an effective and timely response. A key question remains how federal authorities will deal with local first responders, be it state police, firefighters, or hazmat teams, who lack security clearances but who have a dire need for information that's been classified. After the March 11, 2004, terrorist bombing of a Madrid train in which 191 people were killed, the United

States conducted a training exercise where local responders grilled a senior U.S. official about what they should do in the event of a crisis. The official found himself reluctantly revealing classified information that was essential if they were to understand their role and response.

A few days later the official came to William Leonard at ISOO and wondered aloud whether he would fail his next polygraph test for having shared classified information. Leonard explained that a recent regulation allowed, indeed encouraged, federal officials to share vital information, even if classified, with those called upon to respond to a crisis. But the reservations the official experienced reflect a broader inhibition about sharing information with those who have not been cleared. "One of the many lessons of 9/11 is, yeah, you can get into a lot of trouble if you don't share information," said Leonard.

Leonard and others have made that pitch repeatedly in the years since 9/11, but the government has proved recalcitrant. In balancing the instinct for secrecy against the need for an informed state and local cadre of first responders and law enforcement officers, secrecy continues to prevail. In the spring of 2005, city officials in Portland, Oregon, pulled out of an FBI-run antiterrorism task force in no small measure because, they said, the FBI had refused to give either the mayor or the police chief the security clearances necessary to monitor the task force or stay apprised of ongoing investigations. A recent study by the National Academy of Sciences found that federal officials were so concerned over the vulnerabilities of nuclear power plants and their spent fuel that they withheld vital information from the very professionals who were in a position to shore up those vulnerabilities.

As an April 18, 2005, *Washington Post* editorial noted, "Nuclear regulators are hardly unusual in hoarding information so closely that they undermine the very security they seek to enhance. This is, rather, the norm in government."

A *New York Times* headline of March 5, 2005, raised the same fears: "Efforts to Hide Sensitive Data Pit 9/11 Concerns Against Safety." What followed was a litany of examples in which government's apprehension about terrorists learning America's vulnerabilities and soft points outweighed its willingness to fully inform those who might be asked to respond to a crisis. The federal government was then considering removing placards on the sides of railroad tank cars that identified hazardous cargo for the benefit of emergency response teams. Disaster plans and training programs around crisis scenarios involving nuclear plants, dams, pipelines, and other critical infrastructure have been curtailed by those whose concern for security puts collaboration and cooperation at risk.

Government websites containing information even remotely connected with America's infrastructure or hazardous waste are vetted and in some instances redacted, lest terrorists use them as blueprints. Freedom of Information Act requests are delayed, shunted off to the side, or effectively neutered by the imposition of huge fees for the cost of record searches and copying, even where there is a clear public interest in producing the information. Some FOIA requests have languished for a decade. Indiscriminate secrecy has become the reflexive response of those who are petrified of another terrorist attack.

•　　•　　•

But expansive secrecy does not only produce errors in judgment and a tendency toward paranoia. It is the enabling mechanism by which government controls the flow of information to the public and the world beyond. A government freed from fears of being contradicted by facts becomes emboldened to take liberties with the truth. It imagines that news is malleable and bendable to its own purposes. The power to withhold information is the power to create fictions that pass for fact. Protected by secrecy, government may dare to orchestrate and choreograph the news, to airbrush out disturbing images of defeats and setbacks, and ultimately, even to create entire narratives supportive of hapless policies and wayward agendas.

One of the most celebrated triumphs of the war on terror was the capture in March 2002 of Abu Zubaydah in Pakistan. The administration had portrayed Zubaydah as a top Al Qaeda operative and his capture was described as a body blow to bin Laden. But an investigative reporter, Ron Suskind, peeled back the cover of secrecy and discovered that Zubaydah was nothing of the sort, that he was judged to be mentally incompetent and utterly incapable of playing any significant role in Al Qaeda.

Under cover of secrecy, the Pentagon deftly transformed the sad plight of Jessica Lynch, a young American soldier taken prisoner by Iraqis in March 2003, into a stirring saga of heroic grit and guts. Prior to capture she was said to have emptied her M-16 into advancing enemy troops and to have suffered numerous gunshot and stabbing wounds. The truth, which emerged much later, was that her gun had jammed and her injuries were sustained from the crash of her vehicle. But until it was debunked, her story gained wide circulation and became a defining story line of the war in Iraq at a time when morale at home and on the front was sagging.

And it was secrecy that kept from the nation and from the parents of the former pro football player Pat Tillman the truth of his tragic death in Afghanistan in 2004. The Pentagon had said he was killed while barking orders to his fellow Army Rangers as he courageously attempted to storm a disputed hill. In fact, he was a casualty of friendly fire. Yet again, secrecy provided the cover for deception. That death is now under criminal investigation. Likewise, secrecy has concealed alleged U.S. atrocities, including rapes and murder, and has blocked outside scrutiny of investigations into prisoner abuse and civilian casualties, so-called collateral damage.

More secretive than ever, the CIA has nonetheless found time to assign one of its own former covert operatives, Chase Brandon, to act as liaison with Hollywood, part of a broader move to influence—some would say manipulate—the public image of the CIA. And the Agency gladly lent its support to a for-profit Washington museum called the Spy Museum that glorifies the spy business and, though short on the treachery and fiascos of the CIA, is chock full of the paraphernalia and exotica of espionage. It is headed by Peter Earnest, a former Agency covert operative and later one of its de facto spokesmen.

Secrecy also makes it easier for officials to define the political agenda and for battalions of government public information officers—"flaks" as they are known to the press—to stay on message. Not long after the invasion of Iraq, Washington began to sound like an echo chamber of the mantra "Freedom is on the march." Under a regime of secrecy, news is not so much made as managed. Presidential press conferences have become fewer and are less a matter of statecraft than stagecraft. Three years into his administration, George Bush had held only 11 solo press conferences, "fewer than almost any modern president." By that point, his father had held 71, and Bill Clinton, 38.

•   •   •

On February 10, 2006, the CIA's Porter Goss penned an impassioned op-ed piece for the *New York Times* lamenting how leaks had damaged U.S. security and attacking whistle-blowers and leakers who dared challenge America's smothering blanket of secrecy. "Loose Lips Sink Spies" was the article's headline.

That very day a news story appeared in the *Times* whose headline, cynics might suggest, could have been the same. The theme was also abuse of secrecy, though not at all the sort that Goss was railing against. The article pointed to potential chicanery at the highest levels of government. Vice President Dick Cheney's former chief of staff, I. Lewis Libby, it was said, had testified that his bosses had told him that they possessed the authority to declassify information pretty much at will. Libby's testimony emerged in a grand jury investigation into who leaked the name of Valerie Plame, a covert CIA operative, to the press. Her husband, a former U.S. ambassador, Joseph Wilson, had challenged Bush administration claims that Saddam had tried to buy uranium from Niger. (Libby did not suggest that the claimed declassification authority related specifically to the outing of Plame.)

The Plame affair offered an illustration of the sloppiness with which secrets are held and the pandemonium that can result from their exposure. The entire episode, fueled by partisan fervor, had begun with a concern that Iraq allegedly had weapons of mass destruction and ended with the outing of a covert operative who had risked her life to halt the spread of weapons of mass destruction. For months, the White House, Congress, and the press were distracted by a guessing game that focused on who the original source of the leak was. Some saw evidence of a cabal that implicated top White House officials intent upon discrediting a Bush critic. When one of the sources of the story finally was identified as former deputy secretary of state Richard Armitage, himself a critic of the Iraq war, the scandal seemed to deflate for a time. At Libby's trial it was rekindled with testimony that Bush political architect Karl Rove had allegedly confirmed that Plame was with the CIA. Mid-trial, it was still unclear the extent to which inadvertence rather than malice had played a role. The only thing certain was that secrecy itself was a casualty of the affair.

The day after Goss's rant against "loose lips," a news article appeared on the *Times*'s front page that may help explain why some government officials feel they cannot keep quiet. The CIA's own former national intelligence officer for the Middle East, Paul R. Pillar, belatedly charged that the Bush administration had "cherry-picked" intelligence on Iraq to justify going to war, a course of action already decided. Pillar thus joined a growing chorus of those who had been privy to intelligence, witnessed what they described as disturbing abuses of the process, and, only after years of silence, spoke out. He said he had observed firsthand the abuse of secrecy and how policy makers had simply ignored or discounted whatever did not comport with their preconceptions.

But selective attention to secret intelligence is not the only reason that secrecy is held in such low regard. Another part of the explanation may emerge from the stories of two faceless, nameless, and low-ranking officers cited in an obscure report of the U.S. military. Their names are deleted from the report, and so they are presented only in silhouette. One involved an Air Force officer who inadvertently commingled two classified messages with personal mail he was taking to a friend in Prudhoe Bay, Alaska. "Inadvertently" is the operative word, because it contrasts with the overt intention to commit espionage, even though the result of inattention may also be harmful. Still, it reflects the wider casualness with which secrets are handled and the desensitization that comes with being relentlessly deluged with papers stamped "Secret" and "Top Secret."

Upon arriving in Alaska, some 725 miles from his duty station, the report duly notes, the airman discovered the two messages stamped "Top Secret." He slipped them into his friend's desk drawer, apparently intending to bring them back with him upon his return to base. But he forgot about them and it was his friend's roommate who came upon the messages after the weekend and handed them to his supervisor. A military court subsequently judged that the officer had effectively lost the classified materials. He was sentenced to forty-three days of confinement, a reduction in rank to airman basic, and a bad-conduct discharge. So states the report, nearly verbatim.

The second case involved a Marine who inadvertently put some classified information in his desk and then some time later slipped it into a gym bag and later into a drawer in his garage, planning to destroy it at the duty station to which he was being transferred. But as luck would have it, the movers found it first and alerted military investigators. The court determined that the officer had "a continuing duty to safeguard" the information when he discovered he had it in his possession. For his lapse he was sentenced to ten months' confinement and a dishonorable discharge.

Now if the story ended here one might conclude that when it comes to secrecy America is a no-nonsense nation and that others across the spectrum might take heed and come to respect the system that safeguards vital secrets with robust enforcement. But that is not the lesson that is sent to these two young men, and to the hundreds of thousands of other men and women in the military who know of similar cases. Far from it.

No, instead of evenhanded justice, what they see are examples of high-profile hypocrisy and double standards that erode respect for the system and engender cynicism and resentment. In the fall of 2003, they saw Samuel "Sandy" Berger, who was national security advisor to President Clinton, in a secure room of the National Archives, not once, but twice, "inadvertently" (the word that Berger himself used to defend his actions) stuff highly classified documents into his jacket and take them with him as he filed past watchful National Archives employees, whose suspicions were already raised.

"An honest mistake," Berger initially claimed. He had been called to testify before the 9/11 Commission; the documents he took presumably shed light on what Clinton knew about Al Qaeda and what measures he had taken to thwart terrorism. And what did Berger do with the materials? He later shredded them with a pair of scissors at the downtown offices of his consulting firm.

And which stockade did Berger go to? If those within the ranks of the military expected the former national security advisor, one of the most savvy security experts in the nation, to be held to a higher standard, they were in for a letdown. Berger's lawyers and the Justice Department agreed on a $10,000 fine and no jail time. The presiding judge upped the fine to $50,000 and ordered 100 hours of community service. But still no jail time.

Berger is not alone in his ability to slip the bonds of strict accountability. Another senior Clinton security official, John M. Deutch, the director of the Central Intelligence Agency (the ultimate keeper of secrets) from May 1995 to July 1996, was discovered to have taken ultrasensitive classified materials home with him and placed them on his unsecured home computer, a computer with which he connected to the Internet. It may be assumed that Deutch knew better. His previous job was as deputy secretary of defense, the number two position at the Pentagon. Ironically, it may be precisely such experiences within the top rungs of the security apparatus that desensitize individuals like Deutch and Berger, exposed as they are to a ceaseless avalanche of classified documents, many of which are of dubious national security value but of some political sensitivity.

But instead of vigorously going after Deutch for taking home scores of secret documents and putting operations at risk, the Agency dragged its feet, according to a report of the CIA's own inspector general.

The price Deutch ultimately paid for so egregious a violation was a fine of $4,500. No jail, no prosecution. And then, the president of the United States, William Jefferson Clinton, issued Deutch a pardon, an action that disheartened many within the ranks of the intelligence community who saw the Deutch affair as an opportunity to send a message that those who put true secrets at risk will be held accountable. For a time after leaving the Agency, Deutch even retained his security clearance at the Department of Defense, which allowed him to work for defense contractors.

Even those responsible for enforcing secrecy have come to treat it with an insouciance that borders on the reckless. As attorney general of the United States, John Ashcroft, the highest law enforcement officer in the land, was sanctioned for twice violating a gag order imposed by a federal judge. He simply couldn't resist publicly praising a witness in a "sleeper cell" case against four Arab immigrants in Detroit. Never mind that the case later completely unraveled, the star witness was discredited, and the Justice Department admitted "prosecutorial misconduct" in withholding exculpatory evidence. In the end, it was not a case about terrorism at all, but about secrecy run amok. In March 2006, the federal prosecutor in the case, Richard G. Convertino, was indicted on charges of conspiracy and obstruction of justice for concealing evidence—a crime of secrecy.

Other senior officials, too, have been questioned for their handling of sensitive information. In 2000, Martin Indyk, ambassador to Israel, was recalled for allegedly mishandling classified materials. There were reports that Secretary of State Colin Powell may have revealed sensitive information predicated upon intelligence from secret "sources and methods." And, as every Washington reporter who has ever penned a story about intelligence or defense knows, scarcely a day passes when some member of Congress or a "senior White House official" or "informed Pentagon source" does not take it upon himself or herself to unilaterally disclose something of a classified nature to advance a personal or party agenda, or to bring to public light something unsettling. When the opposition to the party in power violates secrecy, it is branded a security breach; when a member of the party in power does this, it is an act of courage or wise discretion. When an enlisted man does it, it is called a crime.

Enlisted personnel could well be forgiven for believing that senior officials who oversee the secrecy establishment carry "get-out-of-jail-free" cards. For those in the ranks, the system is draconian.

Mary O. McCarthy, a seasoned veteran of the CIA, found out the hard way. In April 2006, the CIA fired her as it hunted down the source of a leak to the *Washington Post* that disclosed the existence in Eastern Europe of a network of secret prisons where alleged Al Qaeda operatives were being held. McCarthy was just ten days shy of a planned retirement. (Through her attorney, McCarthy denied being the source for the *Post*'s story.)

Small wonder that more than a few presidential appointees and members of Congress of both parties have come to believe that strict adherence to secrecy is meant only for their subordinates and staff. Those in government's highest echelons imagine they were not meant to be bound by a system with so many foibles and inconsistencies. They rationalize their actions, substituting personal standards for the formal determinations of the establishments they serve and manage. They apply a highly discretionary "no harm, no foul" rule that circumvents the cumbersome and annoying restrictions of classification. Something may be *technically* classified, but, "just between us," they can see it's not a "serious" secret. With such reasoning, they justify taking liberties with secrecy, often for the sake of convenience or career advancement.

That "us" in "just between us" has a remarkable capacity to migrate, to leach into the groundwater of every agency and department in government, and jump the barrier to defense contractors and the entire community of secret bearers. And while junior officers do penance for simple negligence, senior officials guilty of calculated and deliberate violations disregard strictures they swore to uphold.

True, some act out of principle and risk their careers and reputations to bring to light corruption, incompetence, and chicanery. A system of secrecy so bankrupt that it offers safe refuge to those who abuse the public trust, lie, and manipulate invites leaks of the whistle-blowing kind. To those who have demonstrated the courage to expose evils, who made the public aware of Watergate, the Pentagon Papers, the cover-ups of civilian massacres, sweetheart deals, and bribes, the nation is beholden. But the danger is that one man's patriotism is another's betrayal, and leaks, however curative in the short term, are no substitute for transparency and accountability. A nation cannot bank on extraordinary and random acts of individual courage to purge itself of the toxins of systemic secrecy and suppression any more than it can allow that system to degenerate into one dependent upon voluntary compliance, allowing dissenters and opponents to ignore the edicts of secrecy whenever it suits them.

"Discipline has broken down dramatically," concedes James Pavitt, until recently the CIA's head of clandestine operations. In his views on secrecy, like many, he attempts to navigate a complex divide. First and foremost, he believes that secrecy must be honored, but he also remembers what then CIA director William Colby once told him, that there were two kinds of secrets. "There are good secrets," Colby counseled, "secrets which we must keep, and there are bad secrets, which by being kept simply make doing our work more difficult." Says Pavitt, "Our society has become a throwaway society in some ways. We are also a society that believes in certain instances you can throw away secrets and that discipline, perhaps because of the multitude [of secrets], has evolved."

"Evolved" is Pavitt's charitable way of describing what he sees as a dramatic deterioration of discipline. Even in a "throwaway society," he argues, secrets must be kept. He and others recognize that nothing is more corrosive of discipline than the "do-as-I-say-not-as-I-do" mind-set. Cumulatively, double standards take a severe toll, undermining faith in the system and engendering cynicism.

What passes for sloppiness or lack of discipline in the handling of secrets may reflect something deeper—a smoldering resentment, even what psychologists call a "passive-aggressive" response. Unable to assail the system frontally, bureaucrats and subordinates constantly exposed to their superiors taking liberties with secrets may vent their frustration and anger obliquely. Accounts of mishandled secrets are legion: investigators poring through the garbage of a U.S. military base in

Japan retrieved classified reports among the refuse; laptops with highly classified materials have gone missing at the State Department; a briefcase containing classified documents is forgotten on a car top; sensitive documents are left in a file cabinet that turns up at a correctional facility.

At the other extreme, hypervigilance has also caused its share of chaos within the secrecy community. No place has been more discombobulated than the Los Alamos, New Mexico, weapons lab. In the summer of 2004, the entire weapons lab was shut down, idling some 12,000 workers, while investigators searched for two missing disks containing classified information.

(Historically, the United States has always had a hard time imposing the culture of secrecy upon the culture of science. In January 1953, famed Princeton physicist John Wheeler left a sheaf of top secret documents related to the building of the H-bomb on a train traveling between New York and Washington. Eisenhower was irate and the FBI literally took the Pullman car off the tracks and interviewed all the passengers. The documents were never found. Some have speculated that on that same train were passengers on their way to Washington to protest on behalf of Julius and Ethel Rosenberg, who were under a death sentence for nuclear espionage.)

•   •   •

In the past, those who signed on to secrecy signed away their right to profit from it. At Virginia's Mt. Weather, the once-secret underground mountain retreat for the president and cabinet in case of a national emergency, a sign read "What you hear here remains here." How old-fashioned that sort of mind-set now seems.

Today, the culture of secrecy is riddled with inconsistency and contradiction. In the winter of 2004 the CIA forbade a former covert operative, Valerie Plame, from publishing an op-ed article she had written. Numerous other CIA officers, too, have been denied the opportunity to express their opinions in print, even long after their employment with the Agency has ended. Books, op-ed articles, and speeches by former Agency employees are subject to vetting, sometimes with a vengeance. As director Central Intelligence, George Tenet, like his predecessors, held sway over an agency that pressured widows and their children not to speak of those they had lost in service to the CIA, shackling them for decades to cover stories and denying them access to the facts behind their loved ones' deaths. Proclaiming the sanctity of secrecy and security, and the sensitivity of "sources and methods," Tenet's CIA routinely declined interviews and was tight-lipped throughout his tenure.

But for those who, like Tenet, sit atop the secrecy pyramid, the rule of silence appears far more flexible than for those who serve them. Once out of government, officials can and do reap astronomical fees for dangling the promise of rarefied knowledge before the public in the form of lucrative book contracts. The license granted to enrich oneself, once one has departed the marbled halls of secrecy, is now a routine sinecure of high office.

After resigning from the Agency in July 2004, Tenet wasted little time before going on the lucrative speakers' circuit. He signed with the Washington Speakers Bureau (WSB), joining Clinton's national security advisor, Samuel "Sandy" Berger, and former CIA directors R. James Woolsey and Robert Gates. Their fees are not disclosed on the WSB website. That information came in response to an e-mail I sent wearing my other hat, that of a university professor and director of a lecture series. Gates demands $20,000 per talk plus a first-class plane ticket; Berger, $25,000, plus a first-class ticket; Woolsey, $42,500 plus a first-class ticket; and Tenet, a whopping $50,000, plus two first-class tickets. WSB says that for that price, Tenet will speak on any number of topics, including U.S. security and how to lead an organization in transition. Tenet is described as a kind of corporate turnaround artist—not exactly the way he may be remembered either by his peers or by history.

In 2005, the CIA's own inspector general, John L. Helgerson, concluded that Tenet and other top Agency officials had bungled counterterrorism matters prior to 9/11. And it is unlikely that Sen. Richard Shelby, an Alabama Republican and former chair of the Senate Intelligence Committee, will be promoting Tenet's lectures anytime soon. "There were more failures of intelligence on his watch as director of the CIA than any other in our history," Shelby has said. It was Tenet who reportedly declared the evidence for Iraqi WMDs a "slam dunk," and whose service (or was it his silence?) was rewarded by Bush with a Presidential Medal of Freedom.

In December 2004, five months after resigning, Tenet inked a lofty $4 million book deal for himself with Crown Books (he later moved to HarperCollins). On January 18, 2006, HarperCollins announced the deal:

"Now, for the first time, readers will be able to find out what happened during the most challenging times in recent history from the man who arguably knows best. Candid and compelling, *At the Center of the Storm* will not only trace Tenet's life at the CIA but also illuminate the actions of national leaders during times of crisis and war."

Only in a regime of secrecy would citizens be asked to purchase a belated glimpse of what any self-respecting democracy should provide for free, and in a timely manner: information about critical national security issues, the factual basis for key decisions, candor from its leaders. Too late for purposes of assigning accountability, Tenet's book and others by former officials with access to secrets are like the light of stars—they arrive years after the events they describe have moved on.

3

Case Study: A Secret Hell

In October 1997, I got one of the strangest calls of my life. A man named David Day telephoned from California to tell me he had something he had to get off his chest. His story began in 1961, in Germany. It was August, the month the Berlin Wall went up, a time of superhigh tension between East and West. Day said he was then with the Administrative Survey Detachment, a civilian cover for his work in counterespionage with the Army's Counter Intelligence Corps, or CIC. He was, he said, assigned to the Sixty-sixth CIC Detachment, based in Stuttgart. Under the cover name Dieter Dorn, he was running Eastern European agents behind the Iron Curtain. One of these, he said, was a Hungarian named Lurk Havac. The other was Erik Bromski, from Prague. Day said he had come to respect both men and to be fond of their wives and young children.

One morning, Day recalls, his superior, a Colonel Buto, summoned him to his office and informed him that both men had been "doubled," that is, they secretly worked for the other side, the Communists. "Take them to the East Zone and make sure they don't come back," Day recalls the colonel telling him in a none-too-subtle order to execute the men. Day said he protested, but in the end he relented.

Soon after, on September 18, 1961, he persuaded Havac and Bromski

to take a drive with him in his black Opel sedan to Furth im Wald, a remote spot along the German-Czech border, telling them it was the
setting-off point for yet another undercover assignment. Under his coat,
in a shoulder strap, hung his .38. When they reached the forest, Havac
and Bromski took the lead, believing they were to be met by a guide who
would, as before, take them across the border. But when the two were
only steps in front of Day, he said, he took out his pistol and shot them
both in the head. He then emptied their pockets of wallets and keys, and
with a knife cut out the labels from their clothes, making it more difficult
to identify them. He left the bodies to rot in the forest.

On the way back to headquarters, Day threw up and could barely
keep his hands on the wheel. When he told his superiors that the job was
done, they saw in him a man out of control. Then they acknowledged
that there had been little hard evidence that the two men he had just
killed had been compromised—that they were double agents. His handlers' advice to him was to take a couple of weeks off—and get drunk.

Get drunk he did. That day and the days after and the days after that.
David Day said that the murderous incident of September 18, 1961, reduced him to a chronic alcoholic. "I really didn't want to live anymore
but I was too much of a coward to do anything about it," he told me.
"Looking back at it, I was so paranoid, it was unreal. The alcohol just re-
inforced the paranoia. One year I moved eighteen times."

Not until 30 years later did he begin to see a psychiatrist, who recognized the symptoms of posttraumatic stress disorder and to whom he
could confide his dark secret. Eventually, the psychiatrist persuaded him
that because the actions he had taken were under government order, the
government owed him something for all that he had endured as a result
of it: the years of therapy, the nightmares and flashbacks, the alcoholism,
the depression. His life lay in ruins—five marriages, no children, an endless string of nowhere jobs as a bartender, security guard, shoe salesman,
insurance agent, clerk, private investigator, auditor, soap salesman.
Until near the very end, he had not been able to hold down a job or a
marriage.

But convincing the government that it owed him anything would not
be easy. Thirty-six years had passed, and besides, the whole matter was
so sensitive—two cold-blooded murders of civilians in peacetime. The
Veterans Administration turned him down. Eventually, in 1995, he filed
a claim with the Department of Labor, but despite repeated efforts by the

government and by Day, no records could be found to support his claim of having worked for the CIC, much less of having been ordered to commit murder. It was as if he had never existed.

The investigation was further hampered by its extreme sensitivity. Day's case was itself classified, the records stored in a safe in a special room-sized vault. His claims examiner, William Israel, who specialized in security-sensitive cases, wrote: "He had a very unfortunate work experience that undoubtedly led to his illness. . . . Security considerations as well as raw embarrassment may make it difficult to verify the alleged incident actually occurred. Even though we all know such brutal incidents do occur, proving a specific incident occurred can be next to impossible."

Perhaps it was in part some vain quest for evidence that led him to return to Furth im Wald in June 1995 and walk the same forest path where the murders had occurred. But for Day it was also an effort to find peace, to silence the ghosts and the self-recriminations that had dogged him for so many years.

Just when it seemed all records had vanished, some scant few documents were uncovered and confirmations of service found within Defense Intelligence Agency records. With the support of those records and Day's psychiatrist, who was convinced of the veracity of Day's account, the U.S. Department of Labor's three-person Employees' Compensation Appeals Board ruled that Day's story was authentic and he deserved compensation. That was in February 1998. Two months later, Day received a U.S. Treasury check in the amount of $235,746.04, plus he gets another $1,700 a month. To this day, the records of the whole matter remain sealed in a government vault—but what David Day sought from the court was more than money. Call it absolution.

David Day's tortured life ended three years later, on December 14, 2001, when he was felled by a heart attack. The contributing cause of that attack, wrote the attending physician, was stress, the sort that comes from posttraumatic stress disorder. It is said that he died sober and with a measure of peace.

But there is a footnote to the story. My inquiries into the deaths of the two agents David Day said he had shot produced nothing. I could find no record of the alleged victims' lives or deaths. And it should be noted that even the Labor Department panel conceded that there was no documentary evidence of such an incident (which would hardly be surprising under the circumstances). Veterans of the CIC say Day's story is preposterous, that they never received or heard of this kind of order being given, that they doubted any story of assassination. And those who knew Colonel Buto say he went by the book and would never have given such an order.

Could a man like David Day, steeped in the ways of counterespionage and marinated in too much drink and self-pity, have invented such an elaborate tale? To what end? To explain a lifetime frittered away? It would hardly be the first time that secrecy took on a life of its own, the cover story consuming the man, blurring the boundaries between life and imagination. Such is the power of secrecy that it can obscure a person's past not only from others but from one's self.

National Insecurity, Part II: Secrecy Means Not Having to Say You're Sorry

> Left to its own, the system will likely corrode and lose its overall effectiveness, placing in jeopardy all information cloaked in its protective measures. This, of course, has more than theoretical consequences in time of war; especially with respect to the resulting damage to the common defense should such information be subject to unauthorized disclosure. . . . Unfortunately, I have lately found some to use war as an excuse to disregard the basics of the security classification system.
>
> —J. William Leonard, director, Information Security Oversight Office, June 15, 2004

Carved into an interior wall of CIA headquarters in Langley, Virginia, is the passage from John 8:32: "And ye shall know the truth, and the truth shall make you free." The irony that such a passage should appear in the antechamber of an institution consecrated to deception and enveloped in secrecy seems lost on many who walk past. The words seem all the more dissonant when one listens to the message of Porter Goss to students of Ohio's Tiffin University at their May 6, 2006, graduation, which he delivered just one day after resigning as director of the CIA: "If this were a graduating class of CIA case officers," he told them, "my advice would be short and to the point: Admit nothing, deny everything, and make counteraccusations." Only within the realm of secrecy could such candor and such contempt for truth coexist.

Goss's not-quite-joking words advocating denial, deceit, and calculated misdirection, not those of scripture, have set the course of the Agency in recent years, and not just with reference to enemies abroad. At home as well, secrecy has concealed from the American people a multitude of sins and errors, allowing feckless policy makers to escape accountability and to stumble from one blunder to the next. The landscape is littered with misjudgments and transgressions that remain hidden in secrecy or blanketed by denial.

In August 1998, terrorists attacked U.S. embassies in Tanzania and Kenya. Thirteen days later, on August 20, the U.S. retaliated, launching cruise missiles against suspected terrorist training camps in Afghanistan and the Al Shifa pharmaceutical plant in Sudan's capital, Khartoum. The CIA said that soil samples from the Sudan site indicated that the pharmaceutical plant was actually engaged in the manufacture of deadly chemical weapons, specifically VX nerve gas. The nighttime strike left a night watchman dead, a number of people injured, and the factory reduced to rubble.

"Our forces also attacked a factory in Sudan associated with the bin Laden network," President Clinton told the nation. "The factory was involved in the production of materials for chemical weapons." There was no hint of doubt. It was, in the lingo of a successor administration, a "slam dunk." A credulous nation accepted Clinton's words and generally applauded the swift response.

As might be expected, the Sudanese government protested, branding the hit an unprovoked attack on a sovereign nation. It was also, claimed the Sudanese, a tragic error. The factory, they said, was exactly what it purported to be—a maker of drugs—and nothing more. The CIA and White House dismissed Sudan's claims, insisting the plant had been engaged in making chemical weapons.

But inside the CIA's analytical branch, the National Security Agency, and the State Department's Bureau of Intelligence, doubts about the sufficiency of the evidence had surfaced even before the attack. A veteran senior CIA officer who took part in the analysis of the Al Shifa intelligence recalls George Tenet, the CIA director, telling Clinton officials that there were doubts. "At the time that it was presented as a candidate [for bombing] it was presented with caveats," he recalls. "It was not presented with any absolute certainty. The director was quite clear with policy-makers saying 'we don't know everything about this.' The policy guys decided to accept the risk [of being wrong] given the possibility that Al Qaeda could carry out some kind of chemical-based attack. They didn't want to take that kind of risk."

The decision was reportedly spirited through with great urgency and little input from experts in either chemical weapons or terrorism. But in the immediate aftermath, the evidence seemed to soften. Analysts feared that the strike had been a gross error. Six weeks after the attack, when the decision increasingly appeared to have been based on shaky evidence, government officials, trying to fend off challenges at home and abroad, leaked assertions that ownership of the plant was tied to Al Qaeda.

Meanwhile, anti-American protests erupted in Sudan, targeting the U.S. embassy. Sudan appealed to the United Nations. Press reports raised doubts about the attack. Through it all, the White House, the State Department, and the Agency stood firm. (Remember Goss's advice: "Admit nothing, deny everything, and make counteraccusations.") An effort within the State Department to draft a report critical of the decision was killed. So too were efforts to investigate the matter.

A year later, Tenet told an audience at his alma mater, Georgetown University, that the factory had indeed made nerve gas, that it had been a "good target."

That hardly reflected the consensus within the CIA. "Everyone assumes it was an innocent plant," concedes a former Agency analyst. "In retrospect, it may have been." But he and others are not permitted to speak publicly of the decision. To this day, a credulous American public has a wealth of official assurances defending the attack on Al Shifa.

But six months after the attack, a prominent American chemist hired by the plant's Saudi owner, Salih Idris, said no trace of VX precursors in the soil were to be found at the site. And Kroll Associates, an international investigative firm also hired by the owner, reported that it found no link whatsoever between the owner and bin Laden. Meanwhile, Western engineers familiar with the plant say it had little or no security and no areas that were off-limits to visitors; it was exclusively engaged in making antibiotics, antimalaria, and antidiarrhea medicines, as well as veterinary medicines. On May 3, 1999, nine months after the attack, the press reported that the United States quietly and without elaboration released some $24 million from frozen bank accounts to the owner of the plant. Many within the administration saw that as a de facto admission of error, an acknowledgment that the last justification for bombing the plant—the alleged link with bin Laden—had simply dissolved.

Before and since, suppression of the truth in the name of secrecy and national security has undermined both secrecy and security. On the narrowest front, the attack on Sudan further alienated a region already hostile to the United States and provided a bonanza for terrorist recruiters in the region. Imagine the propaganda value of having the United States bomb a pharmaceutical plant that made medicines for the Third World. By one account, which appeared in the *Boston Globe*, the decimation of the plant left thousands of Sudanese without access to much-needed medicines.

Cumulatively the use of secrecy to conceal errors has had an even more insidious impact at home than abroad. It has emboldened those who operate in secret to believe that they can escape accountability and the consequences of foreign adventurism. It breeds sloppiness, a higher tolerance for risk, and a lowering of evidentiary thresholds before taking military or paramilitary action. In an environment where secrecy immunizes decision makers, policy is more likely to drive intelligence, rather than the reverse. The CIA may have gotten away with one mistake in Sudan, but in the realm of national security and intelligence, excessive secrecy blunts the sort of external review process that produces internal reform. Such secrecy perpetuates systemic weaknesses, inviting new catastrophic blunders. Disclosure and confession are not merely good for the soul; they are essential to institutional maturation and integrity. Deeply embedded flaws, left buried, invariably return with a vengeance—and so they did.

The strike on Al Shifa was a response to a terrorist strike by Osama bin Laden. It was justified by two doctrines, one time-honored, one more novel. The first was retaliation, the other, preemption. The linkage between the two was predicated upon the perception—never borne out by reality—that a weapon of mass destruction (a chemical agent) was in the hands of a third country (Sudan) that might provide it to a terrorist (Al Qaeda and bin Laden).

It was the perfect template for the thinking that would drive decision makers and war-planners five years later, but on a far more massive scale. The invasion of Iraq was part retaliation (for 9/11), part preemptive strike, aimed at stripping a third country of weapons of mass destruction (again, *phantom* weapons of mass destruction based on faulty intelligence) that an administration feared could fall into bin Laden's hands.

It may well be that even the most thorough and open investigation of that earlier attack at Al Shifa would not have averted the subsequent invasion of Iraq or deterred those already determined to topple Saddam Hussein. But at the very least, an open investigation would have produced a measure of moral and political accountability. Beyond this, it likely would have provoked debate and discussion about the emerging criteria for decision making in a national-security environment defined by terrorism. Optimally, it would have provided an early and much-needed test of Americans' tolerance for the new and evolving calculus of risk that would later be dubbed "the one percent doctrine." As described in Ron Suskind's book by that title, Defense Secretary Dick Cheney concluded that if there was even a 1 percent chance that a threat from Al Qaeda was real, it would be treated as a certainty and would warrant an appropriate response. That doctrine undermined reliance on intelligence analysis and redefined risk assessment, and, as Al Shifa might have revealed, this attitude was not without precedent.

Between Al Shifa and Iraq there was yet another casualty of obsessive secrecy that would take a toll on American credibility and standing in the world. Just nine months after the Sudan attack, the Agency selected its only target of the Yugoslav air war, a building the CIA confidently identified as the federal supply and procurement center. On May 7, 1999, based on the CIA's targeting selection, three joint defense air munition bombs were dropped precisely on the target the CIA had selected.

It was a perfect hit. The only problem was that the target had been misidentified by the Agency. They had hit the Chinese embassy. Had the CIA checked with its own people who were familiar with Belgrade (not to mention used a current rather than outdated map), the humiliation and tragedy might have been averted. In no small measure, the CIA's fixation with secrecy (its failure to avail itself of experts, even those within its own ranks), combined with a rush to play a role in the air war, kept it from ascertaining the most obvious of facts: that the Chinese embassy had been in that location for three years, that architecturally it in no way resembled a warehouse, and that it flew the flag of China, still reported to be fluttering after the bombings. In the days prior to the bombing an unidentified officer repeatedly tried to alert officials to the possibility of a major target miscalculation, even calling NATO head-quarters in Naples. His warnings went unheeded.

Three Chinese civilians were killed in the attack. Twenty others were injured. The blunder unleashed a furor of anti-Americanism in China and set back U.S.-Chinese relations. So gross was the error that to this day, many Chinese are convinced the bombing was deliberate. And, un-like Al Shifa, the error was on such a grand scale as to be irrefutable. The Agency did not even attempt to suppress the truth. One low-ranking of-ficer was fired, and six others were reprimanded. No senior official was called to account.

Even before Al Shifa and Belgrade, there was Al Firdus, a section of Baghdad. During the first Gulf War, on the night of February 13, 1991, based on U.S. intelligence, two F-117s bombed what was supposed to be the Al Firdus command bunker. It turned out to be an air raid shelter filled with women and children, some 300 of whom were killed. The CIA wrote off the entire episode as one more example of a cynical ploy by Saddam to use a former command bunker to shelter civilians, part of the human-shield strategy. Concealed by secrecy, the CIA was not forced to answer the tougher questions about how its intelligence-gathering and analysis, based largely on electronic surveillance, could have been so wrong about the target, widely known to Baghdad's citizens and at least one American reporter, CNN's Peter Arnett, as a shelter for civilians. Whatever the explanation, the blunder produced one of the most dam-aging barrages of anti-American propaganda in the entire war.

A disturbing pattern emerges: The intelligence community, military planners, and the White House use secrecy to bury the causes of egre-gious miscalculations and errant policies or to avoid altogether asking the tough questions about what produced them. Such an abuse of se-crecy compromises the entire decision-making process by allowing pol-icy makers and the units they manage to know in advance that they will be able to sidestep questions of accountability, and, absent such inquiry, at least salvage their own reputations and careers. Secrecy creates an un-natural divide between the outcome of a mission and the persons who set such events in motion, making the decision maker less a stakeholder than a disinterested third party. That realization lowers the bar on the quality of decision making across the spectrum of government. Like a general indemnification clause, it creates a higher tolerance to risk and breeds audacity. And it virtually ensures that organizations will not learn from their mistakes, but rather will repeat them again and again.

If history teaches us anything, it is that too much secrecy and too little oversight can produce some extreme schemes. Forty years ago, the CIA sought to poison the Congo's Patrice Lumumba with a toxin inserted into a tube of toothpaste. Others secretly administered LSD to their CIA colleagues, to devastating, even deadly, effect.

Military and political leaders routinely rail against the dangers of loose lips and suggest that secrecy is the bulwark of our defense against foreign perils. But there is a long and troubling history of secrecy providing the cover for manufactured provocations. The 1898 sinking of the U.S.S. *Maine*, a provocation that led to war with Spain, comes to mind. So too does the 1964 Gulf of Tonkin incident in which North Vietnamese boats were said to have attacked an American naval vessel, a claim later debunked. The trumped-up incident provided the pretext for the Vietnam War, which cost more than 58,000 American lives.

At the height of the Cold War, secrecy gave cover to a series of frightening scenarios and trumped-up provocations that have only recently come to light. In 1962, the Joint Chiefs of Staff, the military's most senior body, were incensed over the failed 1961 Bay of Pigs invasion, which had been intended to topple Fidel Castro but which had instead produced a mortifying defeat. The nation's senior military planners came up with a plan called Operation Northwoods, a top secret scheme to create a series of pretexts to justify outright war with Castro. The document, dated March 13, 1962, was signed by L. L. Limnitzer, chairman of the Joint Chiefs of Staff. It listed a series of options, including the staging of a bogus Cuban infiltration of the U.S. base at Guantánamo, the capture of false saboteurs inside the compound, the choreographing of riots at the main gate, the blowing up of ammunition, setting fires, destroying aircraft, and the "lobbing of mortar shells from outside the base into base."

But that was just for starters. " 'A Remember the Maine incident' could be arranged in several forms: We could blow up a US ship in Guantanamo Bay and blame Cuba," the memo went on. Other ideas: Create a terror campaign in Miami and Washington and make it look like it was Castro's doing; and then there was this one: "We could sink a boatload of Cubans en route to Florida (real or imagined.)"

Ultimately, the schemes were overruled, but not before they garnered support among senior military planners.

Anyone who imagines that today's government is not so bold as to consider such measures would do well to examine what transpired in a January 31, 2003, meeting in the Oval Office between George Bush and British prime minister Tony Blair. According to a secret five-page memo describing that meeting and circulated among top British officials, Bush is said to have mulled over potential provocation scenarios to justify a war with Iraq, even if no unconventional weapons were found in Iraq prior to the onset of hostilities. Bush reportedly floated the idea of painting a surveillance plane in United Nations colors and flying it over Iraq in the hope that it would draw Iraqi fire. The memo surfaced three years after the war began.

Ordinarily it would be difficult to imagine 35-year-old Veronica Bowers, a missionary, and her seven-month-old daughter, Charity, as targets of a foreign military, but in April 2001 they became just that. In the skies over Peru, the jet carrying Bowers, her husband, James, Charity, their young son, Cory, and the pilot, Kevin Donaldson, came under scrutiny of a CIA surveillance plane on an antidrug sweep, part of a secret operation known as the Air Bridge Denial Program. The Agency plane misidentified the Bowerses' plane as a drug target and alerted the Peruvian Air Force, which promptly shot it down. Bowers's husband, Cory, and the pilot survived to tell the tale, making it impossible to consider covering up the incident. So the CIA paid out some $8 million to the families of the victims.

Some members of Congress suspected that at least four officers of the CIA lied to them about the matter. Some were concerned that the program lacked vital safeguards and had become lax to the point of recklessness. In February 2005, after three years of a secret U.S. Justice Department criminal investigation, the decision was made to drop the inquiry altogether. Secrecy prevailed.

Whether the investigation had ever been anything more than a sop to nettlesome lawmakers is unknown—the whole investigation was itself wrapped in secrecy, as was all the evidence. But for the CIA, the stakes had always been higher than the culpability of the individual officers involved. At issue was whether the Agency would be held accountable, and what message that would send through the ranks of the clandestine service. At Langley, the dropping of the investigation in February 2005 brought a collective sigh of relief.

That same month the CIA remained unbowed by a series of other disturbing disclosures—its role in the Abu Ghraib scandal, its failure to share vital intelligence leading up to 9/11, its erroneous read on WMDs in Iraq, its inability to track down bin Laden, its placing prisoners into the hands of nations known to practice torture. At Langley, the death of a missionary and her daughter, while seen as a human tragedy, had posed the threat of future wider inquiries and possible constraints.

The irony is that the CIA's defense, post-9/11, is that it was already hamstrung by too many constraints, too much oversight, and too many questions asked. What was needed was to let the Agency off the leash— to transform what its former director Porter Goss disparagingly called its "risk-averse culture." Had the Agency been less risk-averse they might have penetrated more terrorist cells and thwarted more attacks, Goss has suggested.

But what Goss and his allies call "risk aversion" simply reflected the inhibitions and constraints that naturally come with the awareness that Agency actions may one day be exposed to public light, that the Agency may be held accountable in the fullness of time. The only way to overcome that kind of "risk aversion" is to further deepen secrecy and remove the prospect of eventual accountability. The decision by the Justice Department not to pursue the Bowers investigation may well have been regarded at Langley as a green light, a reassuring gesture that their work is too important to be constrained by such bothersome inquiries in the future.

But a case could be made that many of the Agency's most spectacular failings are due not to risk aversion but rather to a license that borders on carte blanche. Operating in democracy's shadows, the CIA's only true constraints and the public's only true access to its actions is congressional oversight, and that has been all but shut down in recent years. The intelligence committees nearly always meet behind closed doors and issue no substantive press releases.

CIA director George Tenet had little to fear from the Senate Select Committee on Intelligence. After all, prior to joining the CIA, Tenet had himself been a senior staffer on the committee. They treated him with fondness and deference. Nor did he have anything to worry about from the House Select Committee on Intelligence. It was headed by Rep. Porter Goss, a Florida congressman who was himself a former CIA operative in Latin America. An unabashed cheerleader of the CIA, Goss could not do enough to promote Agency interests and to defend it. As if that were not enough, he not so secretly aspired to become its next director—which is exactly what he did. With the same party at the helm of the White House and both the House and Senate oversight committees, the CIA could rest assured that its secrets were safe and that there would be little interference or meddling, and it would have to share even less with the public.

One need look no further than the elusive weapons of mass destruction in Iraq, which justified the U.S. invasion. The CIA's George Tenet grimly sat behind the right shoulder of Secretary of State Colin Powell as Powell made his impassioned case to the United Nations Security Council on February 5, 2003, offering up what he said was proof positive of the existence of Iraq's deadly arsenal. It was a matter too urgent to be ignored any longer, asserted Powell.

Even after no WMDs were found, Tenet, his own role still safely veiled in secrecy, was unrepentant and indignant at suggestions that he had somehow been complicit in any rush to war, or remiss in failing to resist. He picked a friendly Georgetown audience to defend himself to, declaring that he had never used the word "imminent" to describe the threat posed by Saddam. Such fine parsing of words was more befitting a schoolboy who gives his promise with fingers crossed behind his back than a senior official upon whose advice Americans and foreigners alike were soon to be placed in harm's way. Could anyone in the United Nations that day have interpreted Tenet's presence and Powell's words as anything but an urgent appeal to save the world from the specter of WMDs in Saddam's hands or those of Al Qaeda?

Recently, the CIA rebuffed a suit by the American Civil Liberties Union that sought to force the Agency to disclose documents related to prisoner interrogation and abuse. The Agency refused to either confirm or deny the existence of such documents. In the secrecy trade, such a response is called "glomarization." The term was coined after the salvage ship *Glomar Explorer*, which was used in June 1974 to secretly attempt to raise a sunken Soviet submarine from the floor of the Pacific Ocean in a joint operation involving the CIA and the reclusive billionaire Howard Hughes. To be "glomarized" is to be left totally in the dark. It is a testament to the pervasiveness of today's culture of secrecy that such a word should find its way into the working vocabulary of Washington. These days it is used not merely in reference to specific operations but to entire policies and programs, including those involving domestic surveillance.

•　　•　　•

By now virtually every American is familiar with the humiliating treatment of prisoners at Abu Ghraib prison in Iraq and of the deplorable conditions at the detention center at Guantánamo Bay. But for years, secrecy allowed Americans to close their eyes to prisoner abuse and deprivation, even if just beyond our shores. Secrecy plays an essential role in creating the moral fiction that suggests that what goes on outside America, albeit at the express bidding of the U.S. government, is somehow geographically disconnected from us. It is part of the myth of moral extraterritoriality—that we can distance ourselves from the direct consequences of our own actions. It is as if the arm were to blame the hand and the hand to blame the finger. That is the construct that allows many Americans to live with knowledge of what is euphemistically called "extraordinary renditions." The government's secrecy provides the gossamer-thin veil that allows much of the nation to disavow knowledge of the practice of handing prisoners over to regimes notorious for torture and abuse.

For a true definition of "rendition," that well-scrubbed word, consider the case of Maher Arar, a 34-year-old Canadian citizen, a telecommunications engineer, a husband and father of two. On September 26, 2002, he was in transit through New York City, on his way home from a family vacation in Tunisia. But at New York's John F. Kennedy Airport, he was abducted by U.S. officials, interrogated, and told that secret intelligence indicated he had been associated with Al Qaeda; he was to be deported to Syria.

Cuffed and in leg irons, he was placed by American officials on a private jet bound for Jordan and from there was driven to Syria. The idea was to have the Syrians soften Arar up a bit, find out what he knew, and then share it with U.S. intelligence officials. In Syria, interrogators are not hamstrung by Miranda rights, habeas corpus, or prohibitions on "cruel and unusual punishment."

The Syrians are said to have thrown Arar into a dark, rat-infested cell no bigger than a grave. They beat him and tortured him, striking him with a thick black electric cable. Interrogations lasted eighteen hours. In terror, he urinated on himself. Months after the ordeal began he was still in the same clothes he had been wearing in New York. He had not seen the sun in half a year. He had lost forty pounds.

Finally, he gave his captors what they wanted—a meaningless confession. A year later, in October 2003, finally convinced that Arar knew nothing, Syria released him and allowed him to return to Canada. "I know that the only way I will ever be able to move on in my life and have a future," he has said, "is if I can find out why this happened to me."

Today, haunted by the horrors of his Syrian captivity, he is suing the U.S. government. Like so many others who have endured abduction and abuse, he has never been charged with a crime. But the U.S. government will not apologize to Arar for his Kafkaesque ordeal. In fact, it is challenging the court's right to even hear the case because it would force the government to reveal what it calls "state secrets." The number of people who have endured "extraordinary renditions" and their fates is also a state secret. What is known is that sufficient numbers of individuals have been shunted about and sidetracked through rendition to support a fleet of U.S.-operated aircraft whose comings and goings have been observed and documented across Europe and the Middle East.

But the real state secret, if there is one, is that coerced confessions rarely produce credible intelligence. Experienced interrogators know that prisoners will say anything to end the pain or mental anguish of torture. Consider the case of Ibn al-Sheikh al-Libi, allegedly a terrorist who oversaw a training camp in Afghanistan. Following his capture in Pakistan, it is said, he was "renditioned" to Egypt and there gave bogus information about Iraqi chemical weapons. Later, that information was obliquely cited by Secretary of State Colin Powell in his appeal to the U.N. as evidence of Iraq's WMDs. No doubt, America's enemies saw perverse justice in the notion that intelligence extracted in contravention of civilized norms should be a curse upon those who relied upon it, drawing them into a costly and protracted war.

•   •   •

It is not only foreigners who have become victims of secrecy and inchoate suspicions. A growing number of loyal and hardworking Americans have also been swept up by a prosecutorial system whose secrecy has masked deep-rooted and systemic flaws that produce one injustice after another. The pattern is clear: insubstantial cases move forward and even when they collapse for lack of evidence, the government conceals the weakness of its hand behind claims of national security. In the process, civil liberties are trampled, individual lives destroyed, and the credibility of the justice system shaken.

Among the growing list of casualties is a 37-year-old Muslim and former chaplain at Guantánamo, Army Captain James Yee. A soft-spoken and pensive man who grew up in New Jersey and graduated in 1990 from West Point, Yee was assigned to minister to the Muslim detainees at Guantánamo in the fall of 2002. He was, as he himself later remarked, "the U.S. military's poster child of a good Muslim."

In 2003, following official channels and military protocol, he reported that prisoners were being abused and that the Koran, the Muslim holy book, was being desecrated. Not long after, he came under suspicion of espionage. On September 10, 2003, he was arrested, blindfolded, and placed in shackles. For the next 76 days he was held in solitary confinement in a Navy brig in South Carolina.

In leaks to the media, he was portrayed as the leader of a spy ring. He was told he would face charges of mutiny, sedition, and espionage, and that prosecutors would seek the death sentence. But the evidence against him, always vaguely hinted at, swiftly began to unravel. By the time actual charges were filed, they were far less dramatic than those initially threatened—mishandling classified documents, adultery, downloading pornography. Many argued the charges constituted nothing more than a desperate attempt by the military to save face.

At one point, the proceedings against Yee had to be delayed after it was learned that the government's own legal staff had themselves accidentally mishandled classified documents. Finally, on March 19, 2004, all charges against Yee were dropped. But still Yee could not speak up in his own defense. On April 6, 2004, the Army issued Yee a gag order forbidding him from publicly speaking out.

By then Yee had been vilified in the press, his reputation tattered, his military career in ruins. His wife had threatened suicide, he was deep in debt from legal expenses, and he carried the stigma of suspected traitor.

The military never apologized to Yee, nor exonerated him. Instead it argued that it dropped the case against him because to have pursued it would have compromised national security—once more taking cover in secrecy. Yet it granted him an honorable discharge. Secrecy was to be both the prologue and postscript for the injustice he suffered. The totality of his defense can be read in the title of the book he wrote in 2005, *For God and Country: Faith and Patriotism Under Fire.*

The person who had Yee arrested in the first place was Maj. Gen. Geoffrey Miller, the commander of Guantánamo's detention facility. Miller, too, moved on—to Iraq, where his talents and skills were tapped to organize interrogations at another prison wrapped in secrecy, Abu Ghraib. (In 2006, Miller retired, but not before receiving the Distinguished Service Medal in the Pentagon's Hall of Heroes.)

The Yee case recalled the 1999 prosecution—many would say persecution—of the Los Alamos scientist Wen Ho Lee, who was the victim of government leaks and bogus espionage charges, spent months in solitary confinement, and had his reputation shredded. I will discuss his case in chapters 4 and 5.

Then there was the case against Cyrus Kar, a Los Angeles filmmaker and U.S. Navy veteran who was arrested in mid-May 2005 and held by the U.S. military in Iraq. Kar has said he was held for 55 days in a dingy prison cell where he was variously hooded, threatened, and insulted. His immersion into the ultrasecret realm of American detainment reportedly meant no contact with his lawyers and innumerable failed attempts to get the military and government agencies to respond to inquiries about his status. He was finally released on July 10, 2005. No charges were ever brought against him. Ironically, Kar was in Iraq to complete a documentary about Cyrus the Great, the author of the first human rights charter, a cuneiform cylinder discovered in 1878.

None of this comes as much of a surprise to veterans of the security apparatus. J. William Leonard, director of the Information Security Oversight Office, spent 30 years at the Pentagon, much of the time working in counterintelligence. That experience made him deeply skeptical of acting on the basis of raw suspicion and snap judgments. "I monitored every counterintelligence case we had," says Leonard. "The only thing I rapidly learned is someone would come in and brief me on this case and ninety-nine percent of the time stuff that from that day looked like a slam-dunk turns out not to be the case. I learned in that position that things are never, absolutely never, as they appear. I knew it was not what I was told. Invariably it would never stand up [in court]. It's just the nature of the beast."

No one was more adamant about the need for secrecy than former attorney general John Ashcroft, who made passage of the Patriot Act his personal crusade and who vigorously pursued leaks adverse to the administration. But Ashcroft seemed decidedly less incensed over repeated leaks to the press about Steven Hatfill, a former government scientist at Maryland's Fort Detrick. Hatfill would become notorious as the "person of interest" in the anthrax investigation. "Person of interest" was the legally vague term Ashcroft himself used to describe Hatfill after someone leaked information that a subpoena had been issued to search Hatfill's premises—conveniently, just in time for journalists' deadlines. After that, Hatfill's life was ruined, his job lost, his reputation in shambles. He had been branded a suspect in the nation's first case of bioterrorism.

Four years later, the government has yet to produce any evidence linking Hatfill to the anthrax assault. But the strategy of leaking paid off: it demonstrated to a frustrated and fearful public that the government was aggressively hunting down the fiend behind the anthrax attacks and was making solid headway. The reality, of course, could not have been further from the truth. The Hatfill diversion allowed the tracks of whoever really did launch the attack to grow colder. All along, the real secret is that the FBI was stymied and clueless in the case and that a real and deadly bioterrorist remains at large years later.

The FBI has never apologized to Hatfill, never identified the source of those internal leaks, and never owned up to its own foundering investigation. Instead, it insists that the case against Hatfill remains open, but that the need for secrecy prohibits it from discussing the specific evidence against him.

Norman M. Covert was the public affairs officer and later the historian at Fort Detrick. He is appalled by the government's treatment of Hatfill. Says Covert, "He's a convenient scapegoat. They needed somebody and there he was. He was a monkey up a tree with his pants down. He had nothing to do with this."

• • •

Nearly four decades ago, a young second lieutenant in Vietnam who headed up a platoon of the Ninth Infantry Division remembers watching as every few months a chopper would land at Fire Support Base Danger, located amid muddy rice paddies in Dinh Tuong Province. Out would step a clean-shaven, well-scrubbed officer who would walk past the men and head directly for the battalion commander and executive officer. He would be seen huddling with the senior officers over a map on the hood of a Jeep, or leaning across a table speaking in hushed tones. Two things struck the young lieutenant—the visitor's cleanliness in the midst of such grime, and the visitor's utter lack of interest in what junior officers might have to say.

The visitor was an intelligence officer. Minutes after arriving, he would climb back aboard his chopper and disappear with, at worst, a spot of mud on his boots. But he would invariably leave behind orders that would take the young lieutenant and his men out into the jungles and rice paddies for days at a time, where they would face North Vietnamese regulars, Viet Cong, and treacherous booby traps. The intelligence officer operated in a realm of secrecy, a kind of bubble, to which the second lieutenant and his men were not privy. They would be asked to place their lives in harm's way but could not be trusted with the information held by the intelligence officer. "We would say, 'What are we looking for?' and they would say 'Sorry, can't tell you.' " The men were at risk, but the secret was safe.

"We were marching through the damn swamps having no clue what the hell we were doing exactly or what we were up against. Our first indicator would be when we came under fire or an ambush was sprung on us. . . . I lost men. I lost really good men in the process." That lieutenant determined that one day he would be the guy stepping off the helicopter, so clean. More important, he resolved that should that day come, he would provide those at the operational level, those whose very lives were at risk, with whatever information they needed to know. "I experienced firsthand the failings of the system," he remembers.

In 1970 he became an intel officer. His name is Pat Hughes—Patrick Marshall Hughes. Over time, he rose through the ranks to become a three-star general, oversaw the Defense Intelligence Agency (DIA) from 1996 to 1999, and until 2004 served as chief of intelligence for the newly formed Department of Homeland Security.

"I was fighting the system throughout my time in the military, which was pretty much gauged to continue the process of not informing those who needed to be informed, only informing the elite and the senior people and those who had a right to know because of their position," says Hughes, now vice president for intelligence and counterterrorism at L-3 Communications. But the tragedy of such restrictive and overbearing secrecy, says Hughes, did not end with Vietnam.

"My own view is that that phenomenon was part of the 9/11 failure. We knew things—people knew things throughout the organized intelligence, law enforcement, public safety security system here in the United States and the kind of trite phrase that is often used is 'we failed to connect the dots.' Most of the people working this system are well-intentioned, goodhearted, patriotic want-to-do-the-right-thing citizens who are worthy of our admiration, but the system—the mechanism they were brought up and trained in—told them to keep secrets in an excessive manner and to make it difficult to share information, especially between segments of the professional order."

Hughes believes that some progress has been made. For example, he cites the greater coordination in the Army between the "S-2," the chief of intelligence at the tactical unit level, and the "S-3," the chief of operations, which corrected some of the problems he experienced in Vietnam. He also sees greater sharing of classified information with those in the field. "It's not perfect, but in the context of Vietnam, things [have] improved. . . . Could things be better? Absolutely."

The problems that persist today are due less to official policy and procedure than to failure to put into practice what is already on paper, says Hughes. Cultures remain resistant, individuals cling to parochial views, and a lack of any enforcement regimen to ensure compliance means that the level of information sharing is still largely a matter of individual discretion. Where there has been progress, it has often been because individuals found ways around the system.

"The culture still exists that the CIA or DIA guys won't tell each other. The CIA guys won't tell the DIA guys, but that's not as broadly applied as it used to be," says Hughes. "In recent years I have seen and heard the phenomenon of a CIA guy and a DIA guy becoming friends, as an example, achieving some form of mutual respect and confidence, despite the organizational barrier that might exist; one person from one organization is willing to confide in a person from another organization because they know it's the right thing to do and they know it will further the common cause."

But others continue to hoard information or allow institutional obstacles to stand in the way of vital information reaching those with a need to know. Says Hughes, "They talk the game, but at the working-stiff level, I hear all the time—as recently as yesterday—about problems, and the problems are not appropriate. They should not happen, but they do." ("Yesterday" was August 10, 2006, when news broke that the British had foiled a plot to bomb as many as ten American transatlantic jetliners.) And what, I ask, was the problem yesterday? "I don't want to give you even a remote hint of the actual event," he demurred. "It's too dangerous for the person involved. I might be called upon to explain it and I don't want to have to do that. I also have to take polygraph tests," he said. "I am a creature of secrecy."

But these days, intelligence sharing and connectivity are not the only things that weigh upon Hughes. He is deeply concerned about the convergence of secrecy and technology and the emergence of what he refers to as "this brave new world of technical capabilities." To hear him reel off the list of technological developments and those that may lie just over the horizon is to recognize that not all threats to the United States come from abroad and that unless the country is on guard not only against terrorists but the excesses of surveillance and security, the wave of new technologies could usher in a lifestyle inimical to most Americans.

"It is beginning to call into question morality and ethics, challenging our value system, dredging up Orwellian possibilities. . . . We are being confronted by technical innovations based on nanotechnologies, very advanced computational capabilities, the amassing of data. We are being, I would say, challenged and threatened in some cases, in the context of American civil rights and American civil liberties. . . . So much information is available now in the digital realm, and we don't even know what exists out there on each of us. We aren't in control of it, we aren't in command of it. It is highly mobile, it is manipulatable, it is configurable across the digital realm in ways that most people just don't comprehend."

Such technologies, says Hughes, if not carefully managed and monitored, could imperil the very rights he has spent a lifetime defending. He worries that Americans do not fully appreciate the stakes. He supports a program of communication intercepts only if based on probable cause and direct links with terrorists, but he is vehemently opposed to broad domestic surveillance and monitoring of America's telephone and Internet traffic.

"Conditions are changing, conditions have changed," he says. "These conditions have been changed not by good people but by those who would do us collective ill, and these guys [the terrorists] require some exceptional control measures because their impact can be greater than we can absorb," says Hughes. Striking a balance between the security needs of the nation on the one hand, and on the other, the imperative to preserve America's identity as a place that safeguards civil liberties—this, says Hughes, is the great dilemma facing the nation.

Unbridled surveillance coupled with the new technologies could have effects more far-ranging than many Americans yet grasp. "I think it opens the door to a broader kind of governmental control over our population, which is not what this country was founded on," says Hughes.

" 'If you have nothing to hide,' I hear people say, 'why should I care?' Well, it's not necessarily merely about something to hide in the context of terrorism; it might be something to hide in the conduct of your business, it might be something to hide in your personal relationships, or it might be something in your personal makeup, your personal peccadilloes, or whatever. It's not merely about crime and terrorism. . . . Discovery of these personal characteristics by others can have positive impact and it can also have a negative impact on a civilian population. I think we ought to go down that road extremely carefully. We all ought to know what we're doing, and it ought to be done in the bright sunshine of public debate and collective legislative, executive, and judicial activity that our country is based on. I don't think we ought to compromise on this."

There is something both comforting and alarming about hearing this veteran intelligence figure fret over such issues. For how will the American public know if such technologies are being properly managed and its rights protected, if the entire array of applications is veiled in secrecy? Recent invocations of the "state secrets" precedent, recourse to closed hearings, expanded executive authority, and shrinking congressional oversight do not bode well for "the bright sunshine of public debate." Like Pat Hughes's platoon of long ago, America's citizens may not even know enough to identify the risks they face or recognize that their future may have already been chosen for them.

4

Case Study: Blacked Out:
A Secret the CIA Won't Release

Most CIA officers take their secrets with them to the grave. The few daring enough to consider writing how the clandestine service attempted to shape history must first run the gauntlet of the Agency's Publication Review Board. That's just what Walter McIntosh attempted to do in 2004 when he submitted a brief two-page article for the board's review. A former covert operative for the CIA, McIntosh sought Langley's permission to write about a secret operation the Agency ran in India during the Cold War. He did not have long to wait for his answer. Within weeks the Agency returned his submission, largely gutted. Even the word "station," Agency parlance for its in-country operations headquarters, was blacked out, though the location that preceded the word, "Delhi," survived the vetting process. Oddly, so too did the author's provocative title, which went to the very heart of his story: "Did the CIA Unwittingly Assist the KGB in the Assassination of India's Prime Minister Shastri?"

Given the Agency's heavy-handed redactions, McIntosh gave up on trying to tell the story, leaving the shroud of secrecy intact on an operation that many in India and the United States might well have found surprising, if not objectionable, and that McIntosh suspects may have inadvertently contributed to the death of India's former leader, Lal Bahadur Shastri.

McIntosh knew his piece would get a thorough going-over from the review board, but he did not imagine that it would be eviscerated. A 20-year veteran of the CIA, he served from 1965 to 1985, all of that time in the clandestine service, the Operations Directorate; he rose through the ranks from the Technical Services Division to case officer and finally to chief of Vietnam Operations. But it was a modest covert operation early in his career that he most wanted to write about. He knew it was but a tiny fragment of both India's and America's history, but one that might explain larger events and could certainly serve as a cautionary tale of how covert operations can go awry.

His story begins in January 1966, when the Cold War defined both U.S. and Soviet foreign policy. Both superpowers had elaborate strategies for stalemating the other. The United States exploited the rift between the two Communist giants, China and the Soviet Union. The Soviets sought favor with India as a counterweight to China. India's ruler, Jawaharlal Nehru, had died in office in May 1964, bringing Shastri to power. But from the Soviet point of view, Shastri proved a less reliable friend of Moscow than Nehru. When border fights broke out between Pakistan and India, the Soviet leader, Alexei Kosygin, arranged to bring the leaders of India and Pakistan together in what became known as the Tashkent Conference.

The prospect of such a Soviet diplomatic coup in the region set the CIA to thinking. In the days leading up to the conference, the Agency devised a small covert operation designed to drive a wedge between the independent-minded Shastri and the Soviets. The CIA's Technical Services Division would forge a letter on Shastri's official stationery and place it in a widely read Indian newsweekly, *Blitz*, a publication the Agency saw as decidedly pro-Soviet and a frequent instrument of Soviet disinformation and propaganda. The brief one-page typed note, bearing Shastri's forged signature, was a subtle attempt to cast Shastri in a pro-Soviet light. It was given to a CIA asset on the staff of the newsweekly to be published on the eve of the conference.

The idea was that an irate Shastri, upon learning of the note on his return from Tashkent, would denounce it as a fake, disavow its pro-Soviet stance, and further distance himself from Moscow. Embedded in the letter were said to be subtle errors that would, upon close examination, reveal it to be a fake, thereby implicating the Soviets in what would be seen as a Communist dirty trick.

The letter, dated January 2, 1966, was written on stationery that carried the address "Prime Minister's House, New Delhi" and was addressed to the paper's editor. It read simply: "Dear Shri Karanjia, I wish to congratulate you on your strong drive for a fruitful Tashkent Conference as particularly highlighted on your moving cover picture of 25 December. You can be fully assured that India enters this meeting with a firm resolve to succeed and bring lasting peace. Yours sincerely, Lal Bahadur." The letter, by implication, embraced Karanjia's own earlier pro-Soviet positions and its mere appearance in *Blitz* signaled a position shift. Initially, it seemed that the CIA had scored a hit. *Blitz* featured an image of the note on its front page directly under the masthead; it took up a full quarter of the page. Below it was a large photograph of Shastri flanked by Pakistan's Ayub Khan and Soviet premier Alexei Kosygin.

There must have been particular pleasure in duping so strident a critic of the Agency. Just two weeks earlier, on December 11, 1965, *Blitz* had written, "No cloak-and-dagger organization of espionage, subversion and sabotage in the world today stands so thoroughly exposed and discredited as the Central Intelligence Agency of the United States."

Only things did not quite work out the way Langley imagined.

Two things, says McIntosh, foiled the plan. What the CIA did not know then, and would learn only years later, was that their asset on the Indian newsweekly was a double agent who doubtless apprised the Soviets of the Agency scheme. And on January 11, 1966, just hours after the Tashkent Conference's successful conclusion, in which a cease-fire and pullback were negotiated, Shastri was found dead in his hotel room.

It was said he had had a heart attack, but some suspected the Soviets had a hand in his death, desiring a more dependable and less independent prime minister. As recently as 2000, Shastri's son, Sunil, himself a former prominent Indian official and politician, called for an investigation into his father's death, citing the peculiar circumstances of his father's sudden collapse, unanswered questions about his physician, as well as recently released KGB records shedding new light on Moscow's hand in India's press and politics. Those archives, the so-called Mitrokhin Archives, after the KGB defector Vassily Mitrokhin, contain references to KGB payments to India's press and suggested that *Blitz* in particular was of service to it.

As for the letter that the CIA had expected Shastri to denounce upon his return, it would instead resonate as being among the late prime minister's final words. As if to rub the CIA's nose in its failure, *Blitz*, in a tribute to Shastri following his death, ran the same note again in its January 15 issue, along with yet another photo of Shastri between Khan and Kosygin. Under the headline "He Died at the Height of Glory!" editor Karanjia wrote, "This letter dated the 2nd of January 1966 is of historic significance to the judgment which posterity will be called upon to pass on this splendid little man who rose to be a victor in war and died at the very zenith of glory and achievement. His last letter came to us unsolicited and without any obvious provocation. It speaks volumes for his passion for peace."

Following Shastri's death, Nehru's daughter, Indira Gandhi, came to power. She proved to be a steadfast friend of Moscow.

How was it that McIntosh knew of the covert operation? He was the person who crafted the forged letter as a member of the CIA's Technical Services Division. Now he wonders whether it played into the Soviets' hands, affording them the perfect opportunity to "eliminate" Shastri with pro-Soviet sentiments (albeit the CIA's) on his lips and before he could denounce them. "Secrecy has its place," says McIntosh, "but when it's just covering up embarrassing things, that's not secrecy anymore. That's something else. It seems to me that when you find out that you have had an operation compromised through employing a double agent, that some of this needs to be aired and, if we have any proof or solid suspicions that the KGB did assassinate some foreign leader, it needs to be before the world's public and not covered up because we are embarrassed because of how we learned of it.

"This is one of the follies of the Cold War and of CIA operations in general," says McIntosh. "The blowback or fallout of these things can be incalculable when you do them—how many of them work and how many of them fail and for reasons that can never be foreseen. I am just saying that this particular CIA operation very likely made them [the Soviets] feel even more secure and fell into their hands and that, if they were wavering in any way, this may very well have been the green light. It could have been the deciding factor." Either way, the *full* story was not something the CIA Publication Review Board wanted made public.

"It appears that you can publish almost anything if you say nice things about the Agency, and very little gets published if you don't," says McIntosh.

In 1968, two years after the forged Shastri letter appeared in *Blitz*, the newsweekly ran a story that accused the United States of using bacteriological warfare in Vietnam and Thailand. That story was based on a letter allegedly from the U.S. Office of Naval Research. But that letter, according to KGB files, was itself a forgery, its letterhead lifted by the Soviets from an invitation to a scientific symposium.

Secret History

Who controls the past controls the future; who controls the
present controls the past.

—George Orwell, *1984* (1949)

On September 10, 2001, the last "day like any other" that most of us can
remember, John Steinbeiss, a middle-aged Department of Energy declassifier, was going through crates of dusty old records at the National
Archives and Records Administration in College Park, Maryland. He
was looking for any documents that might contain anything of use to
terrorists. With a top secret clearance, he had spent his entire adult life
with secrecy and the twin themes of vigilance and deterrence. As a
younger man he served in the Strategic Air Command in bombers that
carried nuclear weapons. Later, he was an intelligence officer aboard one
of the EC-135s that was always aloft during the Cold War and ready to
actually launch a retaliatory strike should the nation below be reduced
to cinder by nuclear war. To him, the threat of WMDs was anything but
a vague abstraction.

His job, like that of dozens of other DOE employees and contract
workers, is to sort through mountains of records at the National
Archives, all of them at least 25 years old, weeding out whatever might
contain what his department calls "restricted data" (RDs) and "formerly
restricted data" (FRDs) that could reveal America's nuclear secrets, in-

cluding weapons locations, designs, and yields. Such a job can be thankless work. Historians who rely on the records resent the intrusions and interruptions such searches cause. Other bureaucrats often see it as added work. Some dismiss it as a fool's errand, a search through a gargantuan haystack for a needle that may or may not even exist. Adding to the quixotic nature of Steinbeiss's quest, nearly all the records he searches had long ago been declassified by someone else and made available to the public.

No matter. "I'm black and white," says Steinbeiss. "It's either RD or FRD and where it is doesn't matter. I don't care who saw it, it's still classified."

Among the more daunting tasks he has faced was electronically sorting through some 700,000 already declassified State Department telexes, nearly all of them dating from the early 1970s. Using so-called dirty words that would trigger a closer screening, and a DOE program called Quickcheck, reviewers sought to identify telexes that contained sensitive information related to nuclear secrets. After winnowing down the list to 70,000, he and others then eyeballed each one, one at a time, and finally culled out 21 telexes that raised questions.

Ultimately, after months of exhaustive work, some nine telexes from the original 700,000 were withdrawn from the Archives. Would those telexes have aided bin Laden or his ilk? You be the judge. The telexes contained information related to the positioning of U.S. nuclear weapons on the soil of allies some 25 to 30 years ago. Technically, the documents were a DOE "equity"—a matter of DOE classification—but in reality, the decision to withdraw them was made not out of fear of terrorism—the weapons have likely long since been repositioned elsewhere—but rather out of concern that they might upset U.S. allies who would not want it known that America had ever had nuclear weapons within their borders. Though the documents had been available for years, none of these allies were apparently even aware of their existence.

For bleary-eyed John Steinbeiss, the massive review and culling was worth it. America may not have been made safer by his prodigious efforts, but the regulations had been complied with, and the job of going through America's past to try to safeguard its future was as important as it was onerous.

But on September 11, 2001, moments after he learned of the assault on the twin towers in New York, Steinbeiss recalled one of the boxes he had opened and reviewed the day before. It was devoid of any obvious WMD threat, and he had easily cleared its contents, though it took him longer than usual because he found himself engrossed in the subject. Every now and again history provides Steinbeiss a little relief from tedium.

The yellowing files he perused on September 10, 2001, told of a tragedy some 56 years earlier, when, on the morning of July 28, 1945, a B-25 bomber, lost in a thick fog over Manhattan, crashed into the Empire State Building, then the world's tallest building. The crash killed 14 and sent shudders through the city. Unbeknownst to Steinbeiss, he had looked into the face of the future and a threat not anticipated by his guidelines. Neither "skyscraper" nor "plane" was among his list of "dirty words." In the midst of his search for perils, the true threat masked itself as a mere footnote to history. For Steinbeiss, it was a sobering object lesson in the obscurity of risk and the limits of vigilance.

•   •   •

In March 2003, members of the Society for History in the Federal Government, an eclectic group of some 300 government historians, archivists, and record keepers—the self-described "voice of the federal historical community"—gathered for their annual conference in Shepherdstown, West Virginia. The conference's title, "Federal Records and the Cause of History," spoke to the impact of 9/11 on historians. Eighteen months after the coordinated attack on America, history had become not merely a discipline but a *cause,* and one in jeopardy of becoming a casualty. The title of the keynote address raised the ominous question that was on many minds: "Government Secrecy: Just How Far Will They Go?" Far beyond the West Virginia conference, historians, authors, archivists, and researchers were beginning to feel the first jarring aftershocks of 9/11 as presumptive secrecy spread and, with it, a near paranoia about the release of government records that could in any way be construed as of service to terrorists, could embarrass the government, or could erode public support for the war in Iraq.

What they did not know then—could not have known because it was such a secret program—was that the CIA, Defense Intelligence Agency, and others in that stealthy community were removing from the National

Archives, presidential libraries, and other repositories of history tens of thousands of historical records, some of them already in the hands of scholars or published in official government diplomatic histories years and even decades earlier. At one time readily available as research materials, they had been spirited away and sealed in government vaults.

Some of the records vanished after being in the public domain for a generation. Their handling shows how obsessive the current purge of historical documents has become and how secrecy has been used to alter what Americans may know of their own past as a nation. Many of those records are expected to be returned to the open shelves, but the agencies that carted them off are the same that continue to steadfastly refuse to release other documents critical to our understanding of American history and its place in the world. Matters large and small have been siphoned away in the post-9/11 purges of records, cumulatively affecting the accuracy and scope of the writing of history.

Among the documents withdrawn was a 1948 CIA memo contemplating floating balloons over Iron Curtain countries and using them to drop propaganda leaflets. Another, from October 12, 1950, concludes that it would be highly improbable for the Chinese to cross the border and engage in the Korean conflict. A document marked November 7, 1955, was withdrawn out of concerns that it might contribute to the proliferation of weapons of mass destruction—it suggested considering whether artillery shells might be enhanced with poison ivy smoke as an irritant to incapacitate the enemy.

Another reclassified document was a 1962 telegram from George F. Kennan, then ambassador to Yugoslavia, in which a newspaper article about China's nuclear program had been translated into English. By the spring of 2006 the intelligence agencies had quietly snatched some 55,000 pages from the open shelves of the National Archives. The secret reclassification program, which had been going for five years, only came to light in December 2005 when a researcher noticed that documents he had copied years before were now no longer accessible.

In April 2006, the U.S. government's Information Security Oversight Office (ISOO) completed an audit of the government's previously secret reclassification program at the National Archives. It found that the CIA had deliberately removed unclassified records purely in an effort to "obfuscate" and conceal other more sensitive areas. Some of those materials were the subject of Freedom of Information Act requests that had been dragging on for four years.

That was hardly the only abuse of secrecy revealed. The National Security Archive, a nonprofit organization advocating government openness, found that many of the reclassified documents posed no threat to U.S. security but were merely embarrassing to the intelligence community. One of those reclassified documents was from 1949 and revealed how unaware U.S. intelligence was of Soviet progress toward making an atom bomb and why they were so surprised by its detonation in September 1949.

So secretive was the reclassification effort that not even the archivist of the United States, Allen Weinstein, was aware of it. He learned of its existence from reading the *New York Times*. Weinstein called for a moratorium on reclassification and expressed grave concerns about damage caused by the program. He quoted George Kennan, who cautioned against "the erection of false pretenses and elaborate efforts to deceive." Kennan went on to say: "We easily become, ourselves, the sufferers of these methods of deception. For they inculcate in their authors, as well as their intended victims, unlimited cynicism, causing them to lose all realistic understanding of the interrelationship, in what they are doing, of means and ends." Said Weinstein, "We have a case in point today, with some of the behavior described in ISOO's Audit."

The secret intelligence reclassification program was put on hold in early 2006 as new government-wide criteria for declassification were being considered and promises of greater transparency were offered by the archivist. He even offered assurances that many of the records withdrawn by the CIA would be restored to the open shelves. Of course, such assurances presuppose that, should the CIA choose to resume its review and reclassification of open materials, it will inform the archivist and not leave him in the dark along with the rest of the nation.

The clandestine reclassification effort was only a part of government's drive to filter and restrict information. Others continue unabated, including the Energy Department's efforts as mandated by the Kyl-Lott Amendment. And, as previously described, whole new categories of information control have been invented since 9/11 that are neither classified nor accessible but are part of an ever-expanding netherworld of restricted information. History itself is under siege and those whose profession it is to understand and write about history have been fighting not merely to preserve the records of the past but to retain access to them. Without such advocates, the past could become the exclusive province of those with a high security clearance.

At the National Security Agency, the government's center for electronic eavesdropping, the historian Robert J. Hanyok reviewed the files related to the Gulf of Tonkin incident, which occurred on August 4, 1964. What he concluded, on the basis of classified materials, was that intelligence gathered on the alleged attack by North Vietnamese on U.S. destroyers was deliberately distorted to conceal earlier intelligence flaws and that the episode, which more than any other single event was cited as a provocation and a justification for the Vietnam War, was falsified.

That study, completed in 2001, was of historical significance, except that the government was determined that it not become a part of our historical record, particularly at a time when accusations of skewed and falsified intelligence were swirling around the war in Iraq. To quash the study and keep it out of the hands of historians and citizens alike, the U.S. government classified it, preferring not to face the inevitable comparisons between then and now. But for a leak to the press four years after its completion, that study might never have seen the light of day—which would have suited the keepers of secrets just fine. The Vietnam study offers a glimpse of deliberate efforts by the secrecy establishment to contain and control what citizens may know of our own past. Secrecy has not only cloaked the present, denying citizens access to vital information about current policy and decision making, it has also subverted the past.

What makes the handling of the Tonkin study all the more curious is that its conclusions merely reaffirm what has long been known by those who have studied the period. What made the study so sensitive was not its capacity to elucidate the past, but its potential to enflame the present.

At the National Archives and Records Administration, the foremost repository of historically valuable records in the country and the largest collection of classified documents, the change post-9/11 was palpable. Records that contained detailed structural designs of everything from government office buildings to dams to lighthouses were removed from the shelves, leaving behind a withdrawal slip to mark their place. Researchers in the midst of major projects suddenly discovered that the collections to which they had had ready access the day before were now beyond their reach. The Archives put on a game face and did what it could to operate as it had before, even to the point of largely ignoring a directive from Attorney General John Ashcroft that reversed the Freedom of Information Act's presumption of openness, but it was difficult to pretend that nothing had changed.

Historians and researchers requesting documents from the vast Central Files of the State Department for the years 1967–1969 discovered that they had all been removed from the shelves and would remain sequestered for months and months on end. They were now in the possession of Department of Energy reviewers who reexamined tens of thousands of pages of declassified materials looking for those one or two pages that might, by some leap of the imagination, aid terrorists eager to build The Bomb or get their hands on one of ours. Other massive reviews were also under way. To make matters worse, staff and resources, already spread thin, were diverted from their previous work on declassification. For many historians attempting to chronicle the past, it was a mystery what had happened to the files they had been working on and under what authority they had been removed.

Anna K. Nelson is no stranger to either history or secrecy. The distinguished adjunct historian in residence at the American University in Washington, she served on the JFK Assassination Review Board and has conducted extensive research in five presidential libraries. But she was more than a little surprised in 2003 when, while doing research at the Archives, she opened four boxes she had requested of Nixon-era records from the years 1969 through 1972. Inside there were no documents, just withdrawal slips. It was neither the first nor the last such experience she would have. In September 2003, Nelson requested the declassification of a 1953 National Security Council document she had found at the Johnson Library in Austin, Texas. The subject matter apparently related to Radio Free Europe and psychological warfare during the Cold War. Eighteen months later, in February 2005, she received her response—three entirely blank pages and two with only one cryptic paragraph on each.

"Think of the foolishness of that," says Nelson. "The Soviet Union is gone, the old Iron Curtain countries are now eager to get into NATO, and we are still closing a document from 1953. I think history has suffered badly because we can only write [about] what we can get." Like the good historian she is, she places her lament in historical context. "I feel like we've been through our Prague Spring," she says, referring to the brief period of relative reform and openness that preceded the 1968 Soviet crackdown on Czechoslovakia.

As Nelson knows firsthand from her time reviewing declassified JFK assassination records, indiscriminate secrecy engenders profound and often lasting public distrust and suspicion. "When records are closed," says Nelson, "people imagine all kinds of things. Those conspiracy theories are still with us blaming Johnson and the CIA for Kennedy's death. Young people in college still believe it was Johnson and the CIA. It has permeated the culture."

Steven Tilley oversees the vast paper holdings of the National Archives and by most accounts has done his best to minimize disruptions and defend declassification in a world of changed expectations and demands. He is too savvy a bureaucrat to suggest that massive reviews and reclassification efforts are senseless or wasteful because they are now the rule of the land, to which every government archivist must now answer.

But Tilley will admit that there is to date not a single recorded instance of anyone using the Archives or any historical records for any nefarious purpose related to terrorism. Not one. It is like tearing up an entire garden in search of a single elusive weed. And it is surely not lost on Tilley or the other able government archivists, most of them historians by training and temperament, that every panel and commission that examined the events leading up to 9/11 concluded that too much secrecy and not enough sharing of information—a lack of "connectivity"—may have been responsible for the U.S. failure to discover and possibly thwart the plot.

But in times of crisis, be it the "First Red Scare" of the late teens and early twenties or "Second Red Scare" of the McCarthy era of half a century ago, reaction and overreaction have rarely been tempered by rationality. Familiarity with the events of those periods may strengthen the argument *for* the cause of writing history. "Society's memories" is how Supreme Court Justice Ruth Bader Ginsburg referred to the Archives' records as she swore in the new archivist, Dr. Allen Weinstein, on March 7, 2005. "They make enlightened government possible for us today for, as Santayana famously said: 'Those who cannot remember the past are condemned to repeat it.' "

At the north entrance to the National Archives headquarters building

on Pennsylvania Avenue in downtown Washington is the famous in-
scription from Shakespeare's *The Tempest:* "What is Past is Prologue." At
the south entrance, on Constitution Avenue, are the words "Eternal
Vigilance is the Price of Liberty." The Archives, and by extension the
study of American history itself, are now poised, and sometimes pulled,
between these two eternal verities.

But which force is now dominant in America is unambiguous. In
2004, by the government's own figures, for each dollar the United States
spent on declassification, it spent $148 on creating and protecting new
secrets, investing in vaults, training personnel in security measures, conducting background checks for clearances, and the panoply of other expenses associated with secrecy.

•   •   •

Judith Palya's story goes to the heart of the subject of secrecy and history. On October 6, 1948, she was just seven weeks old, too young to
know that on that afternoon her 41-year-old father, Albert, and eight
other men had died in the crash of a B-29 Superfortress somewhere over
Waycross, Georgia. As an adult she didn't remember anything about her
father, a civilian engineer with the Radio Corporation of America who
had devoted his adult career to enhancing America's security. It would
be years before she would even learn of the crash or of the secrecy that
seemed to swallow it up. On board, it was said, were top secret electronic devices. An uncle suggested that the Russians must have sabo-
taged the plane. Absent any other explanation, this seemed entirely
plausible.

All Judith Palya knew for sure was that she and her two brothers had
lost their father and that her mother had received a modest sum of
$49,000 from the government for the life of Albert Palya. Later still she
learned that her mother and the other widows had sued the government
under the Federal Tort Claims Act, alleging that government negligence
had caused the crash.

The case was rejected because the federal government argued that national security forbade the release of the accident report, even to a federal judge, so sensitive was the information the report contained.
Without the report there was no chance of establishing negligence. The
most senior people in the U.S. Air Force had staked their reputations on

the sensitivity of the accident report and the unspecified dangers that could come with its release. In the end, the U.S. Supreme Court ruled 6–3 in support of the government, and national security trumped the widows' claims.

The ruling created a benchmark legal precedent for state secrecy. The 1953 case, *United States v. Reynolds* (Patricia Reynolds was one of the widows), would be cited scores of times in succeeding years as a reference point in the struggle between secrecy and disclosure, national security and accountability. It would prove to be an invaluable ace in the government's hand when it sought to suppress sensitive information.

Decades passed and Judith Palya made her peace with the past. She had always been willing to accept the government's argument for secrecy as an article of faith. Life moved on. She married and had two sons. A conservative woman, she was a registered Independent but leaned toward the Republican Party, especially on law-and-order issues. She was patriotic and proud of it. The stepdaughter of a Marine, brother of a Marine, mother of a police officer, she took pride in her father's role, albeit a shadowy one, and was devoted to a vision of her country as a place that, as she likes to say, represented "truth, justice and the American way"—words she had memorized from the *Superman* episodes she saw as a girl.

All that changed one evening in February 2000 when she was surfing the Internet and plugged the words "accident" and "B-29" into the search engine AltaVista. Up came a website that listed Air Force accident reports. Among them was a reference to her father's crash. Unbeknownst to her, the report had been declassified in the 1990s and was available for a nominal fee. At last, she imagined, she would learn what her father had been working on, what he had given his life for.

But nothing could have prepared her for the report that arrived soon after. There were no secrets in the report, no sensitive information related to classified systems, no hint of anything that might imperil the nation's security. Instead, she says, what she found were repeated references to negligence in the operation and maintenance of the aircraft. A shield to protect one engine from heat had not been installed. Fire had broken out. Fuel had been cut off to the wrong engine. The report concluded: "The aircraft is not considered to have been safe for flight."

Fifty-two years after the crash, Judith Palya discovered what she believes is the real secret behind the crash of the B-29 that claimed her father's life: it had nothing to do with national security and everything to do with the concealment of negligence and the desire to set a judicial precedent that would protect secrecy above all else. "It was just so wrong," says Judith Palya Loether, now 56. "It was not the American Way."

Reluctantly she began to pursue the matter and contacted the same Philadelphia law firm, Drinker, Biddle & Reath, that had represented her mother and the other widows. Now armed with the declassified accident report and evidence of negligence, she was determined to reopen the case, to get the money that was due her family plus a half century of interest, and, most important of all, to set the record straight by exposing what she believed to be a clear case of government fraud, deceit, and abuse of power. In 2003 the case once more went to court.

But the U.S. government of today, much like that which defended the case in 1953, was operating in an atmosphere supercharged with national security concerns. The Bush administration was loath to part with a precedent that provided latitude and cover in matters of secrecy. The government had no intention of simply rolling over and admitting the errors of its ways. Far from it. U.S. Solicitor General Theodore B. Olson vigorously opposed Palya and the other descendants of the crash victims who had joined her in the suit, arguing, among other things, the virtues of finality and the failure of the plaintiffs to allege a fundamental miscarriage of justice.

Worse yet, the United States argued that even in the original case it had not taken the position that this particular accident report contained "military or state secrets." No fraud, no case. For Olson, the issue of terrorism was no abstraction. His wife, Barbara, was among the fatalities when Flight 77 was piloted into the Pentagon on September 11.

Once again, the government prevailed and once more Judith Palya Loether was left wondering what it would take to get the truth out.

Today Judith Palya Loether has assembled something of a shrine to the father she never knew. Behind the glass of a cherry corner cabinet is a childhood book of his, *Electricity for Boys,* an inlaid wooden checkerboard and cribbage set he made, a wooden bird whose round head may be removed to hold a pipe, and a gray and silver tie that went with the morning suit he wore for his wedding. Over the years, she has come to know the man her father was but has come to understand her country less and less. "Since I found the accident report," she says, "I have been on a journey of discovery, I would almost have to say, about my country, and I hate to tell you, it's not a good one. I may not be as naive about my country as I used to be. It's a sad thing to say."

Judith Palya Loether's personal disillusionment pales beside the impact that the case has had on the nation, and not just in the past, but in the present as well. Despite its murky origins, *United States v. Reynolds* set the foundation for the legal precedent of state secrecy in which the government argues that certain evidence and inquiries, often quintessential to pursuing a case, cannot be sought because they would damage national security. In the 19 years between 1954 and 1973, the U.S. government invoked the state secrets privilege only four times. In the five years since 9/11, it has been invoked at least 23 times, including cases involving allegations of unlawful detainment by the CIA and illegal domestic surveillance.

•　　•　　•

Some invocations of national security barely pass the straight-face test. The landscape of obsessive secrecy is littered with the absurd. One of the most productive record areas for historians (and satirists) to plumb—and one that bristles with government resistance—is that involving investigations of dissidents and other mischief makers who challenge policy. The great irony is that what most of these forbidden records reveal when finally and begrudgingly surrendered is that the legitimate exercise of dissent points to the subversive nature not of radicals but of government itself.

Take, for example, the long-denied FBI records relating to investigations of the musician and political activist John Lennon, now a quarter of a century dead. Surely whatever insidious threat may be contained in the song "Come Together" has long since passed. It took a 20-year legal battle under the Freedom of Information Act to get the FBI to surrender its files on Lennon, and still it held on to some. (Not until December 2006 did it release the final ten documents, none of which even remotely were related to national security concerns.) It's a classic example of "what happens when government substitutes paranoia for law," observed the First Amendment lawyer Floyd Abrams.

One would think that after 9/11 the FBI might have bigger fish to fry, but as of late 2004 it was still resisting the release of some ten pages from

the Lennon files, citing national security and claiming that any such release would compromise a U.S. commitment to an unnamed foreign
government to keep the materials confidential and would expose the
material's source. Another celebrity whose alleged threat to America
was shrouded in secrecy is the singer Cat Stevens (aka Yusuf Islam, of
"Morning Has Broken" fame), who in September 2004 was deported.
Stevens was deemed to be a potential national security concern. His
name appeared on a secret "no fly" list and an unnamed official suggested the singer was barred because he had contributed to charities
with terrorist links—which charities, the government refused to say.
Absent the corrective of history, folly repeats itself like a loop of tape
played over and over again.

Officials charged with protecting America often fall back on the
"slippery-slope" argument, saying that if we were to yield to one request
it would erode the basis for denying the next, as if the irrational could
ever bolster the rational. The oldest classified records at the National
Archives and Records Administration date from 1917 and 1918, to the
war known as the Great War. Those few combatants still alive would all
be centenarians. To say that in the intervening century the technology of
war, espionage, and communications has evolved may be considered
profound understatement. Indeed the Great War predates the CIA by
some 30 years.

But that has not stopped the Agency from invoking national security
concerns in blocking the release of the oldest secrets in the National
Archives. Exactly what are the records that have retained such sensitivity after all these years? They relate to formulas for making and detect-
ing invisible ink used by the Germans in the time of Kaiser Wilhelm,
and, it might be noted, some time before the advent of the Internet, mi-
crodots, and secure satellite hookups. But the CIA argued, in resisting a
Freedom of Information Act request by the James Madison Project, that
revealing those formulas would disclose the basis for currently used invisible inks and thereby compromise the CIA's ability to effectively communicate. (God help us if that is true.) In February 1999, a federal judge
hearing the case mused aloud that he remembered coming upon a recipe
for invisible ink in a cereal box. But ultimately the court sided with the
CIA, denying the release of the documents.

More often than not, if there is a slippery slope at work, it is the one
the government occupies, emboldened by victories like that of the invis-

ible ink case to push the arguments further and further into the realm of the ridiculous, undermining the credibility of a system that has a small core of genuine secrets surrounded by a vast thicket of pretext.

When it comes to secrecy and history, every historian has his own list of ludicrous cases. The James Madison Project's list is as good as any: on it is a Pentagon report classified "top secret" that criticizes the excessive use of classification in the military; the other was a refusal to admit that monkeys had been used in NASA's space program, despite the fact that the National Zoo had already identified the monkeys and displayed a plaque in their honor. The reported reason for the Pentagon's sensitivities: protecting the U.S. relationship with India, where there are sects that practice monkey worship.

For some historians the post-9/11 world has almost literally locked them out. At the Food and Drug Administration, the worry is food safety and bioterrorism. Suzanne White Junod, the FDA's historian and a past president of the Society for History in the Federal Government, says some security concerns have now reached maddening proportions. The government, she says, is constantly changing her password, effectively denying her access to her laptop. To get onto the Internet on her IBM Thinkpad, the FDA requires her to enter three separate levels of passwords, the third and final one requiring that she key in a long series of numbers or letters within a scant ten seconds. "Why does a historian need to have encryption?" she asks. "Getting through the encryption on my laptop has made it worthless, so now we use Blackberries to get around the encryption problem."

•   •   •

Even by the standards of the Library of Congress's Manuscript Room, mine is something of an unusual request. I ask a research assistant for a list of everything that I am not allowed to see. That would include security classified materials as well as materials restricted by deeds of gift to the library. I have been told of the Manuscript Room's vault but am not permitted to see it. Secrecy forbids. In the library's indexes, I have come across a number of tantalizing private restrictions. For example, whatever secrets lie within the papers of the poet John Berryman must wait until they are unsealed on April 7, 2019. Likewise the pocket notebooks of Sigmund Freud, closed for "100 years from the date of creation."

But what about government-classified documents, documents that have been determined to threaten harm to the nation if disclosed? After some minutes, the researcher returns with a neatly printed out list of responses to an internal computer search. The list contains some 104 distinct collections from which have been removed various materials for national security reasons. Some collections seem plausible candidates for containing government secrets. Among these are the papers of former defense secretary Caspar Weinberger, the physicist J. Robert Oppenheimer, and a former national security advisor and secretary of state, Henry Kissinger.

But others raise instant questions about the continued need for secrecy and security. Why, for example, is correspondence by the late Claire Booth Luce from 1953 when she was ambassador to Italy still classified "Top Secret"? What possible harm could their release cause to national security? Or why would a 1946–1948 file on German currency reform from the files of the economist Gerhard Colm (1897–1968) still need to be classified and kept in a vault? Who at the Library of Congress, the Pentagon, or the White House would care to make the case for continued classification of the June 1944 diary (think D-Day) of the long-deceased Carl Spaatz, then commander in chief, Strategic Air Forces, Europe? On and on the classified list runs: papers dated 1941–1942 of Muir S. Fairchild, former vice chief of staff for the U.S. Air Force, who died in 1950; documents of Vice President Henry A. Wallace; materials of the late James P. McGranery, attorney general from 1952 to 1953.

Many of the withdrawn files are more than half a century old and yet they are seen to demand the same rigid security precautions and attention as documents stamped "classified" today. They represent not merely a denial of access to history but an encumbrance on the present. But then, once a secret, always a secret. Long overdue efforts at government declassification, already a tertiary concern of the security establishment, were among the first casualties of 9/11.

But perhaps the most curious records to be withdrawn for reasons of classification came from the donated papers of some of America's leading journalists and authors, individuals who used their pens not to create secrets but to champion openness, transparency, and accountability in government. Now the very records they long ago secured from government and used in their award-winning reporting are once again closed to the public and stamped "Classified." Such documents, whose content contributed to an earlier decade's headlines, are once more treated as if no one yet knows of their existence, part of a grand and continuing fiction that afflicts many keepers of secrets.

Documents have been removed from the donated papers of four distinguished Pulitzer Prize winners, including three former *New York Times* reporters, Hedrick Smith, Neil Sheehan, and William Safire, as well as the papers of the *Washington Post* investigative reporter George Lardner. Other documents have been removed for classification reasons from among the papers donated by the ABC reporter Fred Graham, and by John Osborne, a writer for *Life* and *Time*.

There is little detail in the computer list as to what has been removed, in most cases only vague, generic descriptions. Removed from the papers of Hedrick Smith are "cables, affidavits, notes and biographical material," including some documents relating to his 1976 book *The Russians,* as well as to writings on the Vietnam conflict and Nixon. There is more than a little irony in the fact that materials the coauthor of a book about the Pentagon Papers himself relied upon for research and later left to the Archives are now withheld from the public on the basis of national security.

From the papers of the *Washington Post* reporter George Lardner have been removed two files labeled "Goodwin, Richard, Assassination Plots in Latin America, Research Material, 1961–1963."

The authors and reporters who donated these papers had no inkling they would be treated as classified and removed beyond public reach. The papers were, in each case, given to enhance the public and historical record. Ernest Emrich is the classified-documents archivist attached to the Manuscript Division of the Library of Congress. His phone rings in the walk-in Mosler vault where he is surrounded by shelves of dusty papers, many decades old and stamped "Secret" or "Top Secret." When materials are donated, they are checked for classification and removed without notice to the donor. A simple withdrawal slip marks the place of the documents that have been culled. At that point, no one—not even the original donor of the papers—may have access to the materials until the classifying agency has conducted a thorough review of the records and determined that they have been or can be declassified. Library of Congress personnel say they are bound by protocol and regulation and cannot disregard designations simply on the basis of time passed or previous disclosure. To the custodians of these records, it makes no difference that the substance of these materials may have appeared in Pulitzer Prize–winning stories or best-selling books read by hundreds of thousands of Americans a generation ago. Their task is to squeeze the toothpaste back into the tube as best they can.

•　　•　　•

Roger Heusser doesn't remember the year. It was either 1968 or 1969. He was 27, maybe 28, a young chemist with the Atomic Energy Commission working at the Richlands Operations Office at the Hanford, Washington, site, where materials were processed for America's nuclear arsenal. But one thing Roger Heusser remembers most clearly: his own tears streaming down his cheeks as he read a classified research report chronicling government projects involving experiments on humans. The government, his government, had injected plutonium and other radioactive materials into deathly ill patients and into prisoners to trace the effects of radiation on the human body.

Later, he learned of another study, innocuously dubbed "Project Sunshine," in which the government, working with some of America's most respected scientists (the project's head, Dr. Willard Libby, won the 1960 Nobel Prize), was engaged in a secret worldwide body snatching initiative. The aim of this ghoulish project, begun in 1953, was to gather up as many corpses of stillborn infants and children under three years of age as possible to test their bones for levels of strontium 90 as a way of measuring and tracing the after-effects of atmospheric nuclear testing.

Thousands of bodies were collected through a network of hospitals, physicians, and researchers. Many of the deceased were from poor families. Most bodies were obtained under false pretenses.

Roger Heusser could not put the report out of his mind. "I went to my boss and told him I was concerned about this research and he essentially said not to worry, it's not being done at our site." Heusser was not satisfied with the answer, but neither did he raise the issue again. He understood the strictures of secrecy and kept his mouth shut, though others later spoke of the experiments quite freely. Experiments that involved irradiating subjects' gonads were referred to at the AEC and its successor, the Department of Energy, in shorthand, simply as "The Privates." For officials in the know, it was a matter of "the less said, the better."

A quarter century passed, and Heusser found himself working as a classification officer in Washington, D.C., at Department of Energy head-quarters. One day he was called to a meeting in the conference room of the secretary of energy, Hazel O'Leary. It was late in the day. O'Leary was dressed in gym shoes and sweats. Heusser was sitting among people far senior to him in the department, most of them assistant secretaries. O'Leary wasted no time getting to the point: "Who can tell me about the human experiments?" she asked. The problem had surfaced via a Freedom of Information Act request filed by Eileen Welsome, a reporter with the *Albuquerque Tribune*.

"You could have heard a pin drop," recalls Heusser. No one said a word. The secretary repeated the question twice. Still there was no response. Finally Heusser raised his hand. "Ma'am," he began, "I've known about it for nearly thirty years."

"Well, what was your reaction?" she asked.

" 'When I read the first report,' " he told me he said, " 'I broke down and cried because we were causing pain and suffering to these poor people,' and then she asked me, 'Why didn't you do anything about it?' " He said there was little he could do. With that, says Heusser, there was a brief discussion about how to handle the issue now that parts of it were getting public attention. All the senior officials present argued against releasing materials on the experiments, warning that it would only fuel a widening scandal and wound the department's reputation. O'Leary overruled them. "Let's get it out," she declared, and Heusser, who for all those years had dutifully held his silence, was tasked with spearheading the release. "He was brave in so many ways," recalls O'Leary, now the president of Fisk University.

O'Leary's introduction to secrecy had come more than a half a century earlier. It was just after World War II, and O'Leary was six or seven years old on a train in South Carolina on her way to Hot Springs. She remembers that at a certain point along the way the blinds would be lowered so as to obscure the view of something forbidden. What it was, she didn't know. All she knew was that other passengers on the train did likewise. Years later, it occurred to her that the train had passed near the Savannah River nuclear processing plant. When she became secretary of energy, it would come under her watch, as would the nation's weapons labs.

Now she was in a position to raise the blinds on decades of highly controversial government programs buried by the stamp of secrecy. The release of tens of thousands of human experimentation records was only a small part of what may be remembered as one of the greatest campaigns for openness in the annals of the U.S. government, a recognition that history would have precedent over image, that accountability, no matter how late in the coming, would have its day.

Other sensitive records also underwent review and release. Documents that showed a devastating three-quarters of a million tons of deadly mercury had been released into a tributary of the Poplar River at Oak Ridge's Y-12 nuclear facility in Tennessee, exposing employees and the community at large to a deadly problem; that revealed the existence of some 204 hitherto secret U.S. nuclear tests; that disclosed that as South Vietnam fell, the United States inadvertently left behind a small amount of plutonium at a reactor in Dalat; that a staggering 800 separate human experiments had been conducted. By Heusser's count, they involved some 16,000 human subjects over the course of 40 years.

But those were just numbers. It's the faces behind them that O'Leary remembers, and that day—October 3, 1995—when some of those who had been victims of experiments attended a gathering at the White House called to coincide with the release of the final report on human experimentation. O'Leary recalls leading President Clinton from the podium down among the people who were there to express their gratitude that the truth had finally come out. "I have a clear recollection of the people," she says, "a woman with half a face, a grandmother with her retarded daughter—all of them alleging they had suffered some form of exposure because of government programs. I remember my security force surrounding me and telling me you can't meet with these people, they're crazy." The secret had been lifted, though on that day few Americans paid any attention. It was the day the verdict in the O. J. Simpson trial was handed down.

In 1993, the Department of Energy ordered a review of some 32 million pages of aging DOE documents then held at the National Archives and numerous other record repositories. If stacked on top of each other, said O'Leary, the papers would rise higher than 32 Washington Monuments or stretch some three miles into the sky. What the documents showed time and again was how secrecy was invoked not to protect the nation's security but to conceal nefarious activities from the eyes of American citizens, to avoid controversy, public embarrassment, or ethical review. And as the documents came forth, history was made, literally and figuratively. What was released sometimes shocked the conscience, as when "Project Sunshine's" Dr. Libby declared, "Human samples are of prime importance and if anybody knows how to do a good job of body snatching, they will really be serving their country."

Many DOE staff members, both within its security ranks and within its weapons programs, expressed a sense of liberation from finally coming clean of the past, from setting the record straight and distancing the present from the grim shadow of the Cold War. Heusser and others had felt that by maintaining secrecy around such grim projects they had somehow become complicit in them. What was happening at the DOE was happening elsewhere as well, as government officials began to recognize the costs of obsessive secrecy, a secrecy that had held government in its grip in ways that resembled too closely those of its longtime ideological foe, the Soviet Union.

Much of the impetus for opening the past to review came from Executive Order 12958, which President William Clinton signed on April 17, 1995; it ordered that records of a "permanent historical value" be automatically declassified after 25 years unless they fell under narrowly construed exemptions. The second sentence of that executive order read: "Our democratic principles require that the American people be informed of the activities of their government. . . . The changes provide a greater opportunity to emphasize our commitment to open Government."

Between 1995 and 2001, some 1.5 billion government documents were declassified, providing Americans with a rare and unvarnished glimpse into their own past. Some of what was revealed shook the public, tested their faith in government, and undermined their confidence in a system in which secrecy had sanctioned so many activities that offended basic American sensibilities. "We were shrouded and clouded in an atmosphere of secrecy," Energy Secretary O'Leary declared. "I would even take it a step further. I would call it repression." That newfound openness—what the Soviets would simultaneously hail as *glasnost*—was to be short-lived.

The Soviet Union fell in December 1991. Just shy of a decade later, on the morning of September 11, 2001, terrorists struck the United States, and the "atmosphere of secrecy" descended again. Declassifications plummeted, resources for records review began to dry up, and whole new categories of controlled information surfaced across the breadth of government. Some of what had been public disappeared. Roger Heusser was not surprised. There had always been government officials who resented the new openness; they were opportunists content to bide their time. He called them "the long knives." Their day had come again. Once more, not even history was safe.

•   •   •

Today, the Department of Energy's Office of Declassification has been renamed the Office of Classification. The emphasis on openness embodied in Clinton's Executive Order 12958 has been whittled away by the Bush administration, and as resources for declassification have dwindled, scores of workers have been assigned to find things that should be reclassified.

There was evidence aplenty even before 9/11 that the days of openness that Energy Secretary O'Leary helped promote were numbered. Those who had always preferred secrecy had been patiently stalking Clinton's aggressive policies of historical record declassification. Secretary O'Leary provided the perfect target. On June 8, 1999, Rep. Dana Rohrabacher (R-Calif.) unleashed a vicious personal attack on O'Leary on the House floor, coming as close as one can to charging treason without uttering the word "traitor." Even the late Joe McCarthy might have blanched. But the real target was openness itself. Rohrabacher ranted that O'Leary was "the grand pooh-bah of nuclear openness. . . . This is worse than the Rosenbergs. This is Looney Tunes. This is someone who has a fanatical anti-American attitude in a position to hand over to our worst enemies secrets that put our young people and our country in jeopardy. Those who benefited the most were the minions of the People's Republic of China, the Communist Chinese."

The occasion for Rohrabacher's calculated outburst was an investigation into the case of Wen Ho Lee, the Taiwanese-born scientist at the Los Alamos weapons lab in New Mexico, who was then under suspicion of having helped the Chinese in their nuclear weapons program. Others soon joined in, accusing O'Leary of aiding the nuclear weapons programs of North Korea, Iran, and Iraq (countries that would, a few years later, be dubbed "the Axis of Evil"). Of course, none of O'Leary's accusers apologized after it became obvious that there was no evidence that Wen Ho Lee had committed espionage, nor anything to substantiate their claims that anyone had benefited inappropriately from the release of DOE's historical records. On the contrary, the American people used the information to clean up nuclear-waste sites, address the transgressions of the human experiment programs, retrieve dangerous nuclear materials accidentally left overseas, and write a more comprehensive history of the nation.

Others would soon create their own opportunities to control or prevent the release of records. Once in office, Attorney General John Ashcroft wasted no time before he attacked the crown jewel of transparency, the Freedom of Information Act (FOIA). One month to the day after the attacks of 9/11, Ashcroft sent out a memo to the heads of all government departments and agencies tilting the FOIA's presumption from one of openness to one of secrecy. At the White House, on November 1, 2001, George W. Bush issued Executive Order 13233, which changed the rules of access to presidential papers, neutered the provisions for automatic release of documents, and allowed the sitting administration to largely determine when and whether presidential papers of their predecessors would be released to the public.

In an elegant act of protest, an esteemed historian, Richard Reeves, sent Bush copies of two of his books, one on President Kennedy, the other on President Nixon. "I said that they might be worth something someday as artifacts because it would be impossible to write them under his new order," recalls Reeves.

And at the Department of Energy, openness advocates who had championed the release of historical records were replaced by individuals empowered by the Kyl-Lott Amendment to the National Defense Authorization Act of 1999 to review hundreds of thousands of previously released records to see if there was anything in them that would warrant reclassification. The Kyl-Lott Amendment was framed by lawmakers who viewed the wholesale declassification efforts of O'Leary during the Clinton years as a dangerous and indiscriminate relaxation of security principles predicated upon mistaken notions that because a document was decades old it could be disclosed without harm.

•   •   •

Among the bureaucrats who wield the stamp of secrecy or who reclassify already-declassified documents is Fletcher Whitworth, a DOE declassifier who works in the bowels of the secrecy beast. A dapper 45-year-old bearing a resemblance to the country and western singer Randy Travis, he is a specialist in nuclear, chemical, biological, and radiological threats. He prides himself in being independent—twice he voted for Reagan, once for Perot, and once for Clinton. Never for George W. He is a card-carrying member of both the ACLU and the NRA, and his favorite political speech is a rousing liberal appeal made by the character played by Michael Douglas in the film *The American President.*

Fletcher Whitworth's interest in WMDs goes back to his childhood in Acworth, Georgia, when he wrote his first paper, in the seventh grade, on the atomic bomb. He has 12 years of active duty in the Army and twelve in the Army Reserves, all in preparing for defending against WMDs. One of the original supporters of openness at the Department of Energy throughout the early nineties, he finds no contradiction in his current mission, to secure already declassified documents that contain "restricted data" or "formerly restricted data."

He says he is committed to open government. But Whitworth is convinced that as productive as the open government initiative was under Clinton, its reliance on bulk declassification of records older than 25 years led in some instances to documents being released that should never have been declassified. "I have a son and I want to be able to sleep at night," he says.

Since 1999, the DOE has reviewed more than 460 million pages released under Clinton's Executive Order 12958. A series of surveys and examinations pared the number requiring further scrutiny down to about 200 million, then 30 million, and finally to about 15 million records. This massive quality control, or "QC," effort is ongoing, but in some instances it has meant that records have been pulled from the shelves for months and, in some cases, even years.

Whitworth and his colleagues have scoured not only the National Archives but every presidential library from Truman's through Carter's, searching for nuclear secrets. No records are too obscure to get the attention of government in the post-9/11 environment. In February 2005, the federal government dispatched a team of reviewers to the University of Washington in Seattle to examine the personal papers and records of the late senator Henry "Scoop" Jackson, who died in 1983. Whitworth was a part of that team, along with one colleague each from the DOE, the

CIA, and the ISOO. For several days they pored over the records in the university's Special Collections—some 1,235 cubic feet of them. Whitworth said that he was bleary-eyed when it was all over and that he found nothing that needed to be reclassified. The CIA, however, was said to have withdrawn several pages from the Jackson papers and deleted names. What the CIA extracted it won't say—it's secret.

> There is no more significant pointer to the character of a society than the kind of history it writes or fails to write.
> —Edward Hallett Carr, British historian

The minutes of the ongoing struggle between the writing of history and the expansion of secrecy are to be found in many of government's repositories of historical records, but none are neater than those at the U.S. Department of State. Since 1861, the State Department has published a series of volumes known as the *Foreign Relations of the United States,* or *FRUS,* as it is reverently referred to by historians. To date it runs to some 350 published volumes, an assemblage of narrative and documentation gathered from all of government's foreign affairs agencies. Though virtually unknown to most citizens, it provides "the official historical documentary record of U.S. foreign policy" and is mined by scholars and popular writers of history alike. But today *FRUS* and the effort to record U.S. history are under siege from the forces of secrecy.

That conflict is cryptically chronicled in the minutes of the Advisory Committee on Historical Diplomatic Documentation, a gathering of eminent historians who guide the State Department's Office of the Historian in shaping the *FRUS* series. Much of their energy is spent thrashing out thorny issues of secrecy and classification and butting heads with other agencies and departments that jealously guard their own secrets and their own histories. They search for compromises in an inhospitable landscape in which historians are often viewed as meddlesome second-guessers and trespassers.

Even within this committee of prominent historians secrecy is seen as a vital part of their process, with significant discussion conducted behind closed doors. The *Federal Register* of June 15, 2004, announced an upcoming meeting of the committee and noted without so much as a hint of irony, "The public interest requires that such activities be withheld from disclosure." Even the minutes of open meetings are often so elliptical and diplomatically worded as to leave all but the already informed in the dark.

Sometimes, especially when frustrations run high, the minutes chart the historians' efforts to preserve and present what they can of the nation's historical record. Because they are a kind of clearinghouse for diplomatic history, representatives of numerous agencies and departments appear before them. In September 2003, Nancy K. Smith, director of the Presidential Materials Staff at NARA (the National Archives and Records Administration), told the committee that officials from the Department of Energy and the Air Force were going through the Presidential Libraries' open stacks conducting a review for "quality control." What that meant was that they were examining documents and materials that had already been made public but that, by current standards of national security sensitivities, might be withdrawn and reclassified. The National Archives, Smith said, had already been instructed to "reclassify some *Foreign Relations* published documents." Even some documents that had been previously published in *FRUS* and made available worldwide "may no longer be able to remain declassified," she said.

The concern of the committee members and staff was clear. One staffer noted that DOE reviewers were screening the State Department's vast Central Files. The historian Robert Schulzinger noted that among the types of documents now being challenged were some "published in *Foreign Relations*, which the AF [Air Force] would like to remove from the presidential library shelves on principle."

For *FRUS*, one of the ongoing conflicts in attempting to document U.S. history is with the Central Intelligence Agency. Even before 9/11, State and CIA appeared to be at loggerheads as historians complained that the CIA was simply ignoring them or setting up one roadblock after another. What that meant was that, absent CIA collaboration, some volumes of history would be sadly deficient, lacking a major component, that of U.S. intelligence. For years the CIA had stiff-armed State, as well as the National Archives, providing as little cooperation as possible. Always it invoked the need to protect "sources and methods."

The CIA held the process hostage until the State Department's Office of the Historian agreed to a memorandum of understanding that redefined the working relationship between the State Department and the CIA to safeguard the Agency's "sources and methods." Members of

State's Advisory Committee on Historical Diplomatic Documentation, concerned that State had entered into an agreement that might compromise the entire process, asked repeatedly to examine the memorandum, but were denied access to it. State Department historian Marc Susser also refused to show me a copy of the memorandum or to describe its contents. It is said to be unclassified but marked "for official use only." Glimpses of the agreement emerge from the public minutes of subsequent meetings, as does the pressure the CIA brought to bear in promoting its interests.

One of the provisions of the agreement gives the CIA the right to review not only its own records but the entire *FRUS* manuscript in advance not only of final publication but in advance of conducting its own classification review at the CIA. The Agency argued it needed to know the full context before it could make an informed decision about what could and could not be released. But some within State feared that it would allow the CIA to withhold materials from any volume it saw as unduly critical of, or unsympathetic to, the Agency's position.

The new agreement also gave the CIA the right to review any press releases related to publication and even a say in how the indexes were presented, fearing that they might generate a floodtide of unwanted FOIA requests at the Agency. And while the CIA could not dictate to State whether a particular *FRUS* volume would be published, the Agency had gained a say in determining when it would be published. That meant, for example, that if a publication related to Iran was scheduled to come out at a time of increased tensions, the CIA might block it.

Although the State Department put the best face on the situation, some members of the advisory committee were left with deep concerns. In September 2003, some members balked: "[Warren F.] Kimball said that he was uncomfortable with the increasing amount of time the Agency was using to review manuscripts, and that it seemed to him like there was no light at the end of the tunnel. . . . Kimball raised another point: he wanted to know what compromises or agreements HO [Historical Office] was making to clear documents."

In December 2003, in a closed session, David Herschler from the State Department's Office of the Historian expressed concern: "In particular, the Agency has identified a number of documents from several *FRUS* volumes that were improperly declassified. Herschler asked, 'How do we account for omissions in our volumes when the CIA wants the HO

[Historical Office] to publish redacted versions of already fully declassified documents that have been available at NARA?'"

The problems did not stop there. In September 2004, it is noted in the minutes that the DOE had reclassified documents at the National Archives and that "CIA reviewers claimed the right to remove documents from the open files that, in their view, had never been 'properly declassified.' " All the while, State was publicly hailing what it called the "ever-growing cooperative spirit exhibited by the CIA."

That cooperation had its price. In fiscal year 2004, "the CIA had vetted 13 [FRUS] manuscripts and 1 access guide." No mention is made of what changes, deletions, or additions the CIA made to the manuscripts. And despite the Agency's robust assertions of the need for secrecy, one staff historian at State noticed that the Agency seemed willing to bend its own rules when this served its own purposes. For example, a State Department staffer named David Geyer noted that Ben Weiser, a *New York Times* reporter and author of *A Secret Life*, had "apparently received access to CIA information and subsequently published details that *FRUS* historians could not publish," including "identifications and extraordinary detail from CIA materials." Those materials denied State's historians related to the Warsaw Pact. It was hardly the first instance when the Agency granted selective access to those it favored. Without commenting directly on the matter, the CIA told State that a private book was different from *FRUS*, which was, after all, "an official government publication."

William Roger Louis, who chairs the advisory committee, noted that not all problems came from outside the State Department. The minutes note that "Louis said that he agreed, in principle, with the need to suppress documents that expose intelligence sources and methods. But he objected to having entire documents—even editorial notes—suppressed, often by the Department of State."

The *FRUS* series is pockmarked with examples of how the writing of history has on occasion been subverted, stalled, or censored, by strategic deletions, particularly by the CIA. Such omissions, many of them related to events and crises three and four decades earlier, have rendered some *FRUS* volumes not merely incomplete but distorted. The deletions force researchers to step wide around those very regions and periods where the Agency played its most active and influential role.

The Soviets had a name for such deletions. They called them *byeliye pyatna,* or "white spots," a way to wipe the historical slate clean of pogroms, famines, and purges. But blotting out the past creates its own perils.

The question heard most often after 9/11 was "Why do they hate us?" Nothing could even remotely justify the attack of 9/11, but filling in the "white spots" in the *FRUS* series might help account for some festering animosities toward the United States. The 1990 volume on Iran dealing with the early 1950s left out the CIA-engineered coup that toppled Mossadegh in 1953 and brought the Shah to power. That link between the CIA and the Shah is well known to the people of Iran who suffered under his secret police, the dreaded Savak, and his repressive regime. Omitting such a momentous chapter from America's official history seriously wounded the integrity and credibility of the *FRUS* series. So outraged was the chair of the State Department Historical Advisory Committee at the time that he resigned in protest rather than preside over what he considered to be an affront to history. But that did not bring a halt to the redactions.

In the late 1990s the State Department published *FRUS* volumes on Indonesia-Malaysia-Philippines and Greece-Cyprus-Turkey, examining the period from 1964 to 1968. Though duly printed and bound by the Government Printing Office, the CIA, with cooperation from some State Department insiders, managed to prevent their release for some two years. The Indonesia volume contained documents that detailed how the United States had provided names of suspected Communists to the Indonesian government during a period in which an estimated 100,000 individuals were killed by the dictator Haji Mohammad Suharto. The volume on Greece referred to CIA involvement in the Greek elections, to which the CIA objected. The Agency pushed to have that section redacted or to have the entire press run reduced to pulp. The volume on Greece was finally released just weeks before 9/11.

The volume on the Congo from 1961 to 1963 fared little better, as the CIA spread its cloak of secrecy over decades-old events in a nation whose government and very name had long since ceased to exist. The historian David N. Gibbs blasted the volume, which, he said, "omitted vital information, suppressed details concerning US intervention, and generally provided a misleading account of the Congo crises." That was five years before 9/11.

Now, emboldened by the war on terrorism and the supremacy of security concerns, the CIA has continued to drag out the process of historical declassification. For two years, another volume on the Congo, dealing with the years 1960 to 1968, was held hostage to the CIA's strictures on secrecy.

The State Department's historian Marc Susser argues that despite the tougher security environment, his department and the CIA have ironed out some of their differences and many of the problems that have dogged the *FRUS* series in the past are now resolved. "We don't get everything we would like," concedes Susser, "but we get enough that we still feel we are telling the story in accordance with the law." That law requires that the *FRUS* series provide a "thorough, accurate and reliable documentary record of major United States foreign policy decisions and significant United States diplomatic activity."

But *FRUS* general editor Edward Keefer acknowledges that the specter of secrecy and government resistance persists. A volume on the Congo in the period 1960 to 1968 has been tied up for a year at the CIA and a volume on Japan covering the years 1964 to 1968 was just published after what he called "an inordinate amount of time to clear." It is difficult if not impossible to judge the scope of compromises reached between the State Department and CIA and other intelligence organizations, and doing so is made all the more difficult when the State Department's advisory committee meets in closed session, as it routinely does.

One thing is beyond dispute: If official diplomatic histories fail to meet basic standards of completeness and candor, it could have lasting consequences both here and abroad. Notes from a closed-door session from March 7, 2006, record that an advisory committee member, Edward Rhodes, "remarked that the public perception of the historical accuracy of high profile volumes would make or break the reputation of both the series and the committee. [Robert] McMahon added that the U.S. Government's reputation for openness was at stake as well."

But if the quest for a "thorough, accurate and reliable" history has value, so too does the imperative to protect the nation's security and in particular its "sources and methods." The trick is in maintaining the proper balance between the two and not using secrecy as a way to filter or sanitize history.

The CIA's argument, at least in the abstract, is not without merit. Edmund Cohen, a former director of information management at the

CIA, set forth Agency concerns at a 1998 talk at the National Archives. "Revealing the identification of sources and their deeds at some subsequent time could subject them and their families to personal danger, ridicule, or persecution in their homeland for generations to come, hardly an incentive for cooperating with us. Even more serious is the chilling effect on possible future collaborators who will refuse to assist us out of fear that their names will one day be revealed by the U.S. government."

That sounds eminently reasonable. The problem has been that the Agency has invoked "sources and methods" with such abandon as to cover virtually anything it finds even remotely sensitive or objectionable, including faulty intelligence assessments dating back half a century.

One of the most impassioned defenders of CIA secrecy is "Dr. No," William McNair, a former information review officer for the Agency's clandestine service who was dubbed "Dr. No" by the former CIA director George Tenet. For years McNair dealt with the CIA's Historical Review Group, an outside advisory panel, and fielded scholarly inquiries regarding the CIA's past. McNair, who retired from the Agency in 2003, says it is simplistic and dangerous to assume that because something happened 40 years ago, or appears to be devoid of sensitive information, it should automatically be released. He and other intelligence veterans cite what is known in the trade as the "mosaic theory," in which seemingly innocuous information, when placed in context with other bits and pieces of data, produces a highly sensitive result.

According to McNair, that is precisely what happened as the publicly funded John F. Kennedy Assassination Review Board went about its work and Agency documents were declassified. That effort was hailed by historians, but McNair says it had a darker and undreamt-of consequence. An individual savvy to the ways of correlating disparate pieces of information used a relational database matching up similar phrases, and was able to piece together the identities of some CIA informants. It was a capability that not even the CIA possessed at the time, according to McNair.

As a result, in 1995, though more than 30 years had passed since the assassination, the Agency had to relocate two families at a cost of several hundred thousand dollars. The Agency also made payments to another individual too old to relocate. The money went to bolstering his personal security. The fear was that Cuba would view the individuals as traitors and go after them. McNair will not identify the individuals except to say they had connections to Cuba and had been CIA assets in 1963. While it is impossible to independently confirm McNair's account, it is true that history and secrecy have at times collided, that honoring agreements of confidentiality does not toll with a statute of limitations, and that the mere passage of time does not eradicate the need for prudence.

The CIA's outside board of historians has little real influence with Langley. Some on the board express frustration and complain that the frequent turnover of CIA personnel they deal with is a none-too-subtle strategy designed to keep them off balance and slow down the declassification process, reducing the historians to Sisyphus-like characters. "The CIA kept changing the personnel to erase the institutional memory," says Warren Kimball, a professor of history at Rutgers and a 23-year veteran of Naval Intelligence who served in the active Reserves. He chaired the State Department's historical advisory committee from 1991 to 1999.

Many serious historians also grumble that one of the documents essential to understanding the history of U.S. foreign policy, the president's daily brief, has always been denied them. As long as PDBs are taboo, it is difficult, if not impossible, to know what the president knew or when he knew it, and what was the quality of intelligence he was given. Some of those most familiar with the PDB suggest that opposition to the eventual declassification of the PDBs is concerned less with "sources and methods" than with fear that making them public will expose them as being more pedestrian and less insightful than the CIA is comfortable admitting.

"There are all kinds of rationalizations for hiding stuff, very few of which are honest," says Robert A. Pastor, who has been on the CIA's historical review committee since 1995. Indeed, much of the CIA's resistance to contributing to the historical record is rooted in its desire to maintain a certain "mystique"—the word actually appears in a CIA memo. Members of the Agency's historical advisory panel say they have seen numerous instances in which the CIA has opposed the release of details, including manpower and budget figures, on decades-old covert operations that have long since been exposed and are the stuff of popular legend here and abroad. Insiders familiar with the actual scope of such activities say that many of those celebrated—or notorious—operations were so puny as to be insignificant. "Such selective redactions can lead historians to adopt exactly the opposite historical conclusions of where the truth would take them," says Pastor.

Indeed, Pastor and others suggest, the full declassification of such operations would show the Agency to be at once much less influential but also less malevolent than some journalists and those inclined to conspiracy theories have made it out to be. Pastor says such omissions by the Agency have led to some "pretty grotesque exaggerations in the press."

"Both critics of the CIA and the Agency's own operatives are in this strange conspiracy where they make it appear that the CIA is omniscient and omnipotent; that's complete nonsense," says Pastor.

Such debunking as would result from a fuller historical record is not necessarily seen to be in the interest of the Agency, which has long taken pride in its image of far-ranging potency, the phantom hand of American power that has deftly manipulated regimes to its own advantage. To "neither confirm nor deny" its role in history has created a veritable cottage industry of films and novels, allowing the popular imagination to feed upon fantasy and intrigue. Such a strategy seemed sustainable, and the Agency's true reach remained unknown, until the devastating intelligence debacle exposed by 9/11.

Since then, the Agency has spent much time and energy securing secrets of long ago and effectively editing history by withholding records of its own past shortcomings. But excessive secrecy has a way of clouding judgment and playing havoc with perspective. At times, it seems the Agency might have been better served if its obsession with secrecy had been directed to more immediate matters. In the summer of 2003, the CIA was elated to report that an Iraqi scientist, Mahdi Shukur Ubaydi, had come forward with secret Iraqi plans for a centrifuge capable of enriching uranium. Since 1991, those plans had literally been buried under a rosebush in Iraq. Now they provided the CIA and the administration with evidence, outdated though it was, of Saddam's intent to pursue a nuclear program.

In its enthusiasm to trumpet the find, the CIA was somehow momentarily blinded to its own primary responsibility—the security of the nation. On June 26, 2003, it posted the actual photographs and detailed blueprints of the centrifuge on its official website for all the world to see. In its accompanying commentary, the Agency even noted that "Dr. Ubaydi told us that these items, blueprints and key centrifuge pieces, represented a complete template for what would be needed to rebuild a centrifuge uranium enrichment program."

A few days later, the spy agency came to its senses and realized the sensitivity of that information and removed the photos and blueprints from its website.

"We just took them down," said a chagrined CIA spokesman, Mark Mansfield. "They were up there for a few days and didn't need to be up anymore." In that, he was right.

Within the week the Agency's blunder had made news around the world. A Reuters report appearing in Pakistan's *Daily Times* reported the entire episode and referenced a website where the centrifuge plans and photos displayed by the CIA the week before had been permanently cached and were accessible to anyone interested in building a centrifuge. One might fairly ask if any of the tens of thousands of decades-old documents removed from the archives or withheld from official histories of the United States contained anything as sensitive or potentially damaging to America's national security as that which was so boldly featured on the website of the CIA.

5

Case Study: He Who Must Not Be Named

When reporters who cover the intelligence community gather over drinks or at conferences, they can sometimes be heard to speak of "Jose." Such intimacy suggests perhaps a classmate or old friend. In truth, "Jose" is neither. Most of these reporters have never even met "Jose," though by now that first name is familiar to them and to close readers of the news who take an interest in intelligence matters and national security. Savvy reporters know Jose's last name, but they don't dare say it or print it.

He is like the Harry Potter character Lord Voldemort, referred to by Harry and his friends, out of sheer dread, simply as "He Who Must Not Be Named."

But in this case the one who cannot be named, Jose, heads the nation's clandestine service, that far-flung network of spies.

Reporters' references to Jose are partially the product of misguided patriotism, one more sign that reporters have become comfortable playing footsy with those who have cloaked the business of government in secrecy. But there is also another reason why the press shies away from giving Jose a last name, as I was soon to find out; they have been subtly and not so subtly intimidated by a government obsessed with secrecy.

I called the CIA to ask why I should not give Jose's last name in this book of mine. Michelle, one of three Agency public affairs officers, fielded my question. First I asked whether I might have Michelle's last name. "Depends on the nature of your questions," she responded coyly. And so I asked why Jose could not be given a last name.

"Because he has opted to remain undercover," she said. In other words, it was Jose's decision to be covert. "And what if I were to write his last name?" I asked. "Naming him would be a violation of law," said Michelle. "That would be a matter for the Department of Justice. Did you ever hear of someone named Valerie?" she asked, referring to the covert operative Valerie Plame, whose outing by someone in the administration led to a major criminal investigation and landed a *New York Times* reporter in jail for nearly three months.

Michelle conceded that one might have to go back in history, decades maybe, to find another head of the clandestine branch who was not overt and publicly named. Jose's predecessors as head of HUMINT, or human intelligence, individuals like Stephen Kappes, James Pavitt, and Tom Twetten, were well known to the press and to students of intelligence. Google them and up pop hundreds of links discussing their positions, their roles, and their backgrounds.

But was she, I asked, comfortable with references to Jose?

"That is on your conscience," she said.

Now she is right that it's against the law to knowingly reveal the identity of a covert operative, but ordinarily, when the CIA says someone is "undercover," one imagines someone in the field on secret assignment in Tehran, on a remote Afghan mountainside, in a parlous back alley of Baghdad, or posing as a low-level State Department official in Beijing.

That is not where one would come across Jose. He is to be found in a comfortable, well-appointed office a few minutes' drive from the White House, a bureaucrat who serves as head of the National Clandestine Service (created after 9/11 to coordinate HUMINT). There are few organizations that play a more vital role in the war on terror and few whose decisions and actions have a greater potential impact on the nation's security. Jose oversees what may be called "Spy Central," the headquarters that manages espionage and covert operations within the CIA, but also coordinates such efforts across the U.S. government.

He is a man who oversees thousands of federal employees and who may be expected to have his hands in innumerable critical and often highly controversial operations—snatch-and-grab abductions overseas, renditions, and more.

It is hard to imagine that a person who sits astride such a huge bureaucracy could be known only as Jose. But that is another sign of the slippage, the inexorable slide into greater secrecy. Covert status is essentially a blanket grant of immunity from scrutiny by press and public alike. It's exceptionally convenient, especially when one's line of work is fraught with controversy, moral sensitivities, and legal ambiguities. Jose gets to be virtually invisible, off the screen of public attention, while occupying one of the most prominent management positions in the intelligence community. Such secrecy comes at the expense of public accountability. It means that he will not have to testify before Congress or answer to anyone unless it is behind closed doors.

Yet major news organizations have accepted this stricture without challenge. You will find references to "Jose" in the *Washington Post,* the *U.S. News and World Report,* and the *Christian Science Monitor,* on Fox News, and in other news outlets. In one article, the *New York Times* would not even provide the name Jose, dutifully noting on October 14, 2005: "That official, a long-serving CIA officer with considerable experience in Latin America, remains undercover and cannot be publicly named, the agency said." The *Washington Post* wrote that he is "referred to as 'Jose' because he is still under cover."

Now here's the interesting part. Any schoolchild can search the Web and unmask him without resorting to anything more complicated than Googling "Jose," and "National Clandestine Service." His name is in the European press and appears in such unstealthy venues as the online reference source Wikipedia, complete with a detailed biography of previous posts held. You can also find his full name in the *Asia Times,* which bills itself as "Asia's Most Trusted News Source." In March 2004, his full name was reported by the Associated Press, when it chronicled Jose's visit to Athens to confer with Greek officials on matters relating to the Olympics and counterterrorism concerns. That article went around the world. (And found its way to the *New York Times* website.)

One wonders whether, with all its resources and guile, Al Qaeda might not have the wit and wherewithal to consult Wikipedia for this dark secret denied only to unwitting U.S. citizens.

Still, there may be more to the press's complicity in this matter than meets the eye—or less. Buying into such flimsy secrets does not disadvantage the press. On the contrary, such self-censorship gains brownie points with Langley, as it shows that the press is sensitive to security issues. It may be a small bargaining chip to be parlayed into something more valuable later.

It also artfully conveys to the public the illusion that the press is well connected and has insider access. That kind of "I-know-something-you-don't-know" mentality adds cachet to otherwise pedestrian reports and conveys an impression of sleuthing. This scene-setting is on display in a story run by MSNBC.com on February 6, 2006, written by Robert Windrem, who is identified as "NBC News Investigative Producer."

In the story, Mr. Windrem reveals that the CIA's head of the Counterterrorism Center "has resigned under pressure," saying " 'the head of the CIA's clandestine service has lost faith in my leadership,' U.S. intelligence officials tell NBC News." Spooky. Now comes the really spooky part: "The names of both the official and his boss are classified and they can only be referred to by their first names: 'Bob,' the CTC director, and 'Jose,' the director of the clandestine service." The story then goes on at length exploring how "Bob" and "Jose" didn't get along, all attributed to other unnamed "CIA officials." The public can be forgiven if among all these first names and faceless voices, they mistake this as idle office gossip by the watercooler, forgetting it is about who shall lead America's fight against terrorism.

Within hours of MSNBC.com's story, the *Washington Post* produced its own account of the very same matter, only they identified the resigning head of the Counterterrorism Center as one Robert Grenier. ["Jose" was not even named in the *Post* except as one who "remains under cover."] So too did the *San Francisco Chronicle,* the *L.A. Times,* London's *Sunday Times,* bloggers, and others. So much for "Bob's" cover, except that it is not at all clear that Robert "Bob" Grenier was under cover.

And so it goes, as the press becomes ever more entangled in secrecy—and ever more subject to the increasingly real threat of prosecution. It was hardly the first time that the press has played coy with the name of someone within the CIA. You may remember the book *Imperial Hubris: Why the West Is Losing the War on Terror,* authored by the mysterious "Anonymous."

The identity of that author was hardly a secret to many reporters, but still they participated for weeks in a charade to conceal the name of

Michael Scheuer, a former CIA analyst. Their complicity played right into the hands of what turned out to be, if nothing else, a brilliant marketing ploy that helped catapult the book to bestseller status. All this, and the book had been meticulously vetted and approved by the CIA. Scheuer, aka "Anonymous," then turned up on CBS's *60 Minutes* in November 2004. Other examples abound.

Oh, I nearly forgot. Jose's last name is . . . No, you look it up. I have no interest in squaring off with the Justice Department. The best I can offer is Michelle of Public Affairs' last name. That much she allowed. It's "Neff."

Secrecy and the Press

The Washington leaker, a poltergeist with a phone, is sometimes good and sometimes bad but is almost never caught.
He or she disappears into the Washington souk, an exotic
marketplace where information is traded, character is assas-
sinated and the air is redolent with hypocrisy.

—Richard Cohen, columnist,
Washington Post, Oct. 2, 2003

The Press, Watson, is a most valuable institution if you only
know how to use it.

—Sherlock Holmes, fictional detective,
"The Adventure of the Six Napoleons," 1904

It is one of the crueler ironies of the post-9/11 era that the press, whose
raison d'être is to hold government accountable and promote transparency, should itself have become a casualty of secrecy, its methods and
manners eerily mimicking those it monitors.

Since the 2001 attacks, media critics and administration officials alike
have had a field day chastising the press for its refusal to identify
sources, its habitual reliance on those skulking in the shadows of
power—nameless whistle-blowers, anonymous leakers, traffickers in
classified documents. And to the degree that the press has accommo-

dated government appeals to hold back stories or portions of them, it has rendered itself vulnerable to charges of being compromised, used, or duped.

But to say the press's behavior is indefensible is to miss the point. It was inevitable.

Secrecy has an insidious way of contaminating virtually everything that comes in contact with it. The more government conducts its affairs behind closed doors, the more the press itself is transformed into an unwitting vector and carrier of that secrecy. When all open and conventional channels of information are denied journalists, what choice is there but to rely upon less conventional avenues of access?

Day in and day out, press inquiries are ignored, denied, or dismissed. Cadres of government spinmeisters artfully dodge reporters' questions. Would-be sources are intimidated into silence or face the threat of prosecution or the political equivalent of exile. Government handlers sit in on interviews, screen questions, and chill the exchange. Public officials often equate secrecy and national security, implicitly questioning the patriotism of those reporters who seek answers to critical questions.

That leaves the press with few options: the numbers, resources, and laws all favor government's ability to withhold information. There are few successful frontal assaults to be made against secrecy. Capitulation—resigning oneself to carrying government's water—brings shame upon the press and leaves citizens at the mercy of those who promulgate lies, half-truths, and propaganda. The alternative is to adopt the sort of guerrilla tactics characteristic of asymmetric warfare.

To resist secrecy, one must succumb to it. It is a devilish dilemma: The compromises and countermeasures the press must accept in pursuit of the truth put its reputation at risk and expose it to accusations of hypocrisy.

Damned if it does, damned if it doesn't, the press is led by circumstance to promote transparency by relying on stealth, to advocate openness even as it is driven into government's dark corners and alleyways, and to champion accountability and the rule of law even as it resists disclosure of its own methods, fends off grand juries, subpoenas, and the courts, and takes cover behind a battery of lawyers. To some, its claim to higher authority—the First Amendment—is as suspect as the president's claim to executive privilege. The press runs a gauntlet between disclosures and omissions, something else it shares with government.

At times, the press has demonstrated courage and resourcefulness. It has achieved some stunning victories, pulling back the curtain on torture and abuse, secret detainments, and domestic surveillance. But even these triumphs are tainted with self-censorship and omissions of fact. At its worst—as in its reporting on Iraq's alleged WMDs in the run-up to the invasion of Iraq, its weak coverage of civilian casualties in that country, and its uncritical coverage of alleged spies at home—the press has been judged by some to be complicit, its credulity and its coziness with the institutions it covers profoundly damaging to its stature.

All of this has made the press easy prey for the very individuals who have, by their own calculated actions, placed the press in this unenviable predicament. It is invariably the architects of secrecy who are among the first to impugn the character of the press, to challenge journalists' credibility, to hold its lack of openness against it. In short, the press has painted itself into much the same corner that government now occupies, reflexively invoking secrecy, refusing to cite authoritative sourcing for its statements of fact, and asking the citizenry to accept its word as an article of faith. Caught between the two, government and press, a frustrated public wonders whom to believe and what became of the vaunted transparency that was the hallmark of democracy.

No institution illustrates more clearly the wrenching conflict faced by today's press than the *New York Times,* the nation's preeminent newspaper. Its courage and persistence, its foibles and flaws, are multiplied across the journalistic landscape. Its institutional motto proclaims that it prints "All the News That's Fit to Print." But secrecy has substantially redefined the meaning of "fit," at times casting doubt on the paper's editorial judgment and its candor.

On December 16, 2005, the *Times* printed a blockbuster of a story: in 2002, President Bush had secretly ordered the National Security Agency, without warrant or judicial oversight, to eavesdrop on Americans making international phone calls and to intercept their e-mails, a potential violation of civil liberties and the Foreign Intelligence Surveillance Act.

Within that bombshell was another that was buried in the ninth paragraph: the *Times* had held the story for an entire year. For many Americans that second revelation was no less discomfiting than the first.

Why the story had been held for so long was not disclosed beyond vague references to national security and the need for more reporting to evaluate the government's claim that disclosure would damage

America's ability to track potential terrorists. (Valid as that may sound, *Times* insiders say the outline of the story remained largely unchanged.) Why the story finally ran when it did was never explained. (During that year of self-imposed silence, by the *Times*'s own reckoning, thousands of Americans may have had their phone conversations and e-mails secretly tapped by the U.S. government.)

Whether the *Times* was in possession of this incendiary story prior to the bitter and historically close November 2, 2004, presidential election was not even addressed, though it became instantly clear upon publication that the story had the potential to alter the political landscape. The *Times* has indicated that there are other elements of the domestic surveillance scenario that were also deliberately kept from readers, but it is impossible to know how critical they are to understanding the main story.

Outside the *Times* there were howls of criticism that the paper would withhold such a critical story for so long. If publishing it was an act of public service (the story would go on to win the Pulitzer Prize), then withholding it, in the eyes of many, was a dereliction of duty of equal consequence. Inside the paper's newsroom, too, there was consternation, discomfort, and frustration. America's flagship newspaper had become entangled in the very secrecy that it had long decried.

Internal scandals and turmoil rooted in secrecy have plagued the paper in recent years. Dozens of times between October 2002 and April 2003, a 27-year-old reporter, Jayson Blair, had fabricated and plagiarized stories that appeared in the *Times.* That episode had been perpetuated by the opacity of the paper's editorial process.

The *Times*'s commitment to transparency appeared to end at its own front step. On May 14, 2003, at the height of the Blair crisis, some 600 *Times* staffers filed into Loews State Theater, in Times Square, to confront their beleaguered editors and demand an explanation of how Blair, who had committed more errors in a year than most *Times* staffers committed over several lifetimes, had managed to enjoy the favor of the paper's then executive editor, Howell Raines. Too late, the *Times* would discover that Blair was not merely inexperienced and error-prone but deeply troubled and a serial fabricator. Inside Loews Theater, a *Times* metropolitan editor, Joe Sexton, accused the paper's executives of failing to demand that Blair name his anonymous sources even after they had ample grounds to suspect his honesty.

But what made some inside the room even more uneasy was that the newspaper that championed transparency in government had deliberately excluded the working press from attending the gathering. Security guards posted outside the theater doors made sure no one in the press—beyond the hundreds who worked for the paper itself—got past them.

Later, an in-house commission studied what could be done to restore the *Times*'s credibility and prevent a recurrence. Among the key findings was a call for greater transparency and the need "to make us conspicuously accountable to readers and the public."

Bill Keller, who as a columnist had repeatedly railed against the dangers of government's "obsessive secrecy," as the new executive editor personally signed on to the commission's recommendation to create a "public editor," someone to serve as a liaison between readers and the paper, and even more important, someone "to speak truth to power" (the phrase comes from a 1955 Quaker pamphlet). Keller guaranteed that editors would have access to the publisher.

But by 2005, notwithstanding its public pronouncements about editorial openness, the *Times* had become even more resistant to inside and outside inquiries about its reporting. Byron Calame, the *Times*'s public editor, began his January 1, 2006, column with these words:

"The *New York Times*'s explanation of its decision to report, after what it said was a one-year delay, that the National Security Agency is eavesdropping domestically without court-approved warrants was woefully inadequate. And I have had unusual difficulty getting a better explanation for readers, despite the paper's repeated pledges of greater transparency. . . . The mention of a one-year delay, almost in passing, cried out for a fuller explanation."

But the secrecy that Calame encountered did not end there. He wrote of deliberate "stonewalling," and of editors who were in possession of information "urging everyone else to remain silent." Neither Executive Editor Bill Keller nor Publisher Arthur Sulzberger Jr. responded to Calame's list of 28 questions.

Something else was troubling about the surveillance story. Nowhere in the 3,700-word article was there a reference to another critical fact: one of the *Times*'s lead reporters on the story, James Risen, had a book about to come out that was going to expose the entire domestic surveillance program. Many within and outside the *Times* say it was the threat of a scoop posed by Risen's book that triggered publication and not any change in the paper's prior stance on national security or the adequacy of the reporting. The imminent publication of Risen's book was a fact citizens would learn of not from the *Times* but from other news organizations days later. Even then, the *Times* refused to discuss it.

"It seems to me," wrote Calame, "the paper was quite aware that it faced the possibility of being scooped by its own reporter's book in about four weeks."

If the *Times* stiffed its own public editor, it was even less forthcoming with reporters outside the paper. The spectacle of the nation's premier newspaper and outspoken proponent of government transparency declining comment, conducting its affairs behind closed doors, and shunning outside scrutiny reflects the extent to which the *Times* has itself fallen prey to the very secrecy that it disdains. And in this, it is hardly alone. The *Times*'s handling of the surveillance story is part of a broader pattern that shows what a double-edged sword secrecy can be in the hands of the press, that even as it produces stories of vital importance to the nation, it can wound its own credibility.

Jim Risen is a first-rate investigative reporter, but his methods and those of the paper have courted controversy before. Six years ago he penned a book about the CIA's war with the Soviet KGB. His coauthor on the book, Milton Bearden, had been a covert CIA operative and a key player in the mujahideens' war with the Soviets in Afghanistan. Many believe these CIA activities gave rise to jihadists and Al Qaeda.

What readers of the *Times* were not told is that while Risen wrote about intelligence matters for the *Times,* the portion of his book written by his partner, Bearden, was undergoing vetting by the very agency Risen covered. Risen's six-figure advance and the book it represented were, to a degree, at the mercy of the CIA, about which he routinely wrote. That arrangement was approved by *Times* senior management. Editor Keller said he saw no conflict in having his intelligence reporter paired with a former covert operative or having a portion of Risen's book dependent upon the approval of the CIA.

Risen was also the principal reporter in the paper's investigation of Wen Ho Lee, the Los Alamos scientist who came under suspicion of espionage. When the *Times* first broke its story, it appeared to be groundbreaking. But when the smoke cleared and the facts emerged, the story raised serious questions as to whether, in pursuit of an exclusive, the *Times* had suspended its critical judgment and become reliant upon unnamed government sources with their own agendas. That remains a recurring question facing the *Times*—whether, in attempting to penetrate secrecy, it has become beguiled by it.

The *Times*'s reporting on Wen Ho Lee, and its writing on another government scientist, Steven Hatfill, offer cautionary tales on the power of the press, the allure of secrecy, and the vulnerability of ordinary citizens. How swiftly, these citizens would say, the press can turn from protector to predator.

Wen Ho Lee was a Taiwanese-born American scientist who worked at the weapons lab at Los Alamos, New Mexico. Steven Hatfill was an expert in biological agents who for a time worked at the Army's Fort Detrick facility in Maryland. Both considered themselves patriots, having worked for the defense of the nation. Both were extremely private. Neither read the newspaper. (They had become skeptical of the press even before the personal ordeals that the press helped set in motion.) And both men were to come into the crosshairs of the *New York Times* in ways that would forever change, if not ruin, their lives.

Wen Ho Lee's first encounter with the *Times* came the morning of March 6, 1999. The paper's headline read "Breach at Los Alamos: A Special Report: China Stole Nuclear Secrets for Bombs, U.S. Aides Say." The article alleged that the Chinese had stolen U.S. technology that allowed them to develop small nuclear warheads that bore a suspicious resemblance to America's W-88 warhead. The tone of the story was chilling. One quote referred to whoever was responsible for such espionage as "the worst spy since the Rosenbergs," a reference to Julius and Ethel Rosenberg, who were convicted of providing nuclear secrets to the Soviets in the fifties. (They were later executed.)

Two days later, Wen Ho Lee was fired from Los Alamos. Risen followed up with another article, this one headlined: "U.S. Fires Scientist Suspected of Giving China Bomb Data."

From that time on, Wen Ho Lee was plunged into a Kafkaesque nightmare. It was bad enough that he had been under investigation by the DOE and FBI, but the *Times*, in an instant, helped elevate him to a villain of historic proportions. A June 14, 1999, story offered a quote that Lee "may be responsible for the most damaging espionage of the post–cold war era."

Some six months later, on December 10, 1999, Lee was arrested and imprisoned. For 278 days he was held in solitary confinement. At times he was shackled in irons and allowed but one hour's exercise a week. He faced a staggering 59 counts. Between the government's investigation and the *Times*'s aggressive coverage, augmented by a host of other publications vying to catch up, there were few voices raising any doubts about whether Lee had betrayed his country.

And then, ever so slowly, the case against Wen Ho Lee unraveled. Despite months of innuendo and suspicion, there was no hard evidence that Lee had been a spy. Indeed, there were growing questions as to whether there had been any espionage at all. Despite all the headlines and rushing to judgment by the *Times* and those who nourished the story with leaks, the case was finally unmasked for what it was—utterly unsupportable.

On September 13, 2000, Federal Judge James A. Parker accepted Lee's guilty plea to a single count of using an unsecured computer to download defense information. He was credited with time served and allowed to walk. The other 58 counts evaporated.

One of the great spy stories of the modern era was of no more substance than a soap bubble. Despite the single count to which he pled guilty—a crime of common carelessness, not espionage—Wen Ho Lee became a victim of secrecy and what appeared to him to be a terrifying alliance between the government and the press. Even Judge Parker could not resist remarking on the unfairness of Lee's treatment at the hands of the government. "I believe you were terribly wronged," the judge told him.

To Parker's voice was added President Clinton's on September 14, 2000. "The whole thing was quite troubling to me," said Clinton, "and I think it's very difficult to reconcile the two positions that one day he's a terrible risk to the national security and the next day they're making a plea agreement for an offense far more modest than had been alleged." The White House pointed a finger at the press, and singled out the *New York Times,* suggesting the *Times* editors had, as the paper put it, "propelled an overzealous prosecution by the administration's own Justice Department." Comparisons were drawn with the case of Richard Jewell, who on the basis of anonymous government leaks was implicated in the bombing at the Atlanta Olympics—another victim of secret sources and an overly credulous press.

Members of Congress also weighed in. Rep. George Miller, a California Democrat, saw in the Wen Ho Lee case a matter of concern to all Americans. "Once again," he told Congress in October 2000, "we see that when the incredible power of the government comes down on a single individual, all too often that individual's rights are crushed under the full force. And in this case we saw almost a hysteria that ran through the government, through committees of Congress, within the Department of Energy and Justice and Defense, in a frenzy to try to prove something that they may, in fact, not have had the evidence to prove."

The *Times*, for its part, came under enormous pressure to answer accusations that it had helped railroad an innocent man. On September 26, 2000, two weeks after the judge's apology and rebuke, the *Times* printed a highly convoluted editors' note in which it acknowledged that critics were now charging that "our reporting had stimulated a political frenzy amounting to a witch hunt."

The *Times* expressed pride in "work that brought into the open a major national security problem," even as it acknowledged that it should have "pushed harder to uncover weaknesses in the FBI case" and "did not pay enough attention to the possibility that there had been a major intelligence loss in which the Los Alamos scientist was a minor player or even completely uninvolved." In short, the *Times* acknowledged that it should have given weight to the possibility that Wen Ho Lee was innocent. But as occurred again in other stories to follow, the appeal of exclusivity and the cachet of secret sources had dulled the *Times*'s skepticism.

The October 2000 self-examination, defensive in places, candid in others, grazed another important element of the story that had been given short shrift in the initial Wen Ho Lee stories: the behind-the-scenes political aspects of the case. The Clinton administration had been eager to expand U.S. engagement with China. Many Republican members of Congress were resistant to that initiative and believed Clinton to be both lax on security issues and politically vulnerable. They sought to subvert his China initiatives by focusing instead on China as a potential U.S. enemy and recipient of U.S nuclear espionage.

The Wen Ho Lee investigation played a vital role in that broader attempt to discredit and thwart Clinton's China policy and highlight instead that nation's hostile intentions. The *Times* stories on Wen Ho Lee were instrumental in popularizing that image and putting a human face—a villainous one—on the threat.

The articles were written by two of the *Times*'s most seasoned veterans, James Risen and Jeff Gerth. Neither reporter expressed remorse for the stories.

Lee for his part sued the government for violating his privacy and subpoenaed the *Times*'s Jim Risen (as well as reporters from four other news organizations), demanding that they disclose their sources. The reporters refused, citing the First Amendment. They were held in contempt and in November 2005 a federal appeals court refused to hear their arguments on why they should not be made to comply with the order to disclose their sources.

Finally, in June 2006, after a six-year lawsuit, Wen Ho Lee accepted a $1.65 million payment to settle the case. Of that, $895,000 was from the government to pay for his legal fees and $750,000 was paid by the *New York Times* and the other news organizations. In a joint statement they insisted that the only reason the press paid was to "protect our sources and protect our journalists." There was no hint of regret and no admission of error.

Lee, for his part, simply said, "We are hopeful that the agreements reached today will send the strong message that government officials and journalists must and should act responsibly in discharging their duties and be sensitive to the privacy interests afforded to every citizen of this country."

The *Times*'s handling of the Wen Ho Lee story commands neither sympathy nor support. From the vantage point of Wen Ho Lee, Richard Jewell, and others who have found themselves similarly the subject of suspicion and secret sources, the relationship between the press and prosecutors may appear to be perilously close to one of collusion. The First Amendment was, after all, intended to be a shield against an overly zealous government, not a sword wielded jointly by government and press against hapless citizens.

In such cases, it is questionable whether the collective hands of the press are clean enough to invoke the majesty of the First Amendment. Doing so in the current climate of suspicion and hostility could backfire, endangering far more meritorious cases and ultimately eroding First Amendment protections. Lawyers are fond of saying that hard cases make for bad law. In a judicial environment already distrustful of the press, the Wen Ho Lee case and others like it could well tempt judges to weaken press protections, to render journalists more vulnerable to subpoenas, libel, and privacy actions, and to encourage government lawyers to test the limits of prosecuting the press for disclosing state secrets.

For the press, the question has often been one that the Roman satirist Juvenal raised: *"Quis custodiet ipsos custodes?"* "Who shall guard the guards?" America's answer has been that the press is primarily responsible for watching itself. But if it is widely perceived to have failed in that unique charge, if it is seen to run roughshod over individuals' reputations and to behave as a captive of government, it will invite the intervention of entities already only too eager to weaken it. Collectively, reporting that reflects balance, a commitment to public service, and a high regard for each citizen's liberty and good name reaffirms the need for a robust First Amendment.

Whatever lessons the *Times* and others gleaned from the Wen Ho Lee saga do not appear to have helped Steve J. Hatfill two years later. Hatfill was a medical researcher and former government scientist who, like Wen Ho Lee, through no fault of his own, became the subject of intense attention from both the *New York Times* and the FBI.

Once again, it was one of the *Times*'s most distinguished writers, the Pulitzer Prize–winning columnist Nicholas Kristof, who chose to focus the paper's gaze on an ordinary citizen. The story begins in September and October 2001, when deadly anthrax-laced letters arrived in the mail, killing five, sickening 17 others, and profoundly disrupting the Senate, the Supreme Court, and the postal service. A nation already shaken by 9/11 demanded answers and justice.

But despite intense public and political pressure on the FBI to apprehend the anthrax killer, the bureau was stymied. Weeks passed, then months. With a reported 8,000 interviews conducted and some 5,000 subpoenas served, the largest criminal investigation in U.S. history was going nowhere. Frustrations within the Justice Department and across the nation grew.

One of the harshest critics was Kristof, who wrote a series of columns that did two things: they sharply criticized the Justice Department investigation, and they drew attention to a man Kristof coyly referred to at first as "Mr. Z." On July 2, 2002, he wrote of the FBI's "lackadaisical ineptitude in pursuing the anthrax killer." Later, Kristof called the bureau "unbelievably lethargic." He went on to suggest that "some in the biodefense community"—anonymous sources all—"think they know a likely culprit."

Kristof suggested that the bureau had bungled its investigation of Mr. Z and would do well to refocus its investigation on him. "Some of his polygraphs show evasion, I hear," Kristof wrote. "I hear" is about as indeterminate a sourcing as any ever cited, but enough to draw national attention to the mysterious figure. Kristof went on to provide enough details to set the biodefense community buzzing with suspicion.

Mr. Z turned out to be Steven Hatfill. In June and again in August 2002, someone within the investigation tipped off the press so that it could be present to film a search of Hatfill's residence. On August 6, 2002, Attorney General John Ashcroft announced that Hatfill was a "person of interest," a term just vague enough to thoroughly destroy whatever was left of his reputation, but not so specific that it would require any actual indictment or evidentiary support. That same month, Hatfill was stripped of his job at Louisiana State University, where he was associate director of the university's National Center for Biomedical Research and Training. By then a mob of reporters, fed by anonymous sources, had fastened their attention on him.

Four years after the anthrax attack, not much has changed. Hatfill has been the subject of more than 2,000 articles. No arrest has been made, no charges brought, and there is no suggestion that the FBI is any closer to solving the case than it was when it began its investigation. The *Times* headline of November 3, 2001, could serve today as well as then: "Baffled F.B.I. Asks For Aid In Solving Riddle Of Anthrax."

Many FBI agents once formally assigned to the case are off investigating other crimes. Kristof continues to write his *Times* column but is on to a whole new series of public crusades. He has never hinted that an apology was due Hatfill, nor suggested that his columns were in any way intemperate or imbalanced. (In a column, he did note that Hatfill must be presumed to be innocent, as if that were enough to have shielded him from the tsunami of attention his columns brought.)

For Steven Hatfill, however, life as he knew it is over. A workaholic, he used to be at the lab 14 hours a day. Now he has nothing but time on his hands. His days are spent watching television or conferring with attorneys trying to get answers as to who was responsible for destroying his life and who, in violation of his privacy, shared information from his

FBI files with the press. As with the Wen Ho Lee case, the *Times* invoked the First Amendment and refused to identify its sources. But in October 2006, a federal judge ordered Kristof to reveal the identities of three of his sources, and he faces a possible contempt charge if he refuses—as the *Times*'s attorney, David McCraw, suggested Kristof would. (In January 2007, a federal judge dismissed the defamation lawsuit against the *Times*, but Hatfill's attorney vowed to appeal the ruling.)

During an interview broadcast on National Public Radio in August 2002, Kristof was asked by the host, Brooke Gladstone, about "what appears to be the sweating of suspects by law enforcement through anonymous leaks in the press" and referred to the cases of Richard Jewell, Wen Ho Lee, and Steven Hatfill.

"You know," said a pensive Kristof, "if you look back at how the media's handled various cases, then we really have at times ruined the lives of people by tossing their names out there before they've been subject to any kind of criminal process, and when our presumption has to be that they're innocent and just caught in this incredible nightmare." A moment later Kristof explained why he wrote his columns about Hatfill: "It was," he said, "to light a fire under the FBI." He did light a fire, but instead of illuminating the crime, he helped incinerate a citizen.

•   •   •

Of all the instances in which the press and secrecy have intersected in recent years, none has produced greater public disillusionment than the *Times*'s coverage of weapons of mass destruction in the months leading up to the invasion of Iraq. It is too familiar a story to warrant going into at great length, but it is also too momentous to pass without pausing. One of the principal architects of that coverage was the once-celebrated and now oft-maligned Judith Miller.

A Pulitzer Prize winner, she was hardly alone in accepting that there were WMDs in Iraq. Many leading journalists and many in the military, the intelligence community, and Congress—including those now among the war's strident critics—took it as an article of faith that Saddam Hussein possessed WMDs. To indict Miller alone, or the *Times* alone, is to be as selective with the facts as Miller and the *Times* are themselves accused of being. But in journalism, presumption is a felony and the complicity of others offers neither mitigation nor comfort.

In the debate over WMDs that, once concluded, became the principal justification for going to war in Iraq, no paper had greater stature than the *Times* and no reporter more influence than Miller. Her byline was the reference point to which skeptics were routinely directed by those chafing for invasion and regime change. Miller and the *Times* relied on the whispers of administration sources and unnamed Iraqi exiles to create a persuasive case that Saddam possessed a terrifying arsenal of unconventional weapons.

Miller was very much a creature of America's culture of secrecy. The consummate cultivator of sources, she did not fully realize the extent to which she was being cultivated. The very tenacity that had helped produce solid stories in the past was now pressed into the service of her conviction that WMDs existed and would, with enough reporting, be discovered. She immersed herself in the ranks of those who shared that conviction and single-mindedly pursued the story, believing WMDs to be less a matter of whether than where.

It was later a convenient fiction for the *Times* to suggest that Miller was the root of the problem, that credulity, seductive access, and tunnel vision were her personal excesses, not institutional flaws. But the unusual freedom and perquisites she enjoyed as a reporter—measured in her time spent traveling, her budget, and her independence from editorial interference—were conferred upon her by the *Times*'s most senior editors and it was they who positioned her exclusives on the front page. (Some of those exclusives failed to withstand subsequent scrutiny.) The *Times* later conceded a degree of editorial laxness but, like the captain of a ship, kept suggestively pointing to the loose cannon on the deck, Ms. Miller, whose sobriquet was "Miss Run Amok."

The truth is otherwise. The *Times*'s own editorial page reflected the same predisposition to swallow the government's case for WMDs. Editorial page chief Gail Collins has said that her greatest regret since assuming that position was failing to raise more questions about WMDs.

"If I had it to do over again," she told a writer from the industry magazine *Editor & Publisher* in July 2006, "I would have paid a lot more attention to the people on the board who had doubts. I thought there were weapons of mass destruction and most of the board members did. Frankly, we did not spend enough time debating the issue. . . . We should have argued among ourselves more. . . . Given our readers some of a sense that there was an argument about it; we tended to take it for granted."

Her words are candid but chilling. Unanswered is the question of how one of the nation's most respected editorial boards could have so utterly shirked its responsibility on so grave a matter as that of war and peace.

There have been other occasions when the *Times* has gotten it wrong, though rarely with such dire consequences. "Nothing short of a disaster" would be an apt description of the *Times*'s coverage of WMDs, but it is a phrase lifted from another era. "On the essential questions the net effect was almost always misleading. A great people in a supreme crisis could not secure the minimum of necessary information on a supremely important event."

Those words were written more than 80 years earlier, in another time of secrecy and fear. Then, the paranoia was about the Red Scare, not Al Qaeda. The writers of those words were the journalist Walter Lippmann and Charles Merz, destined to be the *Times*'s editor. Their words appeared in *The New Republic* in 1920, and were an attempt to explain how the *Times* could have been so wrong about the Russian Revolution.

On scores of occasions between 1917 and 1920, the paper reported the imminent demise of the Soviet regime. "They were performing the supreme duty in a democracy of supplying the information on which public opinion feeds, and they were derelict in that duty." Where did they go wrong? In Lippmann's words, the *New York Times* reporters "accepted and believed most of what they were told" by the government. There are no more damning words to a journalist's ears than these.

In an ironic twist for one so adept in trafficking in secrets, Miller was betrayed by someone apparently within the *Times* who leaked to the *Washington Post* an internal memo written by her. That memo identified one of her principal sources as Ahmad Chalabi, the exiled leader of the Iraqi National Congress, a man who had been convicted in absentia in Jordan of embezzling almost $300 million and who in May 2004 was suspected of passing U.S. secrets to the Iranians. Miller, and through her, the *Times* itself, came to rely for inside information on Chalabi, a darling of the Bush administration and a man whose interest in goading America into toppling Saddam would soon help him realize his own political ambitions in Iraq, at least for a time.

Two things are undeniable: Miller did not hijack the paper's WMD coverage; no one forced the paper to put her stories on the front page;

and even when her reporting unraveled, the paper stood stunningly mute.

Not until May 26, 2004, 15 months into the war, did the *Times* run a 1,220-word editor's note on page A10 finally acknowledging what had by then become clear to the entire world—that its coverage of WMDs had been flat-out wrong. In classic understatement, *Times* editors noted that "coverage was not as rigorous as it should have been." Editors, it conceded, had been "too intent on rushing scoops into the paper." But no editors were named. Finger-pointing—what the paper does day in and day out with the rest of the world—is deemed bad manners at the *Times*'s family dinner table.

On October 23, 2005, the paper's public editor, Byron Calame, acknowledged that many of Miller's stories from 2002 and 2003 had "turned out to be inaccurate." And why had *Times* editor Bill Keller allowed Miller's and the *Times*'s reporting on WMDs to go uncorrected for so long—more than a full year after the war commenced?

"I fear I fostered an impression that the *Times* put a higher premium on protecting its reporters than on coming clean with its readers," Keller told the public editor. "If I had lanced the WMD boil earlier, I suspect our critics—at least the honest ones—might have been less inclined to suspect that, this time, the paper was putting the defense of the reporter above the duty to its readers."

On November 9, 2005, Miller and the *Times* finally parted ways when Miller announced that she had "retired," which may itself have been a testament to her formidable ability to see the world as she willed it to be. Fittingly enough, the financial terms of her departure were kept secret.

The *Times* now wishes to put "the Miller matter," as it might like the scandal to be known, behind it. Editor Keller grows testy at the mere mention of her name. Sackcloth has never suited the *Times*. But readers will not relent.

"I've been fairly disgusted with your timid coverage of the Bush administration, especially about the run-up to the war in Iraq, and ESPECIALLY the non-questioning Judy Miller articles. . . . Will you hide behind the lame excuse that you don't want to be part of the story?" a California reader e-mailed the *Times* at asktheeditors@nytimes.com in 2006.

"Sigh," Keller responded. "I can't imagine that there is anything to say about Judy Miller that I have not already said, publicly and to the

Times staff, over and over." He wearily reeled off a truncated explication of the affair, noting that he may be "without any hope of quenching the curious thirst of the Miller-obsessed."

But there is no statute of limitations on the Miller story, and the fatigue Keller and his *Times* colleagues suffer surely pales beside the travails of those still serving at the front in Iraq three years later, or of the Iraqi people facing mayhem, or of the American people drained in so many ways by war. That is the problem with such a story. It will not surrender itself to history, but continues to fuel today's and tomorrow's headlines. It persists with a half-life that goes on and on, and so long as it does, those responsible for it must remain answerable, vigilant, and humbled. It is the least they can do.

One need not be "obsessed" with Judith Miller to worry about whether America's newspaper of record could once again let down its guard, seduced by secret sources and consensus.

•   •   •

For reporters as well as sources, the post-9/11 environment has proved toxic. Increasingly government has proved its effectiveness in choking off access to on-the-record interviews, chilling debate, and raising the specter of subpoenas, prosecution, and incarceration of journalists and sources. Who can blame would-be sources for becoming increasingly skittish and insistent upon promises of confidentiality?

Jack Nelson, a Pulitzer Prize–winning journalist and 50-year veteran of chronicling the news, has never seen anything quite like it before. "This administration," he said in a speech he gave at a Washington, D.C., conference on secrecy in March 2005, "is by far the most secretive administration I have had any experience with at all. They have no shame, in my opinion, in doing things in the dark, and I don't know how we really combat that, except to just keep battering away and filing Freedom of Information suits, talking to people on the Hill, talking to every lower official we can get to talk to us who is interested in the people."

Reporters have been reduced to—but also, seduced into—accepting anonymous sources. This plays into the hands of those in power who seek to discredit the press by suggesting that there is the taint of shame to all this, that sources are afraid to show their faces not because they utter the truth but because there is skullduggery and betrayal afoot. It fuels public suspicions that journalists are shady, biased, or sandbagged.

But accepting secret sources, no matter how loathsome or risky the process, can sometimes be the only way to snatch a glimpse over the wall of secrecy, particularly on sensitive national security stories. Of course, the mask of anonymity is not always donned for high principles alone. At both ends—the reporter's and the source's—it can be used to promote one's career, as high-profile scoops often do, or to gain individual or institutional advantage in a competitive environment, be it journalism or politics. The press is fond of citing its adversarial relationship with government, but the truth is that the relationship between them, no matter how strained, remains more symbiotic than either the press or the government will recognize or admit.

Increasingly the most critical news reaches citizens via disembodied voices and unnamed sources. A 2005 study by the Project for Excellence in Journalism that examined some 16 newspapers and 6,589 stories found that 7 percent of all stories relied upon anonymous sources. It also found that papers are twice as likely to use unnamed sources on their front pages and that the larger, more influential papers among the 16 studied relied on anonymous sources in 20 percent of front-page articles. In short, the more prominent the display of the article, and the more influential the paper, the greater was the reliance on unnamed sources.

Television was worse. The study found that 53 percent of the stories on the three commercial networks that air nightly news were based on tips from unnamed sources, up from 43 percent a year before.

If all stories based on secret sources presented information that was accessible in no other way or that was of critical importance, readers might be more forgiving. But that is often not the case. Bill Kovach, one of the deans of American journalism and a former *New York Times* bureau chief, worries about what he sees. At the March 2005 conference on secrecy and sources, in Washington, D.C., Kovach appealed to his colleagues, reminding them of the observation of the British press baron Alfred Harmsworth, Lord Northcliffe: "Real news is something someone, somewhere wants to keep secret. Everything else is advertising." But today's obsession with secrecy has changed that, said Kovach.

"We have helped create a world in which Lord Northcliffe's dictum is standing on its head. We no longer can feel so sure that what we expose is truly news. As we've all seen to our regret, much of what has been reported from anonymous sources as news was, at best, advertisement and at worse, designed to mislead the public opinion with deceptive and even false information."

Many of today's stories reflect a cynical government's willingness to use secrecy as a screen from which to launch half-truths aimed at political foes and critics. Or simply to avoid being linked to distasteful truths.

On April 2, 2006, the *Washington Post* reported on the collapsing political fortunes of Katherine Harris, a Florida Republican and candidate for the U.S. Senate. A quote critical of her chances to win election—judged by the polls at the time to be astronomically remote—was attributed to "a veteran of Florida GOP politics, who was granted anonymity *to speak candidly* [emphasis added]."

The attribution was an attempt to explain why the person would not allow his or her name to be used, but even as it cloaked the source, it revealed a wider reality: that in the current atmosphere, the price of candor is too high, or the price of secrecy, too low. Easy grants of anonymity breed such inhibitions, even when a source is stating the obvious. A week after the *Post* article appeared, the elders of Florida's Republican Party wrote Harris to say that the party was withdrawing its support, noting, "The polls tell us that no matter how you run this race, you will not be successful." (And they were right. In the November 7, 2006, election she garnered a mere 38 percent of the vote in her doomed race for the U.S. Senate.)

In a May 4, 2006, article, a *New York Times* reporter writing about a disagreement within a film studio noted that her sources "spoke on condition of anonymity because they did not want to be associated with the conflict." Since when is that grounds for concealing the identity of a source? Other such examples abound.

In a July 13, 2006, *New York Times* article, a source described a sensitive document to a *Times* reporter, thereby possibly running afoul of Britain's Official Secrets Act. Without a hint of irony, the *Times* attributed the quote to someone who was not named "because he said he was bound by the secrets act." That was too much for even Calame, the *Times*'s public editor, who observed that such anonymous attributions "strain logic almost to absurdity."

A front-page *Washington Post* story of September 4, 2005, quoted a "senior Bush official" as saying that Louisiana's governor, Kathleen Blanco, had failed to declare a state of emergency in response to Hurricane Katrina. At the time, the administration was coming under withering attack for its inept response to the disaster and sought to shift blame onto the state's Democratic governor. A check of the public record would have revealed that the official was either lying or woefully misinformed. Blanco had in fact declared a state of emergency back on August 26.

The paper ran a correction the next day, but by then both the governor and the *Post* had taken a black eye. As usual, the "senior Bush official" who had been the source for the story was not identified or held to account. And why not? Because protecting a source is a bedrock principle. But should that extend to harboring a fugitive from credibility?

For the *Post,* it might have been worth the embarrassment if the lesson learned was that greater discretion was needed before granting anonymity—or even just to check the facts before quoting. But the very day the *Post* ran its correction, it featured prominent stories attributed to "a senior official," "one top official," "a conservative ally of the White House," "a senior Bush administration official, who spoke on condition of anonymity," and on and on and on. A cynic might wonder whether they were all the same person.

Over time, the press has become so conditioned to operating in a hostile landscape that many reporters now preemptively offer up a promise of confidentiality even to those who have not yet asked for it. It is a kind of auto response that has become part of the preamble to an interview. At the 2005 conference on secrecy and sources, a former White House spokesman, Mike McCurry, said that 80 percent of the reporters who contacted him routinely opened the conversation by pledging not to identify him as a source, a kind of reverse Miranda warning that instantly lets officials off the hook.

Such permissiveness has engendered widespread institutional expectations among government officials that their names will not be revealed. This pas de deux between reporter and official has come to define the culture of both press and government, in which what was once an exception—the grant of anonymity—has become the rule.

Once largely restricted to the White House, State Department, and Pentagon, the practice has now migrated across the entire spectrum of the federal government, and vertically, from federal to state and local authorities. The private sector, too, has taken note, demurring and insisting upon confidentiality. It has almost reached the point where the only on-the-record statements are those in which the information provided advances the source's own self-interest.

"Confidential" is the word journalists prefer to use to define the hallowed (and not-so-hallowed) bond between reporters and sources, but they are careful to distance themselves from the more pejorative word, "secret." The former, they tell themselves, is a necessary price one pays for combating the latter, never mind that both leave the public in the dark.

There are far-reaching consequences to such accommodations. *USA Today*, one of the nation's largest papers, learned the perils of secrecy and anonymous sources the hard way when its ace reporter, Jack Kelley, came under suspicion of having cited made-up sources in his stories. He resigned on January 6, 2004. An independent review panel confirmed *USA Today*'s worst suspicions: Kelley was a serial fabricator. Parts of at least 20 stories were entirely made up and other stories, with parts lifted from the work of other reporters, had been made to appear to be exclusives by the attribution of the lifted parts to "U.S. intelligence sources."

"In reviewing his work," the panel concluded, "it was clear that the editing standards on his use of unnamed sources was appallingly lax. . . . His ability to get away with obscuring any reliable trace of who his sources were is a testament to his ability to deceive and to the inability of his editors to demand that he prove their authenticity."

USA Today's founder, Al Neuharth, says that he has long "preached that anonymous sources are the root of evil in journalism. It's so simple," he says. "Most anonymous sources often tell more than they know. Reporters who are allowed to use such sources sometimes write more than they hear. Editors too often let them get away with it. Result: Fiction gets mixed with fact."

The more a source's information and identity become detached from each other, the more tempted both sources and reporters may be to embroider the facts, float an idea, smear a rival. It is a dangerous game in which one can protect one's own reputation while disemboweling another's.

But there is an even more profound and lasting consequence of anonymous sources. When the face of authority is hidden, authority itself becomes surreal, remote, and suspect. The same may be said of the press itself. The voice of Washington with which we have all grown, if not comfortable, at least familiar, is that which goes by the name of "senior officials" or "well-placed sources."

We would do well to remind ourselves that these faceless individuals so often quoted are *our* elected representatives or are *our* employees paid by *our* taxes to conduct *our* business. But in accepting a regime of secrecy, we first allow our representatives to inhabit the shadows, then to join the ever-swelling ranks of the journalists' witness protection program.

Such anonymity rightly contributes to the public's sense that representative government has deteriorated into a burlesque of democracy, a bureaucracy that is removed and unresponsive, and bears no more personal responsibility for its deeds than for its words. One is reminded of the Wizard of Oz, the voice behind the screen that refuses to reveal itself and wards us off forbiddingly. In the press's tortured effort to expand citizens' access to information, it instead erects more barriers, stripping citizens of their ability to assess the credibility and motives of sources.

Cumulatively, there is something Orwellian about a government that communicates with its people through remote and unidentified interlocutors. It may create transient relief to the pressure of secrecy, but at a stiff price—adding to the malaise and frustration of a people who already sense that the country is overseen by a virtual government where accountability is held in as low repute as truth.

Anonymity is a filter that implicitly suggests that the speaker has something to conceal or something to fear. Routinely resorting to unnamed sources may even inadvertently reinforce government's stranglehold on information by institutionalizing unconventional outlets of expression and by lending weight to the perception that there is indeed good cause for fear. After hearing from legions of nameless sources day after day, despairing citizens are left with the impression that neither government nor the press has the power or capacity to safeguard speakers of truth. Isolated instances of anonymity convey information. Used routinely, they project an overwhelming sense of vulnerability.

The press did not create this regime of secrecy, but its response has helped to define the regime's contours. Coddling officials by allowing them to go off the record even as they spew administration doggerel and indiscriminately handing out grants of anonymity in matters frivolous or of little consequence have played into the hands of government, left dissenters more isolated, and compromised the press's own credibility.

In 2003, after two years of increasing government secrecy and little resistance to it from the press, Bill Kovach, founding director of the Committee of Concerned Journalists and a veteran reporter and editor, expressed his consternation: "For some reason, whether because of 9/11 and terrorist threats or the looming war with Iraq or the popularity of the president or the fear of being labeled unpatriotic, the traditional American press—again with a few exceptions—has virtually looked the other way when it comes to government secrecy."

Most journalists will concede that turning down information because it comes from an anonymous source runs counter to self-interest. In the intensely competitive realm of journalism, such unilateral action is tantamount to cutting one's own professional throat; but mobilizing in concert with others, even against secrecy, runs counter to the very culture of journalism. Campaigns and causes are what reporters write about, not participate in.

Those few willing to take a position against secrecy today often find themselves standing alone, as Ron Hutcheson, then with Knight Ridder and president of the White House Correspondents Association, learned to his chagrin. "Last year," he reminded fellow reporters and editors in 2005, "I led a spectacularly ineffective walk-out at a background briefing, ineffective because I walked out, turned around and there was nobody behind me. And my seat was filled before it was cold."

•   •   •

Government relies upon a mix of carrots and sticks to control the press—promises of enhanced or special access, and threats of exclusion, even prosecution. There have been appeals to patriotism, efforts at suppression, self-censorship, propaganda, and intimidation. An administration that has been intent upon spreading democracy around the globe has shown little regard for transparency at home. It has secretly paid journalists to promote its agenda and planted stories in the Iraqi press. It has emasculated the Freedom of Information Act, reversing its presumption of openness. It has shut down access to all manner of records and even culled the past at the National Archives. Senior officials have felt free to belittle journalists who show the temerity to ask tough questions.

Incensed over leaks, particularly those that revealed a broad program of domestic surveillance and intercepts, the government is even threatening to prosecute journalists under provisions such as Section 798 of Title 18, which makes it a crime to publish classified information about communications intelligence. That worries journalists of all political stripes. In July 2006, the *Wall Street Journal's* conservative editorial writer Paul Gigot fretted: "Now you're a journalist and so am I, and I have to admit that I have on occasion published classified information. And what worries me is that if you—once you start prosecuting journalists, where do you stop? And couldn't this open up a Pandora's box where a political prosecutor anywhere could go after the media they don't like? Where do you draw the line?"

In May 2006, ABC News claimed that calls made by its reporters and others at the *New York Times* and *Washington Post* were being traced by the government in an effort to track down leaks of classified information. Many government sources, perhaps most, no longer feel comfortable speaking to reporters on the phone, especially when the subject is even remotely sensitive. Those kinds of worries on the part of reporters and sources alike have taken their toll on journalism and on what Americans may learn of their government.

"The administration wants journalism stopped," Rep. James A. McDermott, a Washington Democrat, charged on the House floor on May 9, 2006. "It just gets in the way of the administration telling people only what they want them to know. . . . They know that secrecy is the fastest, most effective way to silence dissent."

Such efforts to suppress news and keep secrets under wraps has severely tarnished America's image abroad. Today, five journalists have been detained in American detention centers—four Iraqis are being held in Iraq and one Sudanese, an Al Jazeera cameraman, is at Guantánamo. None has been charged with a crime. The Committee to Protect Journalists says the United States now ranks sixth in the world for the number of reporters behind bars—a tie with the repressive regime of Myanmar (formerly Burma).

Many overseas news organizations and their audiences are convinced that the U.S. military deliberately targets foreign newsmen to suppress the news and keep a lid on information. In November 2001, the United States dropped two 500-pound bombs on Al Jazeera's bureau in Kabul, Afghanistan. Five years later, the Pentagon still has not responded to the Committee to Protect Journalists' call for an investigation into the strike.

On April 7, 2003, as Al Jazeera reporter Tariq Ayub was broadcasting live from the organization's Baghdad bureau, a missile fired from a U.S. jet slammed into the building, killing him instantly. Britain's *Daily*

Mirror reported that in April 2004, President Bush allegedly expressed an interest in bombing Al Jazeera's headquarters in Qatar. (The White House denies the charge.) One month later, in May 2004, an Al Jazeera cameraman, Rashid Hamid Wali, was killed by U.S. machine-gun fire while filming a clash between U.S. troops and insurgents from a rooftop in Karbala, Iraq.

At home, American reporters face the threat of jail, contempt-of-court charges, and fines for refusing to reveal their sources. News organizations cower at the prospect of being hauled before grand juries. False accusations of damage done to national security have been leveled at the press by the Pentagon and White House; one of the most destructive was the canard that the press compromised U.S. counterterrorism efforts by revealing intercepts of Osama bin Laden's satellite-phone conversations. (All indications are that bin Laden abandoned his sat-phone after U.S. cruise missiles struck his Afghan bases in August 1998.)

Grievous as such a campaign against journalists has been, it is the press's self-inflicted wounds that have made America's Fourth Estate a true casualty of secrecy. The line between responsible journalism and self-censorship has been blurred and sometimes crossed. And those in pursuit of secrets have been known to operate in such secrecy as to threaten their own credibility.

Dan Rather failed to adequately authenticate documents related to Bush's service in the National Guard. Robert Novak, knowingly or unknowingly, leaked information that blew the CIA operative Valerie Plame Wilson's secret cover. Bob Woodward, the most famous investigative reporter of his generation, failed to disclose for nearly two years after the Plame affair became a story that an official had told him that Plame had been a CIA operative. He kept that information not only from the *Post*'s readers but from his own editor, even as he publicly disparaged the leak investigation.

Even less comforting was the spectacle of *Time* magazine rolling over for a federal prosecutor and ordering its reporter, Matt Cooper, to comply with a subpoena and reveal his sources in the Plame affair. Time Inc.'s then editor-in-chief, Norman Pearlstine, unilaterally declared that the information *wasn't worth protecting*, as if the precedent *Time* was setting were no more than a matter of simple expedience. (Pearlstine later left the world of journalism to take a lucrative position at a private equity firm, Carlyle Group.) It would be understandable if both *Time's* sources and its reporters were utterly confused as to where the magazine stands in relation to pledges of confidentiality.

Time further managed to trivialize confidentiality when Time Warner's chairman, Richard D. Parsons, in November 2005, announced to a gathering attended by many prominent journalists that the remarks of their guest, Supreme Court Justice Antonin Scalia, were "off the record." That is how conditioned to maintaining secrecy the nation's major newsmagazine has become, and how mixed are the signals *Time* sends about confidential sources.

But then, for all their foot-stomping about transparency in government, the media have shown that it is often a matter of "do as we say, not as we do." Since the summer of 2001, major news organizations have railed against government's secret closed-door meetings. They protested that Vice President Cheney, the former head of the energy giant Halliburton, gave unfettered access to his office to energy executives, while limiting access to environmental and conservation groups opposed to White House energy policies. In editorials, they blasted the White House's refusal to release the records and the content of those meetings.

But as the watchdog group the Center for Public Integrity has pointed out, over the course of eight months, beginning in September 2002, media moguls met behind closed doors with top officials of the Federal Communications Commission more than 70 times to promote their own agenda and interests in relaxing media ownership rules. There was no requirement that the meetings be recorded or for detailed minutes to be taken. During that same period, representatives of two major consumer groups, Consumers Union and the Media Access Project, were limited to only five audiences with the FCC.

Andrew Jay Schwartzman, president of the Media Access Project, said his group and the public interest organizations it represents were routinely rebuffed or given the runaround when they attempted to schedule additional meetings with the FCC and its staff.

Whatever transpired behind those closed doors did not make its way to the front page. What is known is that the ownership rules were relaxed and cross-ownership bans struck down, promising windfall profits to the media giants. The decision was hailed by the likes of News

Corp., owner of Fox Network, and Viacom, owner of CBS and UPN, as well as the Newspaper Association of America, which represents such behemoths as Gannett Inc. and the Tribune Company.

Opponents of the decision warned it would further squelch diversity, create a frenzy of mergers and acquisitions, and lead to greater concentration of the nation's media. Ultimately the relaxation of ownership rules was stayed by the courts in response to a suit spearheaded by the Media Access Project. But some of the same organizations that had lobbied behind the FCC's closed door were among those that had challenged Cheney's closed door. What was good for the goose was, apparently, deemed not so good for the gander.

•   •   •

In times of national crisis, many journalists feel torn between their professional responsibilities and those of citizenship. Whether out of a desire to be patriotic or out of a fear of appearing unpatriotic, more than a few have given government the benefit of the doubt when it comes to issues of national security. Such decisions are rarely easy and often call for balancing equally legitimate values.

But the White House and Pentagon have shown themselves to be particularly adept at exploiting the good faith of the press to hold on to secrets, and the press has shown itself to be remarkably inept in explaining its decisions as to what and when it publishes. Post-9/11, efforts to control what Americans hear and know about the prelude to and conduct of war may well be unprecedented—from insisting that the media not air lengthy excerpts of bin Laden's messages to completely barring the press from seeing flag-draped coffins at the Dover mortuary. Where bad news cannot be outright stifled, the Pentagon settles for tactical delay.

In the spring of 2004, the Pentagon, in the person of Gen. Richard B. Myers, chairman of the Joint Chiefs of Staff, appealed to *CBS Nightly News* not to air a story on prisoner abuse at Abu Ghraib. The general argued that release of the information would inflame passions in Iraq and put U.S. troops and hostages at risk. (Exactly when either of those circumstances might be expected to materially change did not come up.)

So for two weeks, CBS's news anchor Dan Rather, Executive Producer Jeff Fager, CBS News President Andrew Heyward, and others sat on a devastating story of prisoner abuse and humiliation by U.S. servicemen. The network had possession of shocking photos of naked prisoners arranged in humiliating sexual positions, of prisoners facing the threat of electrocution. Some were hooded, some were stacked in human pyramids.

There was little doubt that releasing the photos would have a profound effect on the way Americans and the world would view the U.S. occupation of Iraq and U.S. talk of democratization. No one understood that better than the Pentagon, whose troops daily faced growing anarchy in Iraq and whose officials faced increasingly difficult questions at home.

Only after CBS learned that *The New Yorker* was about to publish a story about Abu Ghraib did CBS decide to air its own Abu Ghraib material. Thus, in the end, the decision to air the story was predicated not upon principle but upon old-fashioned market forces—CBS simply did not want to get scooped on its own story. On April 28, *60 Minutes II* finally shared the story with the world.

Two weeks later, on CNN's *Reliable Sources,* a CBS executive, Jim Murphy, appeared to feel compelled to prove that, notwithstanding the decision to run with the story, he and his fellow CBS newsmen were still good and loyal Americans. "We are like every other American," Murphy said, offering up a gratuitous flag-waving defense. "We want to win this war. We believe in the country." Jeff Fager, the program's executive producer, has called the Abu Ghraib segment "one of the biggest stories ever reported in all the years of *CBS News.*" In nearly the same breath he has argued that "there was no harm in holding the story."

No harm? Even if major abuses at Abu Ghraib had by that time been halted, public exposure of that scandal brought renewed national and international attention to the conditions at detention centers at Guantánamo and in Afghanistan as well as in Mideast countries to which nameless U.S. captives had been abducted and "renditioned"—all of them beyond the purview of humanitarian groups and outside monitors. During the time that CBS held the story, Abu Ghraib came under mortar attack from insurgents and 22 prisoners were killed and 92 wounded. Knowing what conditions were like within the prison might have placed that assault in a different light.

When CBS did finally break the story, it engendered a national debate about what were the appropriate moral and military limits of interrogation. The aftershocks of the story in the two weeks following its airing attest to the profound impact it had and could have had earlier had it been aired when first scheduled: six more soldiers received administrative reprimands, Secretary of Defense Donald Rumsfeld was required to face six grueling hours of congressional testimony, and it was announced that two guards at Guantánamo had been disciplined for using excessive force.

In the comfortable office suites of CBS News in New York, the two-week delay may well have been without consequence, a frustrating scheduling inconvenience, but from the viewpoint of prisoners subjected to interrogation techniques, two weeks might have felt like a lifetime. Such a delay certainly offended the conscience of many Americans and possibly violated the Geneva Conventions.

And then there was the damage done not merely to CBS's own reputation but to that of journalism at large. For many who still imagined the deficiencies of reporting in the run-up to the war with Iraq as either an example of media incompetence or worse—a conspiracy or cabal—CBS's willingness to sit on so explosive a story did nothing to dampen suspicions or bolster confidence in the press. The only thing more disturbing than CBS's decision to hold the story was the reaction of Fox News's Bill O'Reilly, who on a May 3, 2004, broadcast suggested he would never have used the Abu Ghraib photographs. "You can expect even more crazy jihadists to enlist because of this exposition," he huffed.

•   •   •

More than once, demands of secrecy have placed both reporters and government officials in hellish positions. In early October 2005, intelligence officials received word of a possible plan to attack New York's subway system using bombs concealed in briefcases or baby carriages. Jonathan Dienst, an investigative reporter with the local television station WNBC, Channel 4, caught wind of the alleged plot and on Tuesday, October 4, 2005, began to report it out. But New York and Washington authorities intervened and urged the station to hold off on the story, at least until some related operations were conducted overseas.

Dienst recalls that he went to Dan Forman, the vice president of WNBC News, to weigh the government's argument. For Dienst, the dilemma brought back a flood of painful memories. In December 1988 he had been a student in London when terrorists brought down Pan Am 103 over Lockerbie, Scotland, killing all on board. Among the dead were two of Dienst's college friends, John Patrick Flynn and Scott Saunders.

Just days before the flight, Dienst was to learn later, a warning targeting Pan Am flights from Frankfurt to New York had been circulated by the State Department, U.S. embassies, and Pan Am itself, but the warning had not been shared with the general public. After the warnings were disclosed, family members of the deceased were aghast that the alerts had not been made available to the public at large. Some wore buttons demanding to know why they had not been told. That attack and the failure to pass along the warning, Dienst says, helped propel him into a career in journalism. Both were on his mind as he sat across from WNBC's vice president of news.

"People were going to get on the subway and not know," he thought to himself. "People have a right to know, and to make their own choice: 'Am I going to get on the train today?' "

The stakes were potentially enormous. Each day, some 4.5 million passengers take New York's subway system. But Dienst agreed with his superiors to hold off on the story, to defer to the expertise of government antiterrorist officials. The next day, as always, he, too, took the subway to work.

Two full days passed.

Then, on Thursday, October 6, he was cleared to go ahead with the story, which aired at 5 P.M., just 30 minutes before Mayor Michael Bloomberg was to go public with the threat in a news conference. WNBC was praised by city officials for its restraint, but what if a catastrophic attack had occurred within those two days and thousands had perished? How then, Dienst wondered, would the station have explained its actions to the families of the bereaved and injured?

While Dienst and his colleagues fretted over the potential consequences of keeping silent in the face of the threat, others within government itself apparently chose to selectively warn loved ones and friends about the danger. At least two senior officials within the Department of Homeland Security had their security clearances yanked for reportedly sending out e-mails cautioning the recipients to stay away from New York's subways.

One of those early warnings, sent out three days before the mayor shared the threat with the rest of New York, allegedly went to the son of

William L. Ross, then deputy federal security director with the Transportation Safety Administration. The other was allegedly sent by the U.S. Coast Guard's chief information officer, Dr. Nathaniel Heiner, who was said to have alerted a close friend.

"I can appreciate them trying to take care of their friends," Mayor Bloomberg said, "but I thought it was unconscionable that only some people were notified."

In the end, the plot against the subway may have been no more than a hoax or a false lead, but it provided a very real object lesson in what lies ahead for the press in coming to terms with secrecy, and it offers a glimpse into the thicket of ambiguities that rise up between a warning and silence. The station was persuaded by the authorities that delaying the story would allow for measures to be taken overseas that would neutralize the threat without warning the perpetrators. It did what it believed was responsible, but a different outcome might well have cast the station's actions in an indefensible light. The only thing journalists can draw from the dilemma is the near certainty that we will face it again.

•   •   •

In early November 2005, the *Washington Post*'s Dana Priest wrote a stunning exposé disclosing that the CIA ran a network of secret prisons for high-value prisoners in Eastern Europe. The prisons' existence had been deemed an ultrasensitive secret by U.S. intelligence. Conditions within the prisons were unknowable. The clear implication was that these prisoners were isolated and cut off from outside scrutiny so that they could be tortured or abused and no one beyond their immediate captors would know. That suspicion was made all the more plausible by Vice President Dick Cheney's repeated efforts to exclude the CIA from a legislative ban on interrogation techniques that were deemed inhumane or cruel.

But as the *Post* broke one secret it chose to keep another, electing not to identify the nations where those prisons were located. Administration officials had persuaded the *Post* that naming the countries could expose them to reprisals from terrorists and would undermine their cooperation with U.S. antiterrorism efforts.

Honoring such a secret could make the *Post* obliquely complicit in the abrogation of human rights. To what techniques of interrogation were these and other detainees subjected in the days and weeks following the *Post*'s decision not to reveal the facilities' sites in Eastern Europe or elsewhere? And what might the citizens of those countries have to say about their nations' being used as sites of abuse and torture? The U.S. government has repeatedly persuaded top editors to withhold selected information on the basis of national security imperatives, especially in areas that could offend basic American sensibilities or inflame foreign passions against us. Such stories have involved allegations of disinformation, torture, abuse, assassination, and the surveillance of American citizens.

When the government crosses the line in its conduct, be it in abusing prisoners, violating its own laws or international treaties, or conducting indiscriminate domestic surveillance, it is only right for it to fear disclosure. But it is the government's actions, not the press's revelation of them, that may produce a backlash, damage America's image at home and abroad, set back U.S. strategic interests, and even potentially put civilians and soldiers at risk. There are always moral, political, and military consequences to our actions. In morality, as in physics, one can expect that for every action there is an equal and opposite reaction.

Appealing to the press to suppress in whole or in part such stories, to cushion the blow, to delay publication for a more propitious moment is to ask the press to enable such actions and in so doing to put its own integrity at risk. The dread of exposure and the desire to avoid consequences is a stern corrective that should always weigh upon government's deliberations. Detaching consequences from actions only encourages such conduct. The press ought not to be party to changing that calculus of risk.

On the contrary, only by being a predictable force for holding government accountable can the press play its most vital role. In times of great secrecy when process is more easily corrupted, the role of the press is not merely to chronicle government's past or current failings but to stand as a sentinel and a cautionary reminder that may ward off future misadventures and fiascos. It can do this only when decision makers know beyond any doubt that the press is both vigilant and ever at the ready to hold them *fully* accountable.

The press is still entirely free to entertain government's appeals for special consideration if sought on behalf of programs and efforts that would not, if exposed to the light of day, compromise commonly held views of decency and law.

But accommodating government's appeals regarding suspect, unscrupulous, or inhumane actions creates a kind of toxic partnership that can easily be misconstrued by government and public alike as an implicit endorsement by the press. No matter when the story runs, a government inclined to attack the press and divert attention away from its own failings and misdeeds can find ample grounds to blame journalists. Had the insurgents' attack on Abu Ghraib occurred after the publication of the story instead of before (and while the story was being held), CBS would doubtless have been blamed by some for fomenting the hostilities that led to the attack. There is never a good time for bad news.

Holding or delaying a story also may discourage potential sources from taking the risk of coming forward. Running the gauntlet is already daunting enough for whistle-blowers without having to wonder whether the press will have the courage to publish their story. Today, anyone suspected of helping a reporter on a controversial story can expect to be investigated and polygraphed, even fired and prosecuted. Even daring to discreetly raise questions about the propriety of government practices now appears to be a firing offense. In July 2006, Christine Axsmith, a software contractor working with the CIA, had her security badge revoked and her employment terminated. What had Axsmith done to draw such sanctions? She had expressed her personal views on torture and the Geneva Conventions on a secure blog accessible only to those with a top secret clearance. An Agency spokesman would say only, "The CIA expects contractors to do the work they are paid to do."

It was another in a long line of actions and statements designed to demonstrate government's zero tolerance for anyone within who raises questions about such sensitive issues as the conduct of the war in Iraq, the treatment of prisoners, the use of prewar intelligence, the lack of preparedness for the post-invasion governance of Iraq. The name of the game is intimidation; the object, to silence critics and suppress dissent.

In such a high-stakes game, administration and Pentagon officials are ready to pounce upon any publication that makes a mistake, exploiting its momentary vulnerability to long-term advantage in an effort to disable its critics. Even a peccadillo can be made to appear as a mortal wound, particularly where sensitive secrets are concerned.

In its May 9, 2005, edition *Newsweek* magazine reported in the Periscope column that military investigators had found evidence that interrogators at Guantánamo had flushed the holy Koran down the toilet. The story was attributed to an unnamed source—"a senior U.S. government official"—which left the report open to attack by the Pentagon, which vehemently denied the report. Following *Newsweek*'s publication, riots broke out in several Muslim countries, including Pakistan, Afghanistan, and Indonesia, in which at least 16 people lost their lives and dozens were injured.

All this was laid at the feet of *Newsweek* and, by extension, an "irresponsible" press. *Newsweek*'s sin, it was said, was to have relied on a nameless source (as if anyone would have dared go on the record to discuss such a sensitive matter). The editors of *Newsweek,* unable to confirm the story, retracted it (its underlying veracity neither proven nor debunked), apologized for the story, and then revamped its reportorial guidelines to make it tougher to use anonymous sources. The revision of sourcing standards was not a bad thing, though it was unwisely done in a moment of great urgency and stress. The chill that accompanied the change, the sense that another mistake could imperil the magazine's credibility, left it temporarily shaken and vulnerable.

While no one in the press would defend a thinly sourced or inaccurate story, *Newsweek*'s response signaled both a failure by the press and a triumph of those who sought to maim it. *Newsweek,* an aggressive challenger of the administration's version of the truth, had been taken to the woodshed. Now it stood chastened, a lesson to one and all.

An audible sigh of relief was heaved at the Pentagon, as if the administration and those at Guantánamo had been exonerated of this scurrilous charge. The irony, of course, was that there had been numerous reports, many from detainees, in which it was alleged that interrogators had desecrated the Koran, thrown it in the toilet, and sexually humiliated detainees. Less than a month after *Newsweek* was humbled and its report discredited, it was reported that U.S. officials acknowledged that "a Muslim Holy Book" had been splashed with urine—exactly how was not clear—while other reports surfaced that a detainee's Koran "was deliberately kicked and another's was stepped on." It was also confirmed that "water balloons thrown by prison guards" had gotten a Koran wet and that a "two-word obscenity was written in English on the inside cover of a Koran."

Newsweek's real sin was to hand the administration the perfect opportunity to deflect criticism and attention away from the grim facts and to make *Newsweek,* not Guantánamo, the focal point. Republican loyalists took up the cudgel. Rep. Deborah Pryce (R-Ohio) urged people to cancel their subscriptions to *Newsweek.* "Retraction and regrets will not atone for the reckless behavior of an irresponsible reporter and an overzealous publication," fumed Pryce.

This type of intimidation has been a constant and effective strategy of the White House when it comes under fire: if you question the accuracy, the motives, the sources, the loyalty of the press; if you back it into a corner where it is forced to defend itself, the underlying story—intercepting telephone and Internet messages, gathering phone records, collecting bank transactions—will fade from public view.

•　　•　　•

Secrecy has exacted a price not only among the major national news organizations but at the regional and local level as well. Local editors get their backs up when officials close their meetings to the public or withhold records, but they are less attuned to the dangers of a tip whispered into the ear of one of their reporters by an anonymous official. When those tips are reported, the press can become party to the indiscretions of law enforcement officers frustrated with the pace of their own investigations. For every Wen Ho Lee and Steven J. Hatfill, whose privacy and reputation were damaged by the national press, there are countless other ordinary citizens who suffer a similar fate at the hands of the local press. Due process and privacy are both put at risk by the combustible mix of secrecy and the allure of "an exclusive."

Doug Clifton, the able editor of the *Cleveland Plain Dealer,* has waged a vigorous war to gain access to public records and to promote transparency in government. He even served as chair of the American Association of Newspaper Editors' Freedom of Information Committee. But his paper has more than once found itself in the uncomfortable clutches of secrecy.

In the summer of 2005, Clifton wrote a column in which he acknowledged that the *Plain Dealer,* the nation's twenty-first-largest daily, had decided, at least for the time being, not to publish two stories out of fear that the paper would be subpoenaed and the reporters would face possible jail time if they refused to divulge their sources. These were not just any stories, but ones described by Clifton as "profoundly important" and "of significant interest to the public." It was not that Clifton or his reporters lacked the gumption to proceed, but rather that company lawyers cautioned them not to. The chilling effect of secrecy and the fear of courts and prosecutors are being felt coast to coast as reporters in California, Rhode Island, New York, and elsewhere are now under subpoena. No wonder a spring 2006 essay by the executive director of the Reporters' Committee for Freedom of the Press was titled "Courage in Difficult Times."

But if secrecy has muzzled some newspapers, it has also led many down a treacherous path. Like other readers, I missed the *Plain Dealer*'s first article about Joel Rose, a retired 64-year-old former TV and radio personality. It ran on August 3, 2000, a scant 124-word article buried on page 6 of the metro section. It disclosed that a search warrant had been served on Rose. The attribution was simply "sources said." It went on to note, "What was being sought and what prompted the search could not be determined." In short, the story told readers virtually nothing about the crime or Rose's alleged involvement in it, only that he was under suspicion for something.

The next day, the veil of mystery was dramatically lifted in a front-page story headlined "Ex-TV Host Rose Under Investigation In Porn Case." Rose, readers were told, was being investigated for supposedly mailing packages containing underwear and pornography to various women in the area. A DNA sample, consisting of a blood and saliva sample, had been taken. This information was provided by "sources familiar with the investigation." Sources said . . . sources said . . . a source said . . . The mantra of secrecy repeated itself throughout.

Exactly what was the rush to print the story and why place it on the front page? No charges had been filed against Rose and yet someone, presumably within law enforcement, had seen fit to put his name into the public realm and associate him with the offense. The crimes had been going on for some two years, the investigation for nearly a year. Couldn't the story have waited until charges were actually brought or the sources confident enough to have *their own names* attached to the allegations? But the exclusive story was apparently deemed too good to hold even a day longer.

The next day, Rose again made the front page. This time the headline said it all: "Joel Rose Commits Suicide: Former TV Celebrity Leaves Several Notes."

At about 6 A.M. Rose had told his wife he was going out to get the newspaper. Instead, he walked into the woods and put a Titan .38-caliber handgun to his right temple and blew his brains out. The notes Rose left behind declared his innocence.

The next day's *Plain Dealer* editorial page opined on Rose's death and reminded readers that authorities had taken a DNA and saliva sample as well as a typewriter to compare them with the crime evidence. "Rose chose not to wait for the results," the *Plain Dealer* observed. (For that matter, neither had the *Plain Dealer*.) Even the editorial implicitly raised questions about the magnitude of the story. The editorial referred to the crime, even if the allegations were true, as a "strange and apparently petty perversion."

But that was not the end of the story. On August 16, 11 days after Rose's suicide, the story once more made the *Plain Dealer*'s front page. This time the paper reported that the DNA found on the pornographic materials mailed to women did not match that of Joel Rose. Neither did his typewriter produce the letters that accompanied the packages.

There is no way today to prove the negative, to establish Rose's innocence—short of another's confession or conviction—and the *Plain Dealer* to this day takes the position that it was merely reporting the news. But if Joel Rose was a casualty of the story, so too was the *Plain Dealer*, whose editors' judgment and credibility were roundly questioned by the community. The only one who got off scot-free in all this was the source. His identity remains a secret, his reputation intact.

•   •   •

Not long after I joined the *Washington Post* in 1978, the paper ran the photograph of a State Department official with a caption that said this individual had given reporters a background briefing. The man's name appeared neither in the accompanying article nor in the caption, just his face. It was the *Post*'s way of protesting the abuse of background briefings in which government officials offer government's views on events and then insist that their own name not be used. It was a silly dig that changed nothing, but it underlined the absurdity of masking the identity of someone who, standing before scores of reporters, represented the

U.S. government and was being quoted to an audience of millions of citizens.

Following another U.S. government background briefing, a Soviet journalist in attendance identified the speaker to his readers, creating the anomalous situation that Soviet citizens knew who was speaking but not American readers.

What is so deeply disturbing about the use of anonymous background briefings, now institutionalized by practice and expectation, is that they are an official articulation of government policy and position that is deliberately masked so as to immunize those in power from the consequences of their own words and deeds. Anonymity breaks the custodial chain of responsibility, severs the architects of policy from the policy itself, creating the illusion of a government on autopilot, depopulated and fully mechanized. That secrecy can and does routinely cloak the identity of government officials standing at a microphone and podium addressing the nation is a sad commentary on the devolution of democracy. By extension, such spectacle also compromises the press, which is a necessary party to each such charade.

Formal efforts to protest the abuse of anonymity go back decades. Ben Bagdikian, the *Washington Post*'s former assistant managing editor for national news, remembers some 30 years ago when the *Post* declared unilaterally that it would no longer accept information provided off the record or from unnamed sources. It was a bold decision made by Ben Bradlee, then the paper's charismatic executive editor. Bradlee had had enough of government's blatant manipulation of the press, of its floating bogus or half-true stories and then hiding behind unattributed sources, leaving the press chagrined and feeling used. It was the period just before Watergate, when the Nixon administration's penchant for secrecy was in full stride and senior officials such as National Security Advisor Henry Kissinger had elevated the background briefing to a self-serving art form.

The rank and file at the *Post* worried that the ban on unnamed sources would put the paper at a severe competitive disadvantage. They were right. The *Times* and others took full advantage of the *Post*'s principled stand, printing stories the *Post* declined.

Bradlee rescinded his edict after only two days. And it was not long after that the Watergate story, a story built in no small measure upon the famed unnamed source, "Deep Throat," would define the *Post* and the era, bring down an administration, and usher in a period of government reform and accountability.

But for journalists, Watergate left a confusing and contradictory legacy. It demonstrated the significance and centrality of unnamed sources to certain critical stories but it also further opened the door to the use of anonymous sources, with all the intrigue, chicanery, and duplicity that may attend them.

The cachet of Watergate—the fame, the glory, the romance, the altruism—were all read into the relationship between the reporter Bob Woodward and his source, Deep Throat, revealed in 2006 as Deputy FBI Director W. Mark Felt. Within the journalistic ranks, the story became a template for all who followed, and the nobility and courage that attached to that singular unnamed source obscured for many the treachery, the gamesmanship, and the perils that were a part of any indiscriminate reliance on unnamed sources.

Today, once again, editors cringe when they think about the proliferation of unnamed sources and sometimes despair that so long as government is as secretive as it is, they have little choice but to use them. Nearly every newspaper has its policies and guidelines with respect to anonymous sources, attempting to curb their use and to create mechanisms whereby editors become a part of the process that evaluates when they are necessary and when standards of trustworthiness are met.

But such well-meaning rules and principles were not enough to avert recent train wrecks in journalism—the Wen Ho Lee, Steven Hatfill, and Joel Rose stories, and the fiasco of WMD reporting. The problem lies in some measure in the basic culture of the newsroom. First, it is predicated upon trust between an editor and a reporter; second, if that faith is borne out over time, the reporter is rewarded with ever greater freedom and trust; and finally, reporters often idealize the editor as the reporter's advocate and champion, a knight Templar willing to stand up to noisome lawyers or timid publishers. The longer reporters maintain (or appear to maintain) professional standards, the more editors' trust in them grows. That is why so many problems of credibility arise out of the work of veteran reporters, whose fidelity has already been tested.

The danger is that too often safeguards have been misapplied as onetime tests of character. For the veterans, editorial scrutiny is too often pro forma, a mere going through the motions. The credibility test should focus on the story, not on the reporter. Upon each story hangs the paper's credibility, a matter larger than the reputation of any one reporter and not to be defined by the relationship between the editor and the reporter but by that between the press and the public. For the process to become more professional, it must first be less personal.

The *USA Today* panel investigating its star journalist Jack Kelley's reporting over the course of his career recognized this when it noted: "Kelley's ability to routinely abuse rules governing anonymous or confidential sources—and the trusting attitudes of his editors as he exploited their confidence in him—is a harsh reminder that policies drafted on paper are meaningless unless discerning editorial gatekeepers at every level, apply them and enforce their roles as editors."

It is unlikely the press will change government's reliance on anonymity and background briefings anytime soon—and it never will, if news outlets insist on acting individually and in isolated instances of protest. Still, journalists need not aid and abet government's resistance to transparency by preemptively offering to mask its sources or simply submitting like sheep.

Resistance and protest can effect change, at least at the margins. In January 2006, two senior officials of the Mine Safety and Health Administration briefed reporters on the deaths of 12 miners killed in a West Virginia coal mining accident. They insisted that though the information they gave could be used, their names could not. The reporters protested and the officials capitulated, allowing their names to appear in print. It was a small victory but one that should hearten other reporters.

Getting journalists to act collectively is as difficult as herding quail, but it may take no less to persuade government to reexamine its commitment to citizens' right to know. At the very least, reporters should demand in each and every case that government officials who insist they not be identified explain precisely why the American people are not entitled to know their names. And reporters should reflect upon the consequences of their actions, the trade-offs between expedience and principle. The press, driven by deadlines and competition, has settled for tactical rather than strategic victories, for accepting arrangements of anonymity that produce individual stories of often transient significance, but that cumulatively help cement government's deep aversion to accountability. One of the surest ways not through, but around the problem of anonymity is more and better reporting, the development of additional sources, sifting through records, and bringing all resources to bear.

The simple, undeniable fact is that anonymous sources are and will remain a vital part of journalism, particularly in times when process and decision making are veiled by secrecy. And once that bond is forged between reporter and source, it must be honored no matter what the costs, literally and figuratively. For that reason and others, entering into such relationships must be done with sober deliberation, not out of habit or reflex.

After all, there is no statute of limitations on the commitment owed a source. When the Watergate reporters, Bob Woodward and Carl Bernstein, donated their papers to the University of Texas at Austin more than a quarter century after the Watergate scandal unfolded, their gift contained a provision that papers disclosing the identities of unnamed sources must remain sealed until those individuals have died. For today's reporters that is another lesson of the Watergate saga: they ought not to be so eager to grant anonymity. Perhaps the words "Act in haste, repent at leisure" should be posted in every newsroom.

•   •   •

Today's expansive secrecy has caused a fundamental shift in the relationship between government and the press. The *Washington Post* and other news organizations pride themselves on aggressively covering the White House and, while observing rules of civility, have historically not been shy about asserting themselves. But post-9/11, that has changed in some subtle and not-so-subtle ways. In 2003 a senior *Washington Post* reporter told me that the *Post* was feeling slighted. Its reporter was not being called on in White House press conferences. A *Post* editor complained and a White House spokesperson assured the editor that the president would call upon the reporter for the eighth question at the next press conference. Like an obedient child, the reporter waited patiently—only to be skipped over. Said the *Post* editor, "They must have been mad at us."

Reporters and editors bristle at the suggestion that they have been cowed by government, but few would dispute that they now accept arrangements that they would not have even considered a few years ago. By August 2004, the sea change was undeniable. Some 70 journalists planning to travel to Guantánamo to cover military commission hearings signed a detailed five-page contract with the Pentagon. They all agreed to honor the Defense Department's ground rules for coverage. The agreement signed by reporters and bureau chiefs allowed the military to embargo information and censor photographs deemed sensitive. Journalists were barred from publishing any material designated "protected information," a category that vaguely referenced national security but was broad enough to include virtually anything. The determination of what was objectionable was left entirely in the hands of the "presiding officer," who could order a "media embargo."

The agreement even allowed the military to literally look over the shoulders of journalists and insist that they cross out any portions of their *notes* deemed to be in violation of the agreement. Breaching the contract could result in being ejected from the proceedings and criminal prosecution. The agreement had to be signed prior to departing from Andrews Air Force Base for the journalists to be permitted to observe the proceedings. Not one journalist refused to sign.

A year earlier, a *Washington Post* reporter who attempted to find out what conditions were like at Guantánamo instead discovered only the depths of secrecy and containment. During his brief stay at the facility, he was bivouacked on a peninsula that was hemmed in by the sea, minefields, and barbed wire. He was allowed no contact with prisoners, and even when he went to the bathroom he was accompanied by a government handler. He was free to report on whatever he observed, which was exactly nothing. Meanwhile stories seeped out about deprivation of prisoners bordering on torture and of attempted mass suicides by the inmates.

Some 600 prisoners were being held there, and most of them had been held for more than two years. Few had been charged with a crime or given access to counsel.

Two years after the *Post* reporter's fiasco of a trip to Guantánamo, another *Post* reporter wrote about Jumah Dossari, a detainee who attempted suicide after being held in solitary confinement for nearly two years. Reluctantly the military acknowledged in November 2005 that the island detention center had been the site of some 36 suicide attempts. So dire were the conditions that dozens of detainees had been on a hunger strike for months and were being force-fed.

In the summer of 2006, when reports surfaced of three detainee suicides, the Pentagon expelled reporters from the base.

•   •   •

Behind a veil of secrecy, the military and CIA have for several years now resorted to extreme interrogation techniques and rendition—the extradition of detainees snatched overseas and handed over to foreign states far less squeamish than Americans about the methods they use to extract information. All the while, government officials have dangled the prospect of exclusive stories and interviews before the press, seducing some publications into running flattering portraits of government officials and agencies—what journalists contemptuously call "puff pieces" or "valentines." These journalists touted their unique access even as government snowed them. Fox News in particular played host to government officials who used the ever-friendly forum to promote administration agendas.

For example, the October 20, 2003 issue of *Fortune* magazine promoted on the cover the story "Fortune Exclusive: Inside the CIA." Throughout that period the CIA had shunned reporters and refused to answer tough questions on the faulty intelligence related to weapons of mass destruction in Iraq, reports of deep morale problems at the Agency, allegations of torture abroad, and a rising chorus calling for a dramatic reorganization of the entire intelligence community.

In the midst of such woes, the CIA attempted to persuade journalists that things were never better at Langley, that recruitment was up and spirits high. This was the story that *Fortune* magazine bought into. It declared its access as a kind of reportorial coup in a lengthy article so kindly disposed to the Agency and its besieged director, George Tenet, that it was the journalistic equivalent of a wet kiss.

Fortune boasted extraordinary access in writing a piece that compared Tenet to a masterful CEO and corporate turnaround specialist who had reinvigorated Langley. The headline said it all: "How George Tenet Brought the CIA Back from the Dead: Amid controversy and two wars, he's led a classic turnaround by running the Agency like a business." A formal full-page portrait of Tenet featured the director in a business suit, arms crossed, a profile of confidence bordering on smugness.

The spinmeisters at the Agency were jubilant. Of course, that was also not long before Tenet left the Agency in a quagmire of criticism and recrimination. Behind him he left the intelligence fiasco of 9/11, the phantom WMDs, and a blistering congressional assessment of misman-agement. And it was just before much of the CIA director's authority and power were subsumed in a new position, that of national director of intelligence.

In late October 2003—a week or so after the *Fortune* article ap-peared—I called the CIA to get a response to allegations that morale at the Agency was in a tailspin. A senior Agency spokesman dismissed the idea as absurd and as evidence immediately cited the *Fortune* article to refute those allegations. He read whole paragraphs to me over the phone, as if they were from some classified document he was sharing with me. I'd like to tell you the name of this CIA spokesman, but before he would consent to even speak with me, he insisted it was on back-ground. I can't really blame him for not wanting to be associated with that one.

6

Case Study: A Crime of Secrecy?

Notre Dame, not the university of South Bend, Indiana, fame, but Notre Dame College of South Euclid, Ohio, is a quiet Catholic school nestled on 53 leafy acres, a place where 1,200 courteous students come to contemplate questions of theology, literature, or political science. If there is a place safe from the sordid affairs of the world, from crime and secrecy, one might imagine it would look a lot like Notre Dame.

"We strive to insure a safe, secure and pleasant atmosphere, conducive to a positive educational process, in our efforts to protect the College community," reads Notre Dame's mission statement on campus safety. In the college's required annual crime reports to the federal government, it notes that in 2003, 2004, and 2005, there were zero murders, zero burglaries, zero acts of arson, zero car thefts, zero robberies, and, in 2005, one lone forcible sexual assault.

Until March 2006, Patty O'Toole was the college's dean of students, a woman described by former colleagues as someone of deep faith, compassionate, caring, honest, and devoted to the students. But it was, some now say, precisely those qualities that led to her being indicted in June 2006.

That was when the Cuyahoga County prosecutor's office charged her with a violation of Ohio Revised Code, section 2921.22, which makes secrecy—or, to be more precise, failing to report a felony—a crime. Unless protected by some special privilege—such as doctor-patient, lawyer-client, priest-penitent—Ohioans are obligated to come forward and tell what they know. At least, that's the prosecutor's interpretation of the law.

But Patty O'Toole had given her word. She had pledged to a student that she would not report what had happened to the 18-year-old coed who confided in her that she had been the victim of a sexual assault by a classmate. Specifically, the student expressed concerns that her father, a detective, would find out, especially if it were made a police matter.

Those familiar with the case say O'Toole did her best to persuade the student to go to the authorities, but that she would not. She urged her to seek counseling. Others say O'Toole even went to her superior about the matter and was advised that since the student was not a minor, she could not be coerced to go to the police. That superior has reportedly said he has no specific recollection of such a conversation or of giving any such advice.

On October 13, 2005, O'Toole wrote the student, "During our meeting you asked me not to take any legal or judicial action at this time. Based on follow-up that I have done with individuals at the College, at the present time I am able to honor your request (if that changes I will let you know)."

But then, according to prosecutors, it became clear there was not just one secret, but several. In December 2005, campus police investigating a separate allegation of sexual assault came to O'Toole and reportedly learned from her of another incident, involving the same alleged perpetrator, a 19-year-old Notre Dame student, Anthony Carl Wolfe.

On June 7, 2006, Wolfe, a basketball player, was indicted on charges of rape, kidnapping, assault, gross sexual imposition, menacing by stalking, and intimidation of a crime victim. But Wolfe had been expelled six months earlier from Notre Dame and was already enrolled in another school, Defiance College, southwest of Toledo.

"Had she [O'Toole] told the police about the first attack," said Assistant Prosecutor Rick Bell, "none of these other attacks would have occurred."

Perhaps, but if O'Toole is secretive, so too is the administration of Notre Dame. Notre Dame's president, Dr. Andrew P. Roth, won't talk about the case or the situation at the college, which went co-ed only a few years ago. Calls to campus security were not returned. Faculty and staff would speak only if promised anonymity. And after touting the importance of the case in the immediate aftermath of the indictment, the prosecutor's office has suddenly gone silent. "It's a pending case," said the prosecutor's spokesperson, Ryan Miday. "We can't discuss it."

As for Patricia O'Toole, she faced two misdemeanor counts and a possible 30 days in jail. But even before the case went to trial, she had found a new job at Hollins University, in Roanoke, Virginia, where she is, once again, dean of students. At Hollins, O'Toole should not face the same problems—first, because undergraduate studies admit only women, and second, because, as a Hollins spokesman, Jeff Hodges, made clear, the school supports the position she took at Notre Dame: "From our standpoint, we don't think she did anything wrong," said Hodges. Should the same situation arise at Hollins, she would be expected to do precisely the same thing.

Dean Patricia O'Toole is regarded by some on the Notre Dame campus even today as a prisoner of conscience, someone who refused to betray another. By prosecutors she was seen as a criminal, plain and simple. In February 2007, a jury reached its own conclusion, clearing the former Notre Dame dean of all charges, but leaving unanswered the larger question of how secrecy and security may coexist on the nation's campuses.

Secrets and the University

The delicate thing about the university is that it has a mixed character, that it is suspended between its position in the eternal world, with all its corruption and evils and cruelties, and the splendid world of our imagination.

—Richard Hofstadter (1916–1970), DeWitt Clinton Professor of American History at Columbia University

American universities have long extolled the virtues of openness, reveling in the rhetoric of liberty and transparency. College presidents and professors publicly champion openness in government and warn against the perils of excessive secrecy. Many university mottoes are variations on the theme of light and truth.

But these days, at universities and colleges around the nation, presumptions of openness have given way to a permissive secrecy, mirroring government's own move into the shadows. Universities enjoy a privileged position in American society as a result of academic tradition, public deference, and, perhaps, apathy. With what amounts to a grant of extraterritoriality, many universities operate largely beyond all outside scrutiny, maintaining their own regulations and policies, their own government, their own police force, their own judicial and disciplinary systems, their own newspapers.

Even the great state universities, supported by public taxes, have become creatures of secrecy. Invoking privacy concerns, student confidentiality, fear of litigation, and other rationales, many colleges and universities have concealed financial mismanagement, bloated executive salaries, recruiting violations, plagiarism, and a litany of other irregularities. Maintaining a positive public image—critical to fund-raising, attracting students, and standing among one's peer institutions—has become a consuming interest. Ultimately such secrecy undermines respect for the institution, engenders cynicism and suspicion, and provides fertile soil for corruption. At one campus after another, security, public safety, and academic integrity have become casualties of secrecy.

Not that universities have made a calculated decision to withdraw from American society; rather like the society of which they are a part, they have been subjected to a welter of contradictory influences and attitudinal changes that have directly and indirectly promoted secrecy on campuses. Much of the expansive secrecy that grips universities today is a response to these external forces and pressures. Today, campuses are subject to more than 200 federal laws and countless state provisions, many of them complex, some of them ill-defined or seemingly conflicting; a few of them require administrators and their lawyers to walk a constant tightrope between competing societal values.

The ever-greater reliance on technology has also increased the pressure on institutions to be security-conscious and secretive. A single breach in a computer program can produce thousands of cases of compromised privacy, exposure of medical, financial, and academic records, and a rash of identity thefts. One such slip and a school can face a multitude of lawsuits. Much of the increased secrecy at universities today reflects the same defensive posture taken by other institutions facing the same constant threat of litigation.

But new laws and vulnerabilities are not the sole answer to the question of why colleges and universities, so adamant about transparency in government, should be so quick to take to the shadows in their own affairs. Ironically, a portion of the new secrecy may come as a direct response to sunshine provisions, as universities go to sometimes extraordinary lengths to circumvent state provisions requiring open meetings. In 2004, members of a University of Nebraska search committee literally drove 200 miles and crossed the state line into Missouri to secretly meet with seven candidates vying to become the next president of the university. The maneuver to skirt state sunshine provisions did not violate the law, argued the university's general counsel, Richard R. Wood, in part because these were not "interviews," but merely "informal social gatherings." Similarly, leaders of the state university systems of Nevada, North Carolina, Missouri, Minnesota, and Wisconsin, among others, have found themselves at odds with their states' sunshine laws.

At all levels the business of colleges and universities is now conducted behind closed doors. Secrecy envelops student and faculty discipline matters, admissions, promotion and tenure, searches and hires, public safety and financial dealings. Records of governing boards are often sealed for decades. Scandals are buried, accounts of serious campus crime sometimes covered up. Outside inquiries by journalists or legislators are often deeply resented and resisted.

Even as some universities preach the need for candor and disclosure to their students, their actions send a contrary message. In 2003, Rev. Bernard P. Knoth, president of Loyola University in New Orleans, ordered a front-page article in the student newspaper killed. The suppression of the story only made more poignant the intended headline: "Chair's Firing Shrouded in Secrecy." Just miles away, at Tulane University, it was revealed, to the horror of donors, that some cadavers given to Tulane in the expectation that they would be used for research at the med school were passed along to a body broker, who sold them to the Army, which blew them up in land-mine experiments. "I am not at liberty to discuss that," said Dr. Mary Bitner Anderson, chair of Tulane's Department of Structural and Cellular Biology when I called her. "We are still in litigation."

Secrecy is often used to sidestep controversy and discourage public input on sensitive decisions. In 2004, the board of trustees of the University of Utah, a public university, closed its doors in executive session to discuss the issue of guns on campus. That same year it admitted misrepresenting the pay its president received, underreporting by some $143,295 compensation provided from previously undisclosed private funds. Auburn University's board of trustees was found to have violated that state's sunshine law 39 times in three years.

Academic programs, too, are rife with secrecy. In June 2004, an Ohio University graduate student, Thomas A. Matrka, told university officials that he had found evidence of widespread plagiarism among engineering graduate students. He was convinced that the officials ignored or refused to acknowledge the severity of the allegations. But Matrka persisted. By June 2006, Ohio University was calling for the dismissal of the chair of the mechanical engineering department and another faculty member, and found that some 37 former students had committed plagiarism over a 20-year period. Absent Matrka's persistence, it is questionable whether the scandal would ever have been allowed to surface.

There is true cause for concern, says Charles N. Davis, a professor at the Missouri School of Journalism and executive director of the National Freedom of Information Coalition, an umbrella group representing organizations in support of access to information in 39 states. "Overall, universities are endemically secretive," he says. "They are just about as secretive an institution as there is in this country. It's like covering a federal agency like the CIA, there is such a culture of secrecy around academic institutions." He speaks of what he calls "the veneer of democracy" at universities, citing their public devotion to democracy even as they choose their leaders "in a Vatican-like way. The sports information departments have become absolutely authoritarian in nature. They are almost like the Pentagon now."

Mark Goodman, executive director of the Student Press Law Center, has seen student journalists' complaints about access to campus information at public universities and colleges soar from 164 in 2002 to 229 in 2003, the most recent year for which figures are available. The 40 percent leap in a single year may reflect a sea change in attitude or merely a transient response, but it is difficult to ignore the influence of the post-9/11 mind-set. "What happens at other levels of government has an effect on public colleges and universities in terms of their willingness to release information," says Goodman. "When they see state or federal agencies taking a more paternalistic approach toward the release of what would typically be seen as public information, it reinforces their belief that they can do the same."

Universities' conflict between maintaining both transparency and secrecy is perhaps most acute in their handling of serious discipline matters. Not that academic institutions are eager to take on the role of judge or jury, nor that they relish having to conduct investigations and hearings into serious crime; rather, the evolution of federal and other laws, the strings attached to receiving federal funds, the demands of due process, and the harsh realities of crime on campus have left them little choice. They cannot simply throw up their hands and ignore serious crime, especially in cases where victims refuse to go to the authorities and lodge criminal complaints.

Instead, a complex array of quasi-judicial hearing mechanisms has emerged on campuses across the nation in an effort to protect the victims of serious crimes and to provide a measure of due process to the accused. A university can no longer simply expel a student on the basis of allegations. Ideally, the academic adjudicatory process is envisioned to pursue its ends as a parallel system to that of law enforcement, neither one being the exclusive answer. "The official position [of universities and colleges] has to be to encourage and support the reporting of crime to law enforcement and they are obligated to assist if the victim requests that," says Daniel Carter, vice president of Security On Campus, a non-profit organization that works to make campuses safer and promotes the interests of victims of crime.

But in practice, the university is often the exclusive system dealing with crime, and there are serious questions about the adequacy and competence of academicians and school administrators to deal with such serious felonies as homicides, rapes, and sexual assaults. Many campus victims, particularly of sexual assaults and rapes, are reluctant to report the crime to the police. That is not a phenomenon unique to campuses—many rapes go unreported. Particularly when the victim is young, away from home for the first time, and traumatized by the assault, she often chooses to eschew the prosecutorial process and rely on the school for protection, counseling, and justice. But fundamental questions persist about the ability of such on-campus hearings to protect victims, to mete out justice, and to produce a result that promotes campus safety. It is one thing to sit in judgment on drunken frat parties or a cheating scandal and quite another to oversee a hearing on rape or homicide.

Universities and colleges lack the forensic resources to investigate serious crimes, the subpoena power to compel testimony and the production of evidence, the threat of prosecution for perjury, and the sophisticated rules of evidence to ensure due process. But most damaging of all to the credibility of such a process is its reliance on secrecy. There are no reporters, no outside scrutiny of the process, no appellate division to review judicial error, no public record of proceedings.

Institutions of higher learning are torn between the demands of pri-

vacy and confidentiality on the one hand and, on the other, the responsibilities imposed by laws requiring them to report crimes and to alert
students to on-campus risks. Laws that protect the confidentiality of student educational and medical records, such as the Family Educational
Rights and Privacy Act of 1974 (FERPA) and the Health Insurance
Portability and Accountability Act of 1996 (HIPAA) are balanced against
others, such as the Crime Awareness and Campus Security Act of 1990,
the Clery Act of 1998, and the Campus Crime Prevention Act of 2000. As
if the legal landscape were not already complicated enough, the laws un-
dergo review and amendment, creating confusion and misinterpretation
by both government advisors and campus administrators. Throw into
that mix of secrecy, legal confusion, and traumatized victims the institution's own natural reluctance to have its campus crises made public, and
you have a prescription for systemic problems.

No disclosure is more damaging to a university's appeal to prospective students, faculty, and donors than that which depicts a campus as a
high-crime zone. Because of the ubiquitous secrecy that surrounds such
proceedings, it is impossible to know how well the university walks the
line that separates confidentiality from cover-up, compassion from concealment.

For nearly 17 years I taught at Georgetown University in Washington,
D.C., a university committed to turning out students with a fine education and a strong moral compass as well. Georgetown's president, John
J. DeGioia, like many university presidents, has made a point of publicly
proclaiming the importance of free speech and open debate. "We cannot
be a university dedicated to intellectual excellence and at the same time
place limits on what might be said and thought and discussed," he declared before an auditorium filled with Georgetown students in 2003.
And yet Georgetown too is rife with secrecy and will go to considerable
ends to enforce that secrecy.

Just ask Deborah and Jeffrey Shick. Their son David was a junior at
Georgetown, a business major with sandy-colored hair, a wide smile,
and a zest for soccer, skiing, and weight lifting. In the early morning of
February 18, 2000, David was returning to campus with some friends
when they passed another group of Georgetown students in the parking
lot behind Lauinger Library. Words were exchanged. One of the students
sucker-punched Shick in the jaw. He fell to the ground, striking his head
on the pavement. He died four days later. The District of Columbia med-

ical examiner ruled it a homicide. Shick's parents looked to Georgetown for justice.

The Shicks had an abiding respect for Georgetown's principles, and a visceral faith in its ability to represent the family's interest in getting to the bottom of what had happened to their son. Deborah Shick was Catholic and the boys had been raised in that faith. She drew confidence in the fact that the school was Catholic; the Jesuit connection raised her expectations still higher. She and her husband believed the school would conduct a thorough investigation and hold the person responsible for their son's death fully accountable.

They spoke with the D.C. prosecutor, who told them that if convicted, the student who took David Shick's life would face a ten-year prison sentence. "If you try to put the other parents' shoes on, . . ." says Deborah Shick, "yes, the man made a grievous mistake he'll regret for the rest of his life, but I couldn't see what trying to get ten years' prison for him would do. So we talked about it and I basically made the decision." She said she told the prosecutor she would not feel comfortable pushing for a criminal conviction. "I felt very very strongly that the discipline belonged to Georgetown."

In August 2000, some five months after the assault, a university hearing board was to render its decision. But to the surprise of the Shicks, the university told them that they would not be privy to the hearing's outcome unless they first signed a nondisclosure agreement, which would prohibit them from telling anyone of the board's findings and the sanctions it imposed. They would not even be allowed to tell their two other children what they learned.

Incensed, the Shicks refused to sign. Over the succeeding months they spent nearly $100,000 suing both their son's assailant and the university, in an effort to pry out the truth. Even then, they had to agree not to release the assailant's name. In the end, what they discovered in November 2001 shook their faith not only in Georgetown but in the university's entire adjudicatory process. David Shick's assailant had indeed been found responsible for their son's death and guilty of a Category C physical assault (the most serious level), as well as disorderly conduct and a violation of the school's alcohol policy. But it was the punishment that staggered the Shick family.

The young man who killed their son had received a one-semester suspension, was required to get counseling for his drinking problem, and had to write a ten-page paper reflecting on what he had done. A few months later, the sanction was reduced. The brief suspension was rescinded upon completion of the other two conditions. In essence, the student who took David Shick's life received nothing more than a warning. In the end, he would graduate with his class, and, as Shick's mother bitterly notes, miss not a day of classes or a single game of the varsity soccer squad on which he played. She wonders if her son's assailant would have gotten off so lightly if he were not an athlete and his coach had not taken part in the proceedings.

All along, the university cited the 1974 Family Educational Rights and Privacy Act, or FERPA, under which it claimed that confidentiality was paramount. Notwithstanding the gravity of the case, that confidentiality attached to the alleged perpetrator whose educational records—the words "educational" is interpreted very broadly—are protected under FERPA. The idea that a federal bill containing the words "family educational rights" should be invoked in denying the Shick family access to the outcome of the hearing on their son's death only added to their grief and frustration. And contrary to whatever impression the university conveyed to the Shicks, FERPA imposed no such requirement of silence.

When the Shicks finally did go public with what they had learned, some faculty and students at Georgetown could scarcely believe their institution capable of such callousness. In a letter to the school paper, *The Hoya,* a former student, Michael M. Gallagher, class of 2000, wrote, "I write this letter to note a very sad occurrence—Georgetown University's official abdication of its role as the nation's preeminent Jesuit university. . . . The 'punishment' administered by the university is quite simply disgraceful." And Colin Campbell, a former Georgetown professor of public policy, wrote a letter citing "the ineptitude and venality of Georgetown authorities" in their handling of the Shick case.

Had the Shicks' case been an isolated instance, they might never have gone public, but learning what happened to another Georgetown student, Kate Dieringer, just one year after their son's murder convinced them that their silence would only serve the interests of a system they believed corrupted by secrecy and self-interest.

In August 2001, Kate Dieringer was a freshman at Georgetown. She had chosen the school in part because she wanted to be in a big city but not too far from her home in little Bridgeport, West Virginia, population 7,300. Blond and blue-eyed, Kate was the all-American high school girl—a straight-A student, president of the student council, homecoming queen, a devout Catholic. Her father worked for the phone company, her mother for the gas company. Georgetown gave her financial aid, which was supplemented with a modest scholarship from her hometown Elks Club. At Georgetown she set her sights on becoming a nurse in public health.

Like many freshmen, she was anxious. Those normal anxieties were quickly overshadowed by far darker ones. Two weeks after arriving at school, on the morning of September 11, 2001, she looked across the Potomac River and saw smoke rising up from the Pentagon where a jetliner had plunged into its flank. Just four days later, she would face a second, more personal horror.

On the evening of September 15, 2001, Dieringer said she and several girlfriends were partying in the company of a young man who was then a sophomore and was known to them as one of Georgetown's new-student orientation leaders. It was his job to help get new students settled in and ready for the year ahead. He suggested that Dieringer return with him to his residential suite where there was to be a party. Sometime just before midnight, Dieringer said she found herself somehow separated from her girlfriends and alone with the orientation leader at the door of his suite. She was feeling woozy and barely able to stand. The next four hours are utterly lost to her. She is convinced she was drugged.

When she came to, it was 4 A.M. She was naked and on the student's bed. He was lying on top of her and having intercourse with her. His face, filled with anger, frightened her. "He looked like a monster," she recalled. It was her first sexual experience. She pleaded with him to stop. "Fine, be a stupid freshman bitch," he muttered, rolling over and turning his back to her. She searched for her clothes and purse, and ran out, back to her dorm. She showered, got into bed, and tried to block out the images of that night. She felt defiled and ashamed—too ashamed to tell a soul what had happened. For months she was withdrawn, shuttling between the library and her room, where she would lock herself in. She feared her assailant had given her AIDS.

Finally, in January, still haunted by that night, she was tested for HIV and confided in Carolyn Hurwitz, Georgetown's sexual assault coordinator, that she had been raped by another student. Eventually the matter was brought to the attention of Georgetown's Office of Student Conduct, which launched an investigation and held a hearing on April

29 and May 2, 2002. Meanwhile, a classmate of Dieringer's told her and Hurwitz that she too had been raped by the student; however, she was not allowed to testify before Georgetown's adjudicatory body because she had not filed her own formal complaint. Throughout the process, Dieringer felt that the institution was more interested in protecting its own good name and image than in defending hers.

As Georgetown itself acknowledges in its formal policy statement on such proceedings, "Hearings are NOT courts of law. They are seen as fundamentally educational." With the public excluded from such hearings, even in matters as serious as rape or homicide, the university seems preoccupied with "decorum," a word that appears in its official Student Affairs statement. In its official "Instructions for Sexual Assault (Category C) and Sexual Misconduct (Category B) Hearings," the university notes that it frowns upon "staring at the opposite party, laughing, rolling of eyes in an exaggerated fashion, etc." For victims like Kate Dieringer, decorum, public image, and the university's desire to promote "educational" objectives seem to eclipse basic concerns for justice and safety.

Even more troubling, the university told Dieringer that before it would reveal the outcome of the adjudication, she would have to sign a secrecy agreement, promising not to disclose the results. Dieringer says that Judy Johnson, head of the Office of Student Conduct, warned her that if she told anyone the results, it would be viewed as a serious violation of student conduct and would warrant an investigation and possible proceeding against her. If she refused to sign, the university would not tell her what sanctions her assailant faced and whether he would still be on campus. That was not something she could face. She signed the paper as her parents looked on.

Initially, she was told her assailant had been expelled, but soon after, following his appeal, she learned that he had been given only a one-year suspension. Dieringer was outraged. She was also frightened that her assailant would come after her. But she could tell no one. The secrecy agreement strictly forbade it. Instead of once more silently withdrawing into her own little world, Dieringer chose to write about her case for the university paper, though she did not disclose the results of the adjudication. On October 24, 2002, her article, titled "The Girl Who Whimpered Rape," appeared in the *Georgetown Voice*.

In the weeks and months afterward, she said she heard from more than a dozen other students who had been the victims of sexual assault and other serious crimes and had been told they must sign a secrecy agreement if they were to learn the outcome of their assailant's case. (Between 2001 and 2003, Georgetown reported to the federal government some 33 separate acts of "forcible sex offenses." The actual number of sexual assaults may be higher.) One of those who contacted Dieringer was a gay male student who said he had been the victim of a hate crime and been beaten by a Georgetown student. He too had been persuaded to sign a secrecy agreement with the university.

Carolyn Hurwitz, the Georgetown sexual assault coordinator who had worked with Dieringer, was disturbed by what she saw as the university's attempt to silence Kate Dieringer and other rape victims. A former chair of the National Task Force for the American College Health Association and the recipient of several awards, Hurwitz resigned in November 2002 because, she said, she was unable to continue in good conscience under such a secretive system.

On September 12, 2002, Kate's mother, Janet, wrote a letter to Judy Johnson, Georgetown's director of student conduct, and sent copies to President DeGioia and other senior administrators. The last paragraph read: "My daughter asks, 'How could they let this happen?' Sadly that is a question that I will never have an answer to. Life does go on; we still live with this every day. The crying, depression, sleepless nights, the fear, the mistrust, and uncertainty of what to do next are always there. But for now we are trying to pick up our lives and hope that the next victim that has the courage to come forward to the office of student conduct knows what she's plunging into, a sea of disappointment and cruelty."

Such smothering secrecy as the Shick and Dieringer families experienced is hardly unique to Georgetown. Students around the country who have been the victims of on-campus crime have also had to contend with regimes of secrecy. Samantha Collins, a student raped at William and Mary, faced it. So, too, have students at Ohio State. In September 2005, Miami University of Ohio was fined $27,500 for failing to provide six victims of sexual assaults written notice of the outcomes of disciplinary hearings. At the University of Virginia, alleged rape victims have also complained that the university's Sexual Assault Board conducted its hearings in absolute secrecy and allowed perpetrators to receive light sentences for serious sexual assaults.

The matter might have ended there, except that Kate Dieringer was determined not to be made a victim again. She decided to fight the system and bring to public attention what she believed was a double injustice: first, that her assailant had been given only a one-year suspension, and second, that her university had forced her to sign a gag order. In March 2003 she took the issue to the U.S. Department of Education and filed a formal grievance.

That process produced some disturbing disclosures. According to a May 5, 2004, finding of the U.S. Department of Education, at least two of the four members of Georgetown's disciplinary hearing board "were concerned that the respondent [the accused], at the original hearing, showed no understanding of the seriousness of what the Complainant alleged he had done and would repeat his behavior if he were permitted to return to the University." Georgetown justified its reduced sanction in part because "the respondent's file revealed no prior disciplinary offenses," but the Department of Education found otherwise, including "two prior alcohol offenses and a failure to comply in a timely way with the sanctions imposed as a result of one of these prior offenses." And the university, in its internal decision to reduce the sanction, noted that no Georgetown student found guilty of a Category C sexual assault—the most serious offense—had been dismissed. That fact alone might have made Georgetown reluctant to have the outcome of its disciplinary hearings made known.

On July 16, 2004, the Department of Education sent a letter to President DeGioia announcing its formal findings. The Department of Education concluded that Georgetown had no authority to require sexual assault victims to sign "a non-disclosure agreement as a precondition to accessing judicial proceeding outcomes and sanction information," and that its procedures violated the Clery Act, which requires that such outcomes be made available to victims of sexual assault without condition. It pointed out that contrary to Georgetown's position, the Federal Education Rights and Privacy Act, which the university cited as justification for its position, in no way barred the release of such information, but instead specifically allows institutions to provide victims with information related to judicial outcomes and sanctions. It ordered Georgetown to halt the use of such nondisclosure forms and to bring the institution into compliance with federal law. For Dieringer it was a dazzling, albeit belated, victory.

There remained the question of how to remember David Shick, the

Georgetown student who died after being struck in the face. On what would have been his twenty-first birthday, a memorial tablet and small pond were dedicated on the Georgetown campus. On the plaque are the words:

IN LOVING MEMORY
DAVID SHICK
14 OCTOBER 1979–22 FEBRUARY 2000
SON BROTHER FRIEND
THAT HIS MEMORY MAY LIVE AT
GEORGETOWN AS IN OUR HEARTS
BE KIND

But the Shick family is hoping for another kind of memorial. Today a bill is slowly making its way through Congress that would require universities to reveal the results of disciplinary hearings involving violent crime or nonforcible sexual offenses to the alleged victims. If passed, it would amend FERPA and take away the cover of so many secrets. The bill is named the David Shick Honesty in Campus Justice Act, in honor of a young man murdered and a family whose suffering was immeasurably compounded by secrecy.

•   •   •

The University of Central Florida in Orlando likes to boast that it has one of the lowest crime rates of any of Florida's state universities. Senior administrators deny making any such claim, but freshman Alphia Morin and others remember orientation speakers citing the school's glowing record on campus safety and security. Morin was a freshman in 2004 and took considerable comfort in knowing that the university was safe. What she did not know was that the crime statistics were suspect and did not accurately reflect the real risks she faced. For example, the university officially reported that it had only six rapes in calendar year 2004. That's a remarkably good record for a school with nearly 42,000 students.

But only those rapes that were formally reported to the police or by third-party affiliates of the university were included in the report. That same year, the University of Central Florida's Victim Services saw at least 48 women who said they had been raped—eight times the number the university reported. Because most of those women chose not to report the crimes to the police, a common decision of rape victims, or the crimes occurred just off-campus, their cases went uncounted and the boasts of safety went unchallenged. Even a rape of a student that took place across the street from the campus but not in housing run by the university would be excluded from the count.

For Alphia Morin, the beginning of school was the beginning of an odyssey of trauma, disillusionment, and betrayal. On September 17, 2004, the 17-year-old freshman, a virgin away from home for the first time, said she was raped by a fellow student, a football player. The six-foot-one, 255-pound student ignored her pleas to stop and pinned her down, she said. For three days after the assault, she did not leave her room or speak to anyone. When she finally emerged, she went to Victim Services for a pregnancy and HIV test. There she confided in a rape counselor that she had been raped. Because she was a minor, the case was reported to the police.

If the trauma of the rape was not enough, she then had to bear the hearing by the school's Student Conduct Office on January 18, 2005. When it was over, Morin, like Georgetown's Kate Dieringer, was asked to sign a confidentiality agreement that would have prevented her from telling anyone about the outcome of the case. But unlike Dieringer, she refused to sign. As of the end of April 2005, she still had not learned the results. But what she did discover unnerved her even more. Immediately following her hearing, the same assailant faced a second hearing and a second accusation of sexual assault from another student. The outcome of that hearing was also denied her.

Denied the disposition of either case for four months, she did not know whether her alleged assailant was still on-campus. That was almost more than Alphia Morin could handle. The semester before, following the alleged rape, she had gotten a medical leave and dropped out for the fall semester. She had stopped going to classes because of depression, insomnia, and fear. Now she ran the risk of seeing her assailant around every corner of the campus. She tried to schedule an appointment with the university president, John C. Hitt, but was told he only meets with students in a public forum. Finally, in April 2005, unwilling to be gagged and refusing to allow the university to ignore her safety, she decided to take her story to the school newspaper, despite attempts by at least one school administrator to dissuade her from making the matter public, which, she told Alphia, it would be "crazy" to do. The headline on April 28, 2005, said it all: "On a Victim's Journey: More than a Few Bumps." No one told Morin anything more about her assailant's whereabouts or status.

Morin is convinced that the secrecy surrounding her case and that of others is motivated by the school's desire to protect its reputation and to preserve its claim of being one of the safest schools in the state.

Morin's rape counselor, La'Shawn Ruffin, knows the toll such secrecy has taken on Morin and on others. "A lot of victims," she says, "feel like no one is going to protect them." The restraints on information are so tight that, according to Ruffin, not even those conducting the hearings in the Morin case would be permitted to know of other existing allegations, and if they learned of them, would not be allowed to consider them in their deliberations. Thus, multiple allegations and patterns of conduct would be excluded. Because of the pervasive secrecy, it is impossible to know how seriously the university takes the crime of rape, a felony in the state. In 2004, Ruffin handled seven rape cases that went to hearings. Not one of the students accused was expelled, she says. As for the secrecy agreements, Ruffin notes, "It's not helping the victim. In some cases, it's re-victimizing them."

Recently the school, under scrutiny of the watchdog group Security On Campus, said it was going to reevaluate nondisclosure agreements and rethink portions of its student code of conduct, "The Golden Rule," a title that smacks of irony for Morin and others who say no victim of rape would want to be treated as they have been. The school is uneasy talking about such matters even now. My inquiry on the handling of the Morin case was shunted from the Office of Student Conduct to the General Counsel's Office to the Public Affairs Office to the Office of Student Development and Enrollment Services, which oversees student conduct issues. There, a university vice president, Dr. Maribeth Ehasz, said that Alphia Morin's name did not ring a bell and that she would have to review the rules before getting back to me.

As for Alphia Morin, on May 2, 2005—four months after the sexual assault hearing, and after Morin had taken her case public through the school paper—the university finally relented and sent her a letter informing her of the results of the hearing. They were not comforting. The university disciplinary board found her alleged assailant "not in violation for sexual abuse." Once again Morin attempted to speak with the university president. Once more, Morin was forced to settle for an administrative assistant. While the assistant was on the phone to a school administrator, Morin overheard the administrator say that Morin had gone to the media and suggested the assistant not speak with her.

Secrecy and silence persist on the campus. Morin has not been able to learn whether the man she says raped her is still on campus. On April 7, 2005, three weeks before the school sent Morin its letter stating her alleged assailant had been cleared of the charges, Orlando police arrested him and charged him with false imprisonment and battery. The alleged victim was a University of Central Florida coed. A university spokeswoman said the school was unaware of the charge and would not discuss whether the alleged assailant was still on campus.

That question was answered on Friday, May 20, 2005, when Alphia Morin's rape counselor spotted him mixing and mingling at an orientation program reserved for new students. Today Morin's alleged assailant is no longer enrolled at Central Florida but is a student at another university.

•   •   •

Secrecy on campus takes many forms. Federal law requires universities to report all serious crimes. That provision is called the Clery Act and is named for Jeanne Clery, who was raped and murdered by a fellow Lehigh University student. But the reality is that compliance is shoddy at best. Schools, famous and obscure alike, routinely underreport crime. The University of California reported that in 1998 its nine campuses had a total of 90 rapes. But the *Sacramento Bee* reported in 2000 that at least 190 such cases had been documented by campus officials. In 2005, Salem International University in West Virginia was forced to pay a $200,000 fine for failing to report more than 80 crimes, including five sexual assaults and 16 burglaries.

Security On Campus reportedly found at least a dozen cases of rape at Penn State University, which reported that there had been none that year; it was forced to correct the record.

A 2002 study by the nonprofit Education Development Center found that fewer than 40 percent of colleges were in compliance with the Clery Act. Three-quarters of the schools failed even to collect evidence following a report of rape or sexual assault.

Despite cases such as Kate Dieringer's at Georgetown or Alphia Morin's at the University of Central Florida, even universities intent upon finding answers as to what the law expects and demands of them may instead find themselves in a bureaucratic cul-de-sac. In September 2006, I called Leroy S. Rooker, director of the Family Policy Compliance Office at the U.S. Department of Education. He is the government's expert on the Family Educational Rights and Privacy Act as it relates to privacy and what information a school can and cannot release with respect to disciplinary hearings.

Rooker read me the provisions: When the disciplinary hearing concludes that the alleged perpetrator is guilty, the school may—but does not have to—inform the alleged victim or anyone else of the outcome. But if the hearing concludes otherwise, then the school may (again, it is purely up to the discretion of the institution) inform the victim and the victim *alone* of the results. And if it chooses to do so, the student is then expressly forbidden from sharing the information with anyone else, including parents, siblings, or friends.

Sounds clear enough, except that the Clery Act also has something to say about what must be released in sexual assault cases. "We don't answer the Clery piece," says Rooker. "That's not my area." For that, one would have to track down the Clery expert in the Federal Student Aid office, also a part of the Department of Education. "There are no easy answers out there," admits Rooker.

Although that was not the answer I was looking for, it did help explain why institutions, uncertain about the law, have chosen the more conservative course, namely, withhold all information or attempt to silence the victim.

But despite the lingering confusion, the welter of regulations, and the bureaucratic uncertainty of what really is demanded, the law today is unambiguous as to the responsibilities of colleges and universities. "Both the accuser and the accused must be informed of the outcome of any institutional disciplinary proceeding brought alleging a sex offense," says the Code of Federal Regulations, Title 34, Volume 3, Section 668.46(b)(11). And just in case any campus disciplinary hearing officer is still left wondering, the official 2005 Department of Education "Handbook for Campus Crime Reporting" notes: "Disclosure concerning the outcome of proceedings must be unconditional: a victim cannot be required to sign a nondisclosure agreement or to otherwise agree to a prohibition from discussing the case."

•   •   •

Obsessive secrecy defines not only the handling of recent campus crimes but also events from the distant past. In academia, scandals have a half-life that is scarcely diminished with the passage of time. They retain their power to damage the reputations of men canonized by their institutions—be they presidents, faculty, or alumni—and to shake the foundations of schools that have enjoyed carefully sculpted and scripted pasts. When that past does not comport with their public image, they simply seal the files. More than one institution has redacted history.

University archives contain often sordid accounts of political hysteria, racism, homophobia, anti-Semitism, eugenics, inhumane medical experiments—all once sanctioned by the university and reflecting society's own past prejudices and passions. The impulse to smother this history instead of teaching it reveals more about the character of the present than the past.

Consider the University of Colorado in Boulder, a campus of nearly 23,000 full-time students. The school has been embroiled in one scandal after another, most recently facing allegations of sexual assault and recruiting scandals in its beleaguered football program. Its critics say the school has a "circle-the-wagons" mentality, relying on a strategy of secrecy and denial.

But it was the university's past that the governing board of regents seemed most intent upon keeping from public view in 2002. Since 1951, a secret report had been locked away in a vault in the First National Bank of Boulder. Such were the instructions of the university's revered former president, the late Robert L. Stearns, for whom a dormitory is named as well as one of the school's most prestigious awards. The secret report was the product of a McCarthy-era investigation by two former FBI agents, Dudley I. Hutchinson and Harold E. Hafer, into supposedly subversive activities by University of Colorado faculty members. Such inquiries and investigations were hardly uncommon in the period, but it is the efforts half a century later to suppress the details of those inquiries that set Colorado–Boulder apart.

University officials feared that releasing the document could sully Stearns's impeccable reputation and impugn the character of former faculty members who secretly collaborated with investigators, helping to smear their colleagues, often with mere innuendo and the thinnest evidence, thereby ruining lives and careers. The board of regents may also have been concerned with its own reputation. At the height of the "Red Scare," the anti-Communist hysteria of the 1950s, the board was itself instrumental in launching the investigation and demanded that every faculty member sign a loyalty oath to the United States.

In contrast, no one was more interested in having the Hutchinson-Hafer report released than Morris Judd, now 89. His life was forever changed by the report. A 1938 summa cum laude graduate of the University of Colorado, he had gone on to do graduate work in philosophy at Columbia University and served in World War II as a lieutenant in the Navy. In 1949 he returned to teach philosophy at the University of Colorado at Boulder. By 1951, he was a popular lecturer on the campus, well respected by his peers and top-ranked by his department.

But then President Stearns suspected he was a subversive and he became a target of the investigation. The two former FBI agents asked Judd point-blank if he was a Communist. Judd declined to answer, saying his political beliefs were no one's business but his own. "I've never been a Communist, though I still won't admit it publicly," he says.

Judd's refusal to answer the question, together with the idle speculation of others, was all the evidence Stearns needed. Judd's contract was not renewed and in June 1952 he was effectively driven from the university he loved. He would spend the next 15 years working in a Greeley, Colorado, scrap yard wondering how his promising career had come to such a precipitous end. His suffering was compounded by the secrecy surrounding the investigative report, and by his inability to identify his accusers, much less refute their charges.

More tragic still, says Judd, was the fate of his colleague Irving Goodman, a highly respected chemistry professor at Boulder. A distinguished chemist and two-time recipient of a Guggenheim Fellowship, Goodman was in Europe in 1951 when the university contacted him and informed him that because he had been a Communist, he would not be welcomed back at the school. Judd and others believe that Goodman was later offered a job at another university but that Stearns contacted that university and told them Goodman was a subversive, thus scuttling his employment offer. After that, says Judd, Goodman never again found a university position. Instead he settled for work in various labs. He died in 1988.

The instrument of both men's downfalls was the investigative report that was still locked away in the bank vault. Half a century later, Judd, his daughter, Nina, and Paul Levitt, a Colorado–Boulder professor of English who was chair of the Faculty Affairs Committee, among others, requested that the document at long last be released. But the university's board of regents steadfastly refused. The impasse was brought to the attention of a local paper, the *Boulder Daily Camera,* and its reporter Clint Talbott, who petitioned the school for the report's release. Again the regents refused. The paper took the regents to court, but the university's attorneys argued that the report was subject to attorney-client privilege.

At their meeting on April 4, 2002, the Colorado–Boulder Faculty Assembly discussed the regents' intransigence. "The Regents," declared Professor Levitt, "have stated that the event is behind us and that it will serve no good purpose to release the document. These are the same arguments that have been used in the past to keep secret the Tuskegee medical experiments in the United States, the Stalinist purges in the Soviet Union, and the actions of Afrikaners during apartheid." The faculty assembly put its position on the record: "Resolved: that in the interest of openness and the free flow of ideas, and so that we may learn from the past, the Boulder Faculty Assembly urges the Regents to release the Hutchinson-Hafer report, given to President Robert Stearns in 1951."

And still the University of Colorado's regents refused to budge on the issue. But it became clear that the judge hearing the case was skeptical of their claims of attorney-client privilege. On May 10, 2002, the board of regents convened in room 3 of the university's conference center to weigh their increasingly limited options. As if there were not already concern about secrecy, the board immediately retreated into "executive session," leaving the public behind. Emerging from behind closed doors, the regents announced their decision finally to release the report, although they did so in lawyerly language: the board had waived "its attorney-client privilege as to this report only." One board member, attempting to put the best public face on it, patted himself and his colleagues on the back, proclaiming "a time today to celebrate the board and it's a perfect example of its openness."

Five decades had passed and months and months of legal wrangling and resistance. At last, the 126-page report was to be released. It was less a triumph of openness than a testament to sheer persistence and an imminent adverse judgment by the courts.

The report demonstrated the flimsy nature of the case against Judd, Goodman, and other University of Colorado professors. Its substance was innuendo supported by hearsay, and it was based upon confidential informants. Morris Judd had been waiting 51 years to read the report, but as he read it he was "shocked" not by the gravity of the charges but by the poor grammar, the errors in punctuation, and the superficiality of the questions. "The material itself was silly," says Judd. (Among Judd's putative sins: he had once hosted a reception for the outspoken black singer Paul Robeson.)

On November 7, 2002, an embarrassed and contrite Boulder Faculty Assembly honored Morris Judd and expressed contrition for the university's scurrilous past. (Both the university's then president, Elizabeth Hoffman, and the chair of the board of regents, Susan C. Kirk, sent their regrets that they could not attend the ceremony.) Judd was presented with a large brass medal. On one side was inscribed in Greek the university's motto, "Let Your Light Shine Forth." On the reverse were the words "BFA [Boulder Faculty Assembly] honors you for your courageous and principled behavior, presented to Morris Judd by the Boulder Faculty Assembly November 7, 2002."

In accepting his honor, Judd referred once more to history. "In 1656, at the age of 23, fellow philosopher Baruch Spinoza was excommunicated by the Amsterdam Jewish community for the sin of harboring and teaching heretical beliefs. . . . For me, the ban has been lifted and I am here today, by your kind invitation, after only fifty years."

But if the past was behind Morris Judd, it was not behind the University of Colorado. Allegations of sexual assaults, recruiting scandals, and questions of financial irregularities still dog the school. The board of regents continues to avail itself of executive sessions amid concerns about compliance with the state's Sunshine Act. And even those who said that the fate of Morris Judd was a cautionary lesson in the dangers of secrecy and political hysteria seemed soon after to ignore that lesson.

In November 2002, at Judd's award ceremony, University Chancellor Phil DiStefano cited the opportunity "to examine our past—even the difficult adversities of the McCarthy era—so that we may fully understand the tenor of the times and the pressures then facing all associated with the University." Barely two years later, DiStefano chaired a panel investigating Colorado Professor of Ethnic Studies Ward Churchill, who had set off a firestorm of protest after disparaging the victims of 9/11.

While the allegations were of plagiarism and questions surrounding his status as a Native American, many saw the investigation as a ploy by the university to distance itself from a professor with unpopular political views. And in February 2005, Chancellor DiStefano issued a memo to the Colorado faculty informing them that the university was reviewing their files to make sure they had signed their loyalty oaths and pledged allegiance to the Constitution, as required by state law. It was almost identical to the oath Judd and others faced during the McCarthy era, half a century earlier.

• • •

Down through the years, few universities have more vigorously championed the principles of open government and transparency than Harvard. Its motto is simply "Veritas"—"Truth." But like other institutions, it has recently found itself torn between scholarship and secrecy, history and reputation, accountability and privacy. As far back as 1692, Increase Mather, the Puritan president of the fledgling college, and his son, Cotton, a Harvard graduate, cheered on the Salem witch trials in which dozens of innocents were executed or imprisoned. But when the Mathers' role was detailed by Robert Calef in his contemporaneous account, *More Wonders of the Invisible World*, an irate Cotton Mather had the books torched in the midst of Harvard Yard. It would not be the last witch hunt in which a Harvard president would play a critical role, nor the last time that the college would subject history to redaction.

Like other universities across the land, Harvard has institutionalized both disclosure and secrecy. Its relationship with its own past is filled with contradiction—a commitment to preserve the past but not to release information about it until all the participants are safely beyond its reach and the patina of dust is deep enough to insulate them from accountability and embarrassment. What Harvard has done is to accord itself, its administration, and those who attend the school a lifetime grant of immunity from outside scrutiny.

The main repository of the Harvard University Archives boasts some

90,000 linear feet of archival and manuscript material. But official university records are sealed for 50 years. A half century is presumably long enough for anyone with a career at Harvard to have moved on or passed away. Records relating to individual students and personnel are off-limits for even longer—80 years. That, tacked on to the 20 which represents the approximate average age of an arriving student (older for an administrator) adds up to four score and 20—a full life span.

Such secrecy is hardly unusual. Yale's administrative records are closed for 35 years after the date the person leaves office, and personnel and student records are restricted for the life of the individual plus five years, or 75 years, whichever is longer. Yale's governing corporation, which meets behind closed doors, seals its records for half a century. Yale's audit and donor records are "closed permanently." So much for Yale's motto, "Lux et Veritas"—"Light and Truth."

There are of course other, less self-serving arguments for such policies. Harvard archivists assert that making the records of university administrators and professors available earlier might make them self-conscious and induce them to write for history rather than for themselves and their peers. But writing for history is not such a bad thing. The foreknowledge that historians will evaluate and judge them in this lifetime has been accepted in many quarters as a force that elevates both composition and conduct. Review by posterity neither remote nor posthumous may have as much a salutary as a chilling effect. But in choosing between preservation of records and protection of reputation, Harvard has conveniently chosen both.

Nowhere did the two impulses clash more than in the spring of 2002. That's when Amit Paley, a Harvard sophomore and a reporter with the *Harvard Crimson*, the student newspaper, was staring at a computer terminal in the Harvard University Archives, searching the digitized catalog of holdings. Something curious caught his eye. It was a terse reference to a file marked "Secret Court, 1920." There was a cryptic mention of homosexuals, expulsions, and suicide. Nothing more.

Intrigued, Paley duly filled out the usual forms and requested the files. Well versed in the regulations and regimen of the archives, he knew the 50- and 80-year rules on releasing such documents. But these records were at least 82 years old and therefore were subject to immediate release. But instead of a research assistant returning with boxes of dusty documents, the researcher informed Paley that the files could not be released without the approval of a higher-up.

Paley was stunned. He politely cited the rules, but to no avail. The initial denial was to be only the first stop in a long and tortured odyssey in which Paley would face considerable opposition and resistance from Harvard. His request was passed to the desk of the university archivist, Harley P. Holden. Recognizing the sensitivities of the materials requested, Holden passed the matter along to his superiors in the university library system, who in turn brought the dean of the college, Harry Lewis, into the fray. A professor of computer science, Lewis was regarded by the *Crimson* staff as both reasonable and forthcoming. By now, Paley was beginning to suspect that the materials he had requested must be extremely inflammatory to warrant such special handling.

In the past, Harvard had taken the unusual step of placing certain ultrasensitive materials in its vault, an imposing safe such as one finds in banks, with a grand iron door and a combination lock, on the second level of the Pusey Library. The files of senatorial and presidential candidates such as Ted Kennedy and Al Gore had been placed there, lest, as Holden put it, they fall into the hands of the *National Enquirer.* So, too, was the file of the "Unabomber," Theodore Kaczynski, class of 1962. There is even a box containing hundreds of nude photos of Harvard students taken in the early 1940s for Professor William H. Sheldon, who was convinced that body types yielded insight into temperament and intelligence. (Transporting those files from the Smithsonian back to Harvard, Holden was stopped by airport security and ordered to open his attaché case, so jammed was it with nude photos that the X-ray could not penetrate the contents. It is unclear who was more chagrined, Holden or the security officers.)

Months passed and Amit Paley's request to see the files stamped "Secret Court, 1920" went unanswered. He wondered whether the delay reflected Harvard's concern for its own reputation rather than that of students from long ago.

For all the goodwill Dean Harry Lewis enjoyed with the *Crimson* staff, it was he who became the principal obstacle to the records' release. Lewis says his resistance had nothing to do with the university's reputation. Indeed, he says, he never even read the records nor the subsequent articles in the *Crimson.* Rather, his opposition was based on concern for the privacy of Harvard students. An internal memo he wrote at the time that was circulated among several senior Harvard decision makers involved in the matter supports his position.

On June 12, 2002, he wrote, "If the matter were left to my discretion, which I think would be appropriate given what I now for the first time see as the referral to the head of the University department in case of doubt, I would ordinarily not open student disciplinary records for some period greater than 80 years. I do not have a fixed number in mind; certainly I would open records from the 17th and 18th centuries. By extrapolation, I suppose my threshold for opening would be some time period more than 100 years and less than 200." Lewis conceded that "at some point these matters become purely a matter of history," but that time, said Lewis, had not yet come.

As the archivist, Holden, explains, Harvard is generally intent upon "protecting its own." It was a desire to shield from the glare of public scrutiny and embarrassment not only the students of the time, but also their families.

In 2002 there remained a single living member of the class of 1923. Not just any member, either, but one of Harvard's most illustrious, distinguished, and generous alumni. That was 101-year-old Albert Hamilton Gordon, the former head of the investment firm Kidder, Peabody. Gordon had served on Harvard's board of overseers and had given Harvard the field house and indoor track that bear his name. And though Gordon had no link to the affairs of the 1920 secret court, it was a sobering reminder to some that alumni were living longer than the 80-year rule envisioned. (Ironically, on a visit to Harvard's archives a few years ago Gordon requested his own student files and was promptly turned down—it was not out of concern for Gordon but rather for those others whose comments and letters of reference were in his file.)

Following Dean Lewis's denial of the *Crimson*'s request for the "Secret Court, 1920" files, the matter was taken up by an ad hoc committee that included Lewis, the head of the library, a representative of Harvard's governing corporation, the secretary of the administrative board, and others. There, Lewis's concern for student privacy was seen as somewhat overextended by other committee members, though other issues of concern did surface. Among these was the recognition that the university's McCarthy-era records were imminently passing out of the protection of the 50-year rule and would themselves doubtless be subject to a flood of requests by journalists, historians, and those who suffered during the "Second Red Scare" at Harvard. How the "Secret Court" records were handled might well set a precedent for those and other sensitive record groups.

But the *Crimson*'s persistence and the committee's realization that Harvard could not ultimately withhold the files without violating its own rules and policy left it little choice but to release the documents. Still, there was one more obstacle the committee could erect—the redacting of all students' names in the files. One administrator involved in the decision said that it was done for the protection of the lads named in the files and their families. But when the records were finally released—some 500 pages in all—Paley and others came to suspect that the redactors' motives were not all so altruistic. It seemed to them that whatever shame and embarrassment might be suffered with the release of the records belonged to Harvard, not the long-since deceased students or their families.

For months after the files were released, Amit Paley and his colleagues at the *Crimson* painstakingly investigated each and every lead, cross-checking and correlating references in the materials in an effort to put a name and a face to the students whose redacted identities had been reduced to the likes of "S1" and "S2." What the Harvard records revealed and the *Crimson* research unearthed was a secret inquisition directed by Harvard's august president Abbott Lawrence Lowell and overseen by senior Harvard administrators and staffers.

The mission of the secret court was to root out students who were homosexual or who had associated with students believed to be gay. This it did with a vengeance and a callous efficiency that left Paley, his colleagues on the *Crimson,* and the Harvard community at large aghast. Lowell's secret court prosecuted at least nine students, literally banishing them not only from the campus but from the city of Cambridge itself. Never mind that the inquisition possessed no such extraterritorial authority—it had the unspoken power that went with the threat of public exposure and scandal.

At least two of those targeted by the court took their own lives. The others packed and left without making any explanation to their friends and classmates. Not content to drive them off, Harvard systematically pursued them, hounding them for years and torpedoing their careers. Even this was not enough. A conscious effort was made to erase their very existence from alumni publications and class notes. They were treated as pariahs for decades. The irony that 80 years later the same institution would attempt to block the release of these scurrilous proceedings supposedly to protect the reputations of those whose lives it had ruined struck Paley and others as a kind of perversity in its own right.

But the secrecy that surrounded the 1920 court and the subsequent effort to suppress those records seemed to some Harvard watchers to be consistent with the ongoing efforts by the university and the regime of its then president, Lawrence Summers, to manage how it was covered in the news and to restrict press access.

The conflict between the *Crimson,* as a proxy for the Harvard community, and the administration was drawn more than once on the pages of the *Crimson.* Its reporters and editors complain that deans in the College of Arts and Sciences will not meet with them unless in the presence of Robert P. Mitchell, the college's director of communications. Mitchell, a onetime PR man for Nike and a former press secretary for the mayor of Philadelphia, denies that Harvard is secretive and insists that the *Crimson* enjoys "extraordinary access." But Mitchell too has been seen by some to be a part of the attempt to manage the news that emerges from Harvard. It was Mitchell who in May 2005 blocked TV cameras from filming a student production reenacting the abuse of Iraqi prisoners at Abu Ghraib prison. Mitchell said he was merely enforcing university policy with regard to media at student productions and that it had nothing to do with fear of controversy.

In February 2004, the *Crimson* ran an editorial cowritten by the paper's managing and associate managing editors, bluntly titled "The Iron Curtain Lowers over U. Hall." David H. Gellis and Kate Rakoczy wrote of "the thoroughly scripted party line" and said, "We saw a level of secrecy enshroud the governance process of the Faculty of Arts and Sciences like none we had witnessed before. Information control has become a preoccupation within the Harvard administration, one that seriously threatens to stifle meaningful discussion and debate over the policy decisions that shape this university."

Four months later, in June 2004, Amit Paley, former president of the *Crimson,* wrote an editorial titled "In Search of a More Open Veritas." Wrote Paley, "The university's culture of secrecy extends beyond shameful episodes like the Secret Court of 1920. Harvard administrators today make every effort to keep even simple decision-making processes hidden from public view." Paley cited the *Crimson*'s lawsuit against the Harvard Police Department, filed in an attempt to gain access to crime records, as well as "the information blackout concerning budget shortfalls and layoffs. And the proliferation of spokespeople-cum-spin-doctors has made it impossible for reporters from the *Crimson* to properly cover even the most benign topics."

One eminent Harvard professor, too fearful to allow his name to be used, called President Lawrence H. Summers's regime the Ministry of Truth, no reference to "Veritas" intended. And at a February 2005 meeting with the faculty, Summers came under withering attack for what, according to the *New York Times*, was said to be "an autocratic management style that has stifled debate." *Times* reporters were not permitted to attend the meeting, nor were any other press representatives, except those from the student-run *Crimson*.

As for the story of Harvard's secret court of 1920, it was cited by the U.S. Supreme Court in *Lawrence v. Texas*, and led to a call by the *Crimson* staff that those who had been expelled should receive posthumous honorary degrees. In a December 2002 editorial the *Crimson* pointed out that once again, even after the secret tribunal had been exposed, Harvard's continuing insistence on secrecy stood in the way of justice and projected the stigma of the past into the present:

"The university still refuses to release the names of the students, making it difficult to grant them diplomas. But this position ignores the crucial issue—that the students in 1920 had done no wrong and that they were victims of a witch hunt. By not revealing the students' names, the University implies that they were accused of some legitimate transgression; nothing could be further from the truth. The university can never compensate these students for their cruel persecution. Granting the students honorary diplomas is the best way Harvard can make amends today for one of the darkest moments in its history." Eloquent as the appeal may have been, it fell on deaf ears. Harvard still will not identify those it subjected to the secret court. Some at Harvard surmise that the university fears granting posthumous degrees to students who have been expelled could set an unmanageable precedent; others say the university is simply reluctant to draw still further attention to the scandalous 1920 court of inquisition.

Today, Paley, the *Crimson* reporter who first broke the story, writes for the *Washington Post*.

In February 2006, Harvard's beleaguered president announced he was resigning. Not long after, Timothy Patrick McCarthy, former director of the Harvard Alumni Association, opined in the pages of the *Crimson* that Summers had "worked to maintain a fortress of secrecy around him. . . . Together, we must work to make Harvard the institution it can and should be—a place of higher education . . . where transparency replaces secrecy." That same exhortation would be welcomed at campuses around the nation.

To be sure, the uprising against Summers was not merely about secrecy, but also about what was perceived to be his abrasive manner. Nor could his departure be seen as an unqualified celebration of transparency. After all, the Harvard Faculty of Arts and Sciences that delivered the vote of "no confidence" in Summers did so by way of a secret ballot.

7

Case Study: A Case Unsealed

Until that moment on September 4, 2002, the case before California's Placer County Superior Court had focused exclusively on Sarah Davis. She was a passenger in a Honda Civic that was involved in a rollover accident in March 1999 that had left her a quadriplegic. At 17, a willowy blonde who loved to ride horses, she would never again walk or even be able to feed herself. Her mother had just suffered a recurrence of brain cancer and, distraught over her daughter's condition, elected not to have further treatments but to spend her remaining time—a matter of months only—alert and caring for her disabled daughter.

All that remained now was the civil suit against Honda, whose defense was that Davis had failed to wear a seat belt. Had she been wearing her seat belt, argued Honda's attorney, Paul Cereghini, she would not have suffered such devastating injuries. In essence, much of the blame lay with Sarah Davis, not Honda.

But on the afternoon of September 4, 2002, all eyes shifted from Sarah Davis to Honda's expert witness, Robert Gratzinger, a former engineer for General Motors and a veteran of numerous product liability cases. At an Auburn, California, yard, Gratzinger was examining the seat belt in the right rear passenger seat where Sarah Davis had sat. What happened next is very much in dispute. Plaintiff's attorney Kirk Wolden would tell the judge that what he witnessed so stunned him, he was momentarily at a loss for words.

As Judge James D. Garbolino later wrote in his opinion, Wolden said that Gratzinger removed from his pocket a reddish-colored grease rag and began to rub the seat belt's latchplate, as if buffing it. "Frozen in astonishment"—Judge Garbolino's words—"Mr. Wolden briefly did nothing in reaction to Gratzinger's action. But when his mind registered that Gratzinger was possibly damaging the 'witness' marks on the latchplate [evidence that might show the belt was worn at the time of the accident], Mr. Wolden ordered Gratzinger to 'Stop,' and shortly thereafter, 'Stop it.'" Gratzinger was said to have then stopped what he was doing and tucked the rag into his front pants pocket.

Never happened, says Gratzinger's attorney, Mark O'Connor. Indeed, says O'Connor, it would have been physically impossible to remove such a mark merely by rubbing it with a cloth.

Moreover, there was testimony that the victim had not worn her seat belt, testimony corroborated by an expert who was not called to testify. Gratzinger was never given the opportunity to testify on his own behalf, and the court afforded Honda only one half of a day to defend itself and Mr. Gratzinger against these allegations. Critically, the plaintiffs did not produce any expert at trial to support the allegation that the seat-belt marks were wiped away by Mr. Gratzinger.

Nevertheless, attorneys for Sarah Davis argued that the "witness" mark that they had earlier observed, and that, they argued, constituted evidence that their client had indeed been wearing her seat belt, was now gone. Judge Garbolino too appeared persuaded that Gratzinger had altered a critical piece of evidence.

In a 36-page opinion, Garbolino railed against Honda's expert. He turned his attention to Honda's attorney, Paul Cereghini, who he said had been directed to preserve the rag, as it, too, had now become a piece of evidence. The attorney had failed to do so, said the judge, thereby compounding the initial problem. The judge appeared convinced that Gratzinger had altered the evidence and that the rag subsequently produced in court was not the one said to have been used to wipe clean the seat belt and latchplate.

The only just solution, Garbolino ruled on October 3, 2002, was to find Honda liable for the accident, which ensured that the company would not benefit from any alteration to the evidence. It would then be up to the jury to determine the amount of damages.

But the matter never reached the jurors. A week later, Honda settled the case with Sarah Davis for an undisclosed but sizable monetary award—said to be over a million dollars. And as a part of that settlement, Judge Garbolino, the same judge who expressed concern about the conduct of Honda's defense expert, took a step that was itself remarkable.

On October 10, 2002, pursuant to the terms of settlement between the lawyers, he agreed not only to seal the case, but to vacate his 36-page judgment sanctioning Gratzinger. The judge went even further. He barred publication of the judgment, and prohibited any and all reference to the matter in any subsequent legal action. All outstanding copies of the decision were ordered destroyed. In essence, Garbolino's decision to vacate the judgment was tantamount to declaring that nothing untoward had happened and that no one was to speak of the matter again. What one day he had viewed as egregious conduct, one week later he caused to be utterly erased from memory. The slate as regards Gratzinger was now completely clean.

In the months and years after, Robert Gratzinger went on about his business representing other major auto manufacturers in product liability cases around the nation, the earlier allegation protected by the sealed order, which prohibited anyone from testifying about Gratzinger's alleged conduct in *Davis v. Honda*.

The impact of Garbolino's order was felt soon enough. A year after Garbolino sealed the case, the attorney, Cereghini, and the expert witness, Gratzinger, represented Kia Motors America, Inc., in an action in the Sonoma County Superior Court that involved the death of 21-year-old Marissa Beck, killed in September 1997 when her SUV rolled over in a crash. The suit was brought on behalf of Beck's son, six years old at the time of litigation.

One of the attorneys representing the boy's interest was Barbara Bozman-Moss. She had learned of Gratzinger's alleged misconduct in *Davis v. Honda* and with her co-counsels had decided that it was crucial that the jurors, too, be privy to information on Gratzinger so that they could assess his credibility. But, intimidated by Judge Garbolino's sweeping orders, she decided not to speak of the evidence issue that surfaced in *Davis v. Honda* in open court but rather in the private chambers of Judge Laurence K. Sawyer of the Sonoma court. "We were pretty timid about it," recalls Bozman-Moss. "We were probably more timid than we should have been."

But no words would likely have changed Judge Sawyer's mind. He cut off argument citing Garbolino's edict and denied Bozman-Moss the right to ask Gratzinger before the jurors whether he had ever been sanctioned for tampering with evidence. Because it was an in-camera meeting, no notes were taken, no record was kept. The order was discussed behind closed doors and there it remained. In September 2003, the jurors ruled for Kia, clearing the automaker of liability in the accident.

Attorney Bozman-Moss says she is disturbed by what she views as pervasive secrecy in the handling of cases, particularly in the realm of settlements. "All of these secret settlements turn my stomach every time," she says. "I love working on these issues and working to make the world a safer place and every time you hide evidence and information in a settlement about a defective product the public is compromised not knowing that it's a defective product."

There was some consolation, she says. Kia Sportage SUVs were later redesigned. Of course, that made no difference to the six-year-old whose mother was killed in the vehicle and who lost the case against Kia.

As for Gratzinger, he would go on to testify on behalf of other auto manufacturers in product liability cases. Not until October 26, 2005—three years after the Honda case was sealed—did anyone dare question the secrecy order. Trial Lawyers for Public Justice, representing the Center for Auto Safety, challenged the provisions and convinced the court to revisit the issue. The judge in that case was none other than Judge Garbolino, who had authored the original decision. Acknowledging that his earlier decision to seal the record had been a violation of the rules of the court, he unsealed his own sanctions decision.

Today Judge Garbolino says he is still unable to discuss the case. But he did offer this thought on secrecy and the courts: "Litigation belongs to the litigants, not to the court," he said. "One may be a champion of a cause but when the parties decide they want to settle the litigation, it's for them to settle it. You deal with the parties in front of you, not the fallout that may be later on."

Garbolino's position represents the prevailing legal philosophy of attorneys and judges around the country. Sarah Davis's lawyer, Kirk

Wolden, estimates that he has handled hundreds of cases in his 18 years of legal practice, but only 5 percent have gone to trial. Many of the rest were quietly settled out of court, and of these, he estimates, half contained secrecy or confidentiality provisions. Does it ever give him pause that such provisions could have wider implications for the safety and well-being of society at large? The question has occurred to him, he says, but he chooses not to address it, at least not publicly.

Mark O'Connor says his client, Gratzinger, was also very much a casualty of the Davis case. O'Connor says his client was denied the opportunity to defend himself against the allegations and was tainted by unfounded suspicions that lingered on even after a fully vacated judgment. Gratzinger still must fend off those who seek to introduce into evidence conduct that he steadfastly denies ever occurred, which is kept alive in no small measure by the notion that it was once veiled in secrecy. O'Connor argues that the issue of Gratzinger's conduct in the Davis case was not a secret, that it was reported in the media before and after it was sealed, and that it was not secrecy that barred that information from being presented to future jurors, but rather, the proper application of the rules of evidence.

Ultimately the full truth of what happened in *Davis v. Honda*—particularly the central issue of liability—may never be known. The case is but one of tens of thousands of confidential settlements and sealed cases nationwide, most of which go unchallenged, their contents unknown and unknowable.

Secret Courts

Secret Justice is a contradiction in terms.
> —Editorial in *Louisville Courier-Journal,*
> September 8, 2002

Everything secret degenerates, even the administration of justice; nothing is safe that does not show how it can bear discussion and publicity.
> —Lord John Emerich Edward Dalberg Acton
> (Lord Acton), historian (1834–1902)

Lady Justice is often depicted as blindfolded, to symbolize impartiality, but today, she might just as well be portrayed as bound and gagged, hostage to a system that relies increasingly on sealed settlements and sealed lips.

Secrecy in the courts is rampant, and with that secrecy comes the increasing risk that public perils will be suppressed and miscarriages of justice concealed. Civil suits involving product liability (tires, cars, prams, airplanes, appliances, medicines), civil rights, free speech, discrimination, police brutality, fraud, and innumerable other issues of vital interest to public safety and well-being are now routinely settled out of court, their outcomes sealed and relegated to a vault beyond citizen scrutiny or regulatory inquiry. Civil trials that go to jurors are an increasing rarity. Secret settlements predicated upon promises of silence are now the standard.

Long-held American ideals of open justice and of public reviewability and accountability are yielding to a system that is opaque and defined by the narrow self-interests of the parties and of judges only too eager to avoid time-consuming trials. In civil courts, the entire universe of jurisprudence is geared to resolving disputes between two opposing parties. Considerations of public interest rarely, if ever, even surface. From the beginning, law schools prepare aspiring lawyers to conceive of the legal profession exclusively in terms of service to the litigating parties. Their job, they are taught, is to represent their client's interests—period. How that parochial interest intersects with broader societal interests is a subject that seldom comes up in the classroom or the courtroom. Secrecy and confidentiality are presented as the necessary lubricants to dispute resolution. Judges now speak of trials as if they were some sort of pathology, a disease to be avoided at all costs.

The popular and revered image of American justice has always been the open trial, especially trial by jury. But such trials in both the federal and state courts are now in drastic decline. Lawyers and jurists now refer to what is commonly called the "vanishing trial" syndrome. The American Bar Association held a symposium on the subject in 2003 and a working paper by a University of Wisconsin law professor, Marc Galanter, detailed how the number of civil trials has dropped precipitously in recent years, transforming the American system of justice.

In 1972 the percentage of federal civil cases disposed of by trial was 9.1 percent; in 1982, 6.1 percent; in 1992, 3.5 percent; in 2002, 1.8 percent. As for the "causes of the trial implosion," Galanter notes that "alternative dispute resolution"—mediation and arbitration—account for a portion of the decline. Both are steeped in secrecy. But he also notes that "the great majority of almost every kind [of case] in both federal and state courts has terminated by settlement." Some 50 to 60 percent of civil cases in federal court today will end in a settlement, and many of these will have confidentiality clauses and secrecy provisions attached. Trials in state courts reflect the same pattern of marked decline and a concomitant rise in secrecy. Fewer criminal cases, too, are finding their way to trial. In 1962 there were some 33,110 federal criminal cases, of which 15 percent went to trial; in 2002, the number of cases was 76,827, but fewer than 5 percent made it to trial.

The decline of trials and the reliance on settlements with their secrecy provisions has changed the fundamental character of American justice. Increasingly, litigation comes down to what some have called "bargaining in the shadows." Legal considerations become subordinated to negotiation, concerns of publicity, and bartering for confidentiality.

"Judges preside over routine settlements that reflect not legal standards but the strategic position of the repeat players," says Galanter. The practice may have improved judicial efficiency, but it has severed the once-sacred connection with jurors, whose participation in the process reflected societal values and who represented a link with the wider community. Jurors were there not merely to adjudicate the case but to represent public standards and interests. Judges, instead of applying the law, have increasingly become administrators and processors of a private and secret system. Two hundred years ago, the English jurist Sir William Blackstone noted, "It is not to be expected from human nature that the few should always be attentive to the interests and good of the many."

The routinization of secrecy and confidentiality, considered by some to be necessary to securing settlement agreements, may obviate the need for protracted trials and help clear crowded dockets, but it comes at a steep price. "The evidence trials generate may be of value not only to litigants and the courts but to the public at large," writes the DePaul University College of Law professor Stephan Landsman. "The risks posed by asbestos, cigarettes, and a host of other items would not have been broadcast without the sharing of information obtained in litigation and disseminated at trial. . . . The absence of trials renders the law a private affair despite the strong public interests that may exist. Private processes like mediation and arbitration cannot provide an effective substitute for trials because secrecy is their hallmark."

Landsman and other legal scholars who have studied the justice system believe the impact of secret arbitrations, secret negotiations, and secret settlements is profound. They argue that it impedes the development of American law because the factual patterns of risk and behavior that emerged from the nation's courtrooms and once helped determine the shape of law are now sealed and sequestered. "You now find the erosion of lawmaking where you drain off the facts through settlement or alternative dispute resolution," says Landsman. The production of publicly available evidence from trials also once provided invaluable road maps for other attorneys pursuing complex litigation against corporations in product liability cases. Secrecy has absconded with the records and removed the road maps, giving a decided edge to corporations.

Perhaps most damaging of all to the public interest, because secrecy in all its myriad forms—arbitration, mediation, and secret settlements—has become the default position of American justice, is that it is no longer possible to monitor or assess the integrity of America's courts and system of justice. "It's about the judiciary losing the people's trust because we don't see them at work," says Landsman. "We have had an erosion of our trust in judges."

In lieu of a public process, we are left with private resolutions arrived at behind closed doors, where terms are secret and liabilities unresolved. No longer is American justice composed of public trials and open courtrooms. "We have moved into gated communities," says Landsman. "That is the real danger."

Justice Oliver Wendell Holmes suggested that the law sharpens the mind even as it narrows it. One of the narrowest edges of the law is its apparent disregard for the wider implications of secrecy. To challenge the culture of secrecy that lies at the core of tort litigation and product liability cases would require a fundamental change in the culture of legal practice, in the mind-set of litigants and judges, and in a public vision that looks beyond the myopic benefits of quick-fix solutions that leave citizens in the dark. It is a notion of "tort reform" of a far more radical and sweeping nature than the current notion, which aims at merely limiting defendants' damages and exposure to liability.

These are not mere abstractions, especially not for James Lammey, who has been a plaintiff, a lawyer, and a judge. On January 16, 1999, he and his wife, Maria, of Bartlett, Tennessee, were getting ready to go to a child's birthday party. While they gathered their things in the house, their three-year-old, Anthony, climbed into the front seat of the family's Lincoln Town Car and apparently bumped the transmission on the steering column, somehow putting the car in reverse. The ignition, the Lammeys say, was off, the gear shift on "park." But suddenly the car went into reverse and began to roll down the steep driveway. Little Anthony jumped out. An instant later the two-ton behemoth ran over his head. His brother rushed into the house wailing, "Anthony is dead!"

His mother, a nurse, ran outside and kneeled beside her injured son. His head was a gaping wound, his eyes vacant, and he was not breathing. She began to administer CPR. Anthony stirred back to life. A med-evac helicopter took him to a nearby hospital, where he would endure the first of several protracted surgeries.

Ultimately he would survive the ordeal with some minor disfigure-ment and problems with balance. His father, then a Memphis prosecu-tor, sued Ford, the maker of the Lincoln, in U.S. District Court for the Western District of Tennessee. He hired a local Memphis attorney, Todd Kaplan, who worked in a small three-person firm. Ford retained a Nashville attorney, John Randolph Bibb Jr., then with one of the nation's largest law firms. "Randy" Bibb was ranked one of America's top lawyers and was a seasoned defender of Ford in product liability cases.

That much can be gleaned from court records. But what happened next is not something anyone beyond the judge, the Lammeys, the two attorneys, and Ford are privy to know. Following a series of pleadings and exhibits, the trail of court records ends abruptly with a notation in the file that the matter was settled and sealed from public view. Neither Lammey nor his attorney is comfortable discussing the case. If Ford had a problem with the transmission, as Lammey and his attorney alleged, it was never adjudicated and Ford vigorously insists it was not responsi-ble for the accident.

Like thousands of sealed settlements entered into around the nation each year, its contents are a binding secret. It may have brought a mea-sure of relief to the Lammeys and it ended Ford's legal exposure for the accident, but it left the public in the dark as to what happened and whether there was a problem that merited further attention.

Months after the accident, little Anthony Lammey would be pro-nounced the year's "miracle case" and was featured in a fund-raising telethon. His father, now a criminal court judge, says he is unable to comment on the case because of the constraints of the settlement agree-ment.

Because of such settlements, and the imposition of secrecy that often attends them, patterns of product liability are harder to discern, and life-threatening defects stand a potentially greater chance of going unde-tected and uncorrected. Whether there was a problem with the transmission, as argued by the Lammeys and denied by Ford, is impos-sible to know. Such cases, quietly resolved between the parties, seldom produce any sort of warning to the wider public.

What the Lammeys did not know—could not have known—was

what happened four years earlier to a Boston woman. For her, there was no miracle, no happy ending. In February 1995, 49-year-old Grace Iantosca was getting out of her Lincoln Town Car in her driveway, when, according to her husband, the car slipped out of park into reverse and began to lurch down the steep driveway. Iantosca tried to jump out but got caught between the door and the vehicle and then was pinned against the side of the house. The momentum of the massive car crushed her aorta. She died two days later, on Valentine's Day 1995. She left behind her husband, Charles, a postal clerk, and two sons, Charles Jr. and Paul.

The family sued Ford, whose attorneys argued that Grace Iantosca had failed to set the parking brake and didn't put the vehicle into so-called park latch—in essence, that it had never been fully put in "park." But in 1998, the company settled—a year before Anthony Lammey's near-fatal accident. Included in the settlement agreement was a promise of confidentiality. Charles Iantosca Jr. was uneasy about the settlement. He wanted Ford to explain what had gone wrong and to assume responsibility for his mother's death. That didn't happen. And widower Charles too felt some discomfort with the agreement.

On December 9, 2002, seven years after the Iantoscas' loss and four years after the Lammey accident, Tim McGrath's wife, Carol, was in her Waltham, Massachusetts, driveway reaching in to turn off the ignition of her Lincoln Town Car when, it is said, the vehicle apparently slipped into reverse and dragged her to her death. She was 46. Iantosca heard about McGrath's accident and contacted her husband, Tim, to express his condolences.

As Tim McGrath recalls, Iantosca also said he felt somehow partially responsible because in accepting Ford's money and the promise of silence he had perhaps denied the public knowledge of a dangerous and even deadly defect. Ford initially offered McGrath $150,000, but he said he turned the money down and is preparing to take Ford to court. But McGrath, a former special agent for the U.S. Department of Homeland Security, acknowledges that he may not be able to resist a generous settlement offer, even one predicated upon his silence.

And so the pattern of secrecy continues, with everyone involved— plaintiffs, defendants, and judges—participating (some might even say "complicit") in a system that is singularly committed to self-interest, whatever the cost to society. No one wants to stand in judgment of those who have faced grievous losses and trauma, as the Iantoscas and the Lammeys have, nor can we equate settlements like those proffered by Ford and hundreds of other corporate defendants with admissions of responsibility. Ford denies it has a wider problem with the Lincoln Town Car and says the vehicle's safety record is laudable. And there is no reliable way to know how many cases like the Lammeys' and Iantoscas' have been settled and sealed.

Bibb, the attorney representing Ford in the Lammey case, says that over the past 27 years he has represented Ford in some 100 cases involving allegations of "false park." The car is safe, says Bibb; it is the operator of the vehicle who is at fault. "The vehicle is not defective," he says. "It's someone's inattention that caused the accident." Bibb says public interest groups and government watchdog agencies monitor the landscape and that it is the responsibility of litigants solely to resolve their differences, not to concern themselves with society at large. As for himself, he has never found cause to report any alleged defect to the government, nor, to his knowledge, have any of the scores of plaintiffs' attorneys he has faced.

"The plaintiffs say it's so dangerous but they don't notify the government," says Bibb. "These people are in it just for the money. They are not out to protect the good of mankind. If they start recalling those products, they'd [the lawyers would] be out of a job." Nor, says Bibb, has a judge even once questioned a confidentiality agreement out of a concern for public safety or well-being.

Indeed, the judges who sanction these secret arrangements have their own strong self-interest in what is called "judicial efficiency," the imperative to keep the cases moving and avoid costly and time-consuming trials. The simple truth is that today, justice is a matter solely between the litigants, and as they reach their clandestine accords, the party asked to leave the room is the public. The notion that such cases are like a canary in a coal mine—providing timely warnings of wider danger—is rarely borne out in the day-to-day process of tort and product liability litigation.

For Ford the problem of cars slipping from park to reverse may seem like déjà vu. In the 1970s, a rash of such cases, particularly a jury verdict for $4.2 million, brought public attention to the problem, then labeled "illusory park." Case filings suggest some 90 people were injured or killed by the defect. Ford is credited with having taken corrective action to fix the problem. The case is even cited as an example of how open product liability litigation can bring life-threatening defects to public light. Back then sizable verdicts in open courtrooms drew the attention of lawyers, journalists, and government alike. When cases are settled without a jury verdict, without media coverage, and without government awareness, there is the growing risk of defects going undetected for years, while casualties mount.

The most economically vulnerable plaintiffs—made all the more so by injury, mounting hospital and legal bills, and the loss of family wage earners—are in no position to resist a settlement offer, no matter how repugnant the terms of secrecy may be. The alternative is often to weather the opposition of a topflight law firm funded by a deep-pocketed corporation and to run the very real risk of an adverse judgment by a jury.

Where secrecy prevails, it is often virtually impossible to decipher even the most basic facts of a case. Consider the case of *Farr v. Newell Rubbermaid,* filed in U.S. District Court for the Northern District of Alabama on April 18, 2000. What is publicly known of the case is precious little: that Judge Paul W. Greene presided, that the plaintiffs were Billy C. Farr, Tina Farr, and their minor daughter, Destiny Farr. The Farrs sued Newell Rubbermaid, whose subsidiary Graco Children's Products, Inc., manufactures a product that allegedly had injured Destiny Farr.

The case was closed on August 27, 2001, when the two parties agreed to a sealed settlement. What makes the case even more of a mystery is that the entire case file was sealed and placed in the courthouse vault. There is no hint of which Graco product was involved, how serious the injuries were, or anything else that might have shed light on the case. So completely was the case erased that the clerk of the court told me that, upon reflection, she should not even have acknowledged its existence.

The attorneys in the case refused to discuss it with me, as did Judge Greene. Through his law clerk, Neva Webb, Judge Greene said he had no intention of explaining why he had allowed the entire case file to be sealed, but that it was my right to ask him to review the decision and petition him to unseal the case. It was suggested I first consent to not disclosing anything I subsequently learned about the case, as part of such a formal proceeding. I declined the offer. I had no wish to make myself a further party to secrecy.

The Farr case may be much ado about nothing—or it may not be.

In recent years Graco has been the subject of at least a dozen major

U.S. Consumer Product Safety Commission warnings and recalls of its products, including beds, strollers, cribs, high chairs, walkers, swings, and bath sets. Injuries reported to the Consumer Product Safety Commission and associated with Graco products have ranged from deaths to skull fractures to concussions to broken arms, legs, and noses to hundreds of bruises, scrapes, and cuts.

It is impossible to know where on that spectrum of injuries Destiny Farr was—or whether she was even counted in the tally—but it is relatively easy to make a case that excessive secrecy leaves at risk a broad swath of the American population, including its most defenseless members, its infants and children.

This is hardly idle speculation. In March 2005, Graco agreed to pay the government $4 million after the government accused it of failing to report defects promptly. It was the Consumer Product Safety Commission's largest fine ever and came after more than 12 million units involving 16 different Graco products had to be recalled in the years between 1992 and 2002. That was the time period in which Destiny Farr was injured, and a period in which Graco products were implicated in the deaths of at least six children and the injuries of more than 900 others.

R. Bradford Wash represented Destiny Farr's parents in their case against Newell Rubbermaid and its subsidiary, Graco. He says he barely remembers the case and that, even if he could recall the details, he is barred from speaking of them by the confidentiality agreement that was a part of the settlement. A practicing attorney for 27 years, he, like many of his peers, has grown completely blasé about secrecy as a condition of settlement agreements. He routinely sees confidentiality made a part of agreements in larger settlements and mediations, particularly those involving product liability cases.

A grandfather himself, he acknowledges that a jury verdict might well draw public attention to the potential hazards of a defective product, but adds that this is not his role as an attorney. His only concern, he says, is getting his client the best settlement he can. If secrecy is part of the price to be paid, then so be it. Not once does Wash recall alerting the Consumer Product Safety Commission about product defects that, he alleged, injured or maimed his clients. He says that it would have been unusual—even, arguably, contrary to the interests of his client—to do otherwise.

And in all his years of practicing law, Wash says no judge has even raised a question about the secrecy agreements and confidentiality clauses that are a part of settlements, whether they barred the plaintiff and attorney from going to the media, prohibited the lawyer from writing about the case or mentioning it in a professional seminar, or sealed the entire court file from public view. Not even one judge.

But Bradford Wash has never met Judge Joseph F. Anderson, chief judge of the U.S. District Court for the District of South Carolina. Judge Anderson remembers well his first encounter with secrecy in the court. The year was 1986. At 36, he had been on the bench less than a year and was facing a protracted and complex six-month civil trial involving a groundwater-contamination case. It was not something he was looking forward to. *Whitfield v. Sangamo Weston* involved residents around a lake who alleged that PCBs had been dumped in the water.

As he prepared for the case, the attorneys informed him that the more than 300 plaintiffs and the defendant had reached a $1.2 million settlement, worth some $4,000 to each of the plaintiffs. The news brought the judge a certain sense of relief, but there was a catch. The parties wanted him to put a gag order on the case, to seal up the settlement and ensure that all the defendants' documents would be returned to them. The information that had been procured, such as how many PCBs were in the water, was to be subject to the gag order.

Judge Anderson granted the request, but says now that he had misgivings even at the time. "That just bothered me, to be a part of that process that had been so laboriously extracted in discovery. I looked back on it and regretted it later. I am pointing a finger at myself as well."

Unlike so many of his peers on the bench—federal and state court alike—Judge Anderson resolved to do something about it. In the years after *Whitfield v. Sangamo Weston* he became aware of the vast scope and corrupting influence of secret settlements and of gag orders, of how pervasive secrecy eroded the standing and authority of the court and ill served the public. He heard of cases in which, as a term of settlement, defendants would even get the plaintiffs' attorneys to promise never again to represent clients in such cases against the defendant company. "You're just buying off the plaintiffs' lawyer," he thought. Plaintiffs' attorneys, he said, know that defendants will pay a premium in the settlement for the promise of secrecy, a kind of hush money. "It's a pecuniary sweetener," says Anderson.

But what troubled him most was the spectacle of judges lending their authority and that of the court to sanction such secrecy by presiding over such a system. "Secrecy," says Judge Anderson, "is being bought and paid for right under the judge's nose and with the judge's complicity. It's a commodity that has a market value."

Determined to challenge the system, Anderson proposed a radical solution—ridding the system of confidential settlements and gag orders, except in the most meritorious of circumstances. His first attempt to create access to all settlements was in 1994. His efforts were swiftly vetoed. But by 2000 the climate had begun to change. The local Columbia, South Carolina, newspaper, *The State,* wrote about malpractice suits so cloaked in secrecy that not even the defendants' names were public. The headlines in *The State* told of the casualties of secrecy: "Medical Mistakes Kept Secret," "Medical Errors Kill, Injure S.C. Patients." The first account told of a South Carolina doctor, identified only as "Dr. 169186," whose malpractice insurance company paid $9.9 million to the doctor's victim and "whose ineptitude was hidden from the public by nature of a protective order." The second story described "a patient's death after obeying a doctor's orders to take a fatal combination of drugs."

Across the nation there were similar tales of court secrecy run amok and of the public placed in jeopardy. People were beginning to take note of the rash of fatalities and crippling injuries associated with Firestone tires and the Ford Explorer, the emerging scandal of the Catholic Church and child molestation cases, and the secrecy surrounding corporate giants like Enron, companies that imploded with devastating results. Anderson was hardly alone in wondering whether eight years' worth of sealed settlements in the Firestone and Ford Explorer cases had contributed to the enormity of the suffering by delaying and suppressing the public's awareness of the problem.

The time was right. Judge Anderson's crusade to end secrecy in his federal court won the day. But it remains the only federal court in the nation that is outright hostile to sealed settlements and to seeking judicial approval for such secret agreements. Judge Anderson's changes were opposed by an onslaught of corporations and defense attorneys who predicted that without such secrecy the courts would become choked with cases and that dispute resolution between the parties would grind to a halt.

"You would have thought we were going to abolish the Bill of Rights, the nerve it struck," says Anderson. But the truth is that cases that went to trial were rare before Anderson's sweeping change—of 3,856 cases brought, only 35 went to a verdict—and they are just as rare today, three years later. The dire predictions never materialized. Judge Anderson couldn't help but gloat in an October 25, 2004, letter to his fellow judges on the South Carolina court.

But any such change riles those accustomed to the secretive and largely privatized system of justice in which the judicial impulse for resolution and the parties' appetites define the outcome. Plaintiffs' attorneys know that many defendants will pay a premium to have the matter settled "discreetly"—what cynics call "hush money"—and corporations facing product liability or discrimination cases know that public trials can call unwanted and costly attention to them. It is the so-called blood-in-the-water scenario, where open trials, public verdicts, and media attention attract other would-be litigants. Anderson's move to open the courts was also seen as a threat to federal judges around the nation who are often resistant to change and averse to risk taking. They, like the corporate defendants who come before them, are the beneficiaries of a "business-as-usual" mentality that has become increasingly dependent upon secrecy as a prerequisite to settlement, while parroting the judicial mantra of efficiency.

As if to defend this position, the Federal Judicial Center (FJC) released a study in 2004 that noted that fewer than 1 percent of the cases brought before the federal bench resulted in sealed settlements. As Judge Anderson noted in a letter to his judicial colleagues, "Implicit in this report is the suggestion that those who worry about court-ordered secrecy are wasting their time because confidential settlements are so rare, they cannot possibly be a problem."

Anderson fired back: "It has been well documented that confidential settlements are underreported. There is no one method of coding docket entries where secrecy has been ordered, and statisticians working on the FJC study simply manually reviewed docket sheets from a small number of selected districts [52]. If they had contacted me (which they did not), I could have cited several cases where secrecy was ordered in cases that adversely impacted the public interest, and the only way one would learn that anything was sealed would be to ask to see the file, where annotation was made outside of the envelope sealing the record. In other words, the docket sheets revealed nothing."

Besides, as Anderson and his supporters point out, it is not only about the number of cases but the types of cases in which secrecy and confidentiality most often occur. "Sure, no one is going to ask for any type of court-ordered secrecy in a case involving an intersection fender bender or a student loan default," he wrote his colleagues. "But in a case where a child is killed in an allegedly defective go-cart, and the model go-cart is still on the market; or a teacher is accused of molesting a child, and that teacher is still in the classroom; or a car dealer is found to have rolled back odometers and the dealer is still in business—those are the ones where secrecy will often be sought and where secrecy is not in the public interest."

In fact, the very study Anderson questions makes his point persuasively. Of the 1,270 sealed settlements cited in a sampling of federal court cases between 1997 and 2001, some 40 percent were "of special public interest," to quote the study itself. These included cases involving the environment, product liability, professional malpractice, public party defendants, and sexual abuse. Excluded from the so-called public interest cases that were sealed were another 38 percent of the cases that involved civil rights, discrimination, labor practices, and antitrust issues—matters that many Americans would consider to be "of special public interest." Together the two groups of cases account for some four-fifths of the sealed settlements.

Among the sealed settlements is one alleging the failure of the Memphis School Board to protect children from physical and sexual abuse by their special-education teachers; a North Carolina case against a nursing home alleging medical malpractice and wrongful death "resulting from the insertion of a feeding tube into a patient's trachea instead of her esophagus, resulting in her lungs receiving feeding solution"; a New York case brought by a widow against Dow Chemical Company alleging that her husband had died from a cancer caused by exposure to vinyl chloride in the workplace; a Missouri case brought against American Telephone and Telegraph by an African American woman with epilepsy, for race and disability discrimination; a Michigan case against the city of Detroit alleging a wrongful killing by a police officer.

The list of defendants reads like the Fortune 500—Ford, General Motors, Deere and Company, Amazon.com, Goodyear Tire and Rubber, DaimlerChrysler, Sunbeam Corporation, America Online, Sprint,

Bridgestone/Firestone Inc., Mitsubishi, McDonnell Douglas, and scores of other prominent corporations. It is asserted that such settlements avoid costly and time-consuming trials and promote judicial efficiency, but the practice of settling cases one at a time in secret, hushing up the results, and avoiding findings of liability and the publicity that goes with public trials—acting as a kind of public alarm system—has contributed to a corporate mind-set that can dismiss isolated instances of injury and death as just one more cost of doing business.

Other cases that were sealed in secrecy in the federal courts involved allegations of police brutality, rape and murder, sexual abuse by clergy, and discrimination against blacks, women, the elderly, and the foreign born. And as Judge Anderson points out, this disturbing sampling of cases is but a fraction of the larger universe of grievances that were settled in secret that the federal courts may never have even been made aware of. Thousands more such cases crop up in state courts and just as quickly disappear without a trace.

Anderson may be a formidable foe of court secrecy, but he is no match for the deep-pocketed opposition nor the resistance of his peers on the bench. "I waited to see if we had any people follow our lead," he said, "and very few have. We are still out there alone." (Fewer than half of the state courts have made any attempt to restrict secrecy in civil litigation, and none have approximated the prohibition of the federal court in South Carolina.)

The secrecy that Anderson faces in the federal courts is deeply embedded throughout the judiciary, so much so that it is even reflected in the software used to manage and keep track of cases. That system is known as CM/ECF, shorthand for Case Management/Electronic Case Files. For several years it has been in use in 94 bankruptcy courts and a similar number of federal courts, as well as a dozen federal appellate courts.

In publications, the Administrative Office of the United States Courts hails the system and speaks of its advantages to the bar and public alike. What it does not publicly proclaim is that the electronic case management system is set to a default position that responds to all outside inquiries of cases that are sealed with the message "Case Does Not Exist." An internal March 31, 2006, memo that went out to all clerks in federal district courts discusses "the increasing scrutiny by the media of the practices in district courts related to the management of sealed cases." It notes that the system is designed to produce the "Case Does Not Exist" message or another that says the docket number entered is invalid. (Some courts, the memo notes, are not even bothering to enter sealed cases onto the system at all, which also generates a "Does Not Exist" message.)

The memo informs the courts that they are free to substitute a message of their own choosing, but it neither encourages nor discourages such a change. In fact, the decision to deny the very existence of such cases was made by a working group within the federal court system that decided this was the optimal way to shield such cases from prying eyes.

The stakes are not insignificant for those who care about transparency and justice. The CM/ECF system holds some 26 million cases and has been used by at least 200,000 attorneys nationwide. The number of sealed cases that have vanished with the help of the system is unknown and perhaps unknowable. Cyberspace can be perfectly tailored to keep a secret.

Gary Bockweg oversees the technical side of the case management system for the federal courts and reluctantly expresses a hint of misgiving over the message, referring to it as "inaccurate" and "unfortunate." But in the realm of secrecy, it is not only sealed cases that are sensitive but also the inner workings of the federal courts. "I shouldn't be talking to you without getting clearance from public affairs," he says, offering me the number of Karen Redmond, a spokesperson for the Administrative Office of the United States Courts. She says she will set up other interviews but is reluctant to weigh in on the matter herself beyond saying, "If a sealed case says 'sealed case,' it doesn't exist for me." Her offer of other interviews comes to naught. I never hear from her again.

The larger question as to whether there is a moral issue in having the federal courts mislead if not outright lie to the public is, Redmond suggests, a "philosophical question" best left to others. But it seems odd to have federal judges, clerks, and members of the bar complicit in a program that misleads the public when truth-telling is at the heart of every court and perjury a punishable offense. "Case Does Not Exist" sends a message that goes well beyond a particular case, and raises broader institutional questions about the justice system's regard for truth.

•   •   •

Secrecy often reflects a convergence of self-interests that come at the expense of the public at large. Nowhere is that more in evidence (actually, literally, *less* in evidence) than in the area of health care, where pharmaceutical companies, physicians, and HMOs facing malpractice or product liability litigation want to avoid publicity and where attorneys representing injured plaintiffs look no further than their own and their clients' interests. Judges for their part are only too eager to reduce their dockets and settle cases. Lawmakers are not immune to the influence of political contributions from the medical community, which is eager to see legislation that favors secrecy and confidentiality.

Consider Carol Forte, a respected New Jersey litigator. On her website, she cites cases that have netted sizable settlements for her clients. It's a form of advertising. In the spring of 2002, her website featured a headline that read "Settled a Case Against a Drug Company for $5 Million." Beneath the headline are two brief and cryptic sentences: "The plaintiff had a very serious injury, which she alleged was caused by using a certain drug. Further details are prohibited by a confidentiality agreement."

Forte says the confidentiality agreement with the pharmaceutical company was so restrictive that she could not say which drug or even which court was involved. She may not even be permitted to acknowledge the existence of the case, though that did not dissuade her from citing it on her website. Her secretary, apparently unaware of such sweeping prohibitions, suggested I was referring to the "fen-phen case." Fen-phen was a combination of diet drugs that injured many.

Like many plaintiffs' attorneys, Forte sees nothing wrong with having files sealed and cases virtually disappear. Many of her cases involve medical malpractice, and these, too, often end in settlements tethered to confidentiality provisions. "I have a job to do and that job is to represent my client," she says. "That's my first obligation." First, yes, but what about those who may be unaware that the same unnamed drug could harm them or thousands of others? Is that something to be considered? "Whether it is or it isn't," says Forte, "as long as my client wants me to do it and that's who I'm representing, if that's what has to be done, that's what has to be done. . . . I guess there is no way for me to know of a case settled subject to a confidentiality agreement that could have prevented another person's injury. How would anyone ever know?"

It seems a reasonable question to ask, especially of Forte. Before she was a trial attorney, she was a nurse.

•   •   •

It is not just lawyers as advocates who maintain the veil of secrecy over the medical field. Distinguished judges too have become enablers of a medical system shrouded in anonymity, confidentiality, and sealed records. Take, for example, a 2002 case before California's State Court of Appeals for the Fifth District, in Fresno. The case was listed on the court docket as *Unnamed Physician v. Board of Trustees of Saint Agnes Medical Center*. A note by the court seeks to explain a curious docket entry, "Unnamed Physician": "Because of the sensitive nature of the allegations made by the hospital and the pendency of the internal peer review process, we deem it necessary to protect the physician's professional reputation at this juncture and will refer to him in this opinion as an unnamed physician, or appellant." But does such judicial solicitude for the reputation of the doctor leave patients and the public in the dark?

The case grew out of questions raised by a hospital peer review committee (PRC) consisting of five physicians who conducted a ten-day evidentiary hearing into the quality of care provided by the unnamed physician. When the doctor came up for reappointment, reviewers found what they believed was a disturbing pattern: his patients had suffered a "significantly higher" infection rate than patients of other physicians with the same specialty. "For the period of January 1, 1999, to September 30, 1999, appellant had a 14 percent infection rate for one procedure and a 7.9 percent overall infection rate." Postoperative infection rates appeared to be quadruple those of his peers' patients.

An external reviewer for the hospital concluded that the medical charts he reviewed "demonstrated some type of situation that might be deemed a quality of care issue. Foremost among these is an apparent excessive number of postoperative infections."

The reviewer wrote: "There is a pattern in this [physician's] operative technique which is detrimental to good patient care. Whether it be lack of attention to sterile technique or careful attention to hemostasis the result is that an unusual number of patients have had disastrous outcomes from apparently well intentioned surgery. As such the present situation should not continue and some changes should be made. . . . There is sufficient concern about patient outcomes and the surgical management and judgment of this practitioner to warrant a reduction or removal of staff privileges." By July 2000, following a formal internal investigation, the doctor's privileges were said to be "severely" limited.

An October 2000 document stated that the doctor's "acts and omissions caused complications and infections through either poor surgical technique or poor post-operative assessment or poor post-operative management." Two patients suffered bleeding that could not be controlled after surgery and another was said to have developed third-degree burns from a heated bag placed by his neck.

The unnamed doctor brought the matter before the Court of Appeals in Fresno, challenging the procedures and process by which he had been evaluated.

The court focused narrowly on due-process questions. Ultimately, the doctor's name was deleted and the entire file placed under seal. In January 2002, the doctor lost his appeal. The presiding justice who wrote the opinion and granted the physician anonymity was James A. Ardaiz, a thoughtful and well-regarded 25-year veteran of the bench. But he is a captive of a system of secrecy that reaches from the hospitals to the state legislature and into his very chambers. The medical lobby in California persuaded the state's lawmakers to allow the medical profession to police itself and to conduct peer review within the strictest confines of confidentiality. The patients and the public at large do not have access to these secret proceedings, nor to complaints filed with the Medical Board of California, nor to investigations by the board, nor to misdemeanor convictions. Only "hospital disciplinary actions that resulted in the termination or revocation of the physician's privileges to provide health care services" generate a public document or alert from the state medical board.

In this case, the hospital's judicial review committee (JRC) concluded that "Dr. 257 [the doctor in question is identified only by number by the hospital's review committee] was deficient in his professional care in a manner reasonably likely to be detrimental to patient safety in 10 of the 12 cases reviewed by the JRC."

Given that such reviews are confidential, Justice Ardaiz extended the curtain of secrecy a little further—from the operating room to the courtroom. He says the case turned on technical questions of due process, not the competency of the physician, and besides, the state legislature had already validated the confidentiality of doctors' peer review. Judge Ardaiz is not one to duck the tough questions. He is a judge, but also a husband and a father. Given what he knows about the unnamed physician, how comfortable would he be having one of his own loved ones treated by the unnamed doctor? "Can I tell you, taking off my judicial robes, in reading this, that I would not have some reservations? No, I can't tell you that. Are you kidding me?"

Today, the unnamed physician continues to practice surgery in the Fresno area and enjoys surgical privileges at three hospitals, including Saint Agnes. There is no record that he has been involved in any subsequent problems and his record appears to be otherwise clear of criticism. He declined to return phone calls or be interviewed, nor would Saint Agnes Medical Center comment on the case.

There is a footnote to this story that illustrates the complexities of secrecy as it applies to peer review and to the case at hand. The peer review committee's recommendations, which included a higher degree of monitoring of the physician, were deemed insufficient by Saint Agnes's medical executive committee, which had initiated the peer review and which took an even sterner view of the matter and sought to have more stringent restrictions imposed. They even considered alerting the California Medical Board.

In 2004 the doctor challenged those tougher restrictions, and this time he prevailed. The same judge, Ardaiz, on December 21, 2004, determined that the medical executive committee had overstepped its authority and failed to follow the hospital's own bylaws, substituting its judgment for that of the peer review committee.

The "Unnamed Physician" is not talking, but his attorney, John Harwell, is. Harwell says he has represented hundreds of doctors in peer review cases. "It is the front line of protection for the quality of care in the United States," he says. " 'Secrecy' is not the word I use. I use the word 'confidentiality.' I am a doctor's lawyer. I am not a hospital's lawyer. I only represent the accused in this process."

Harwell is convinced that the peer review process, though steeped in "confidentiality," ultimately does serve the public's interest. He notes that following the peer review process, the physician's infection rate plummeted to zero. He suggests that the doctor, the hospital, and the patients benefited from the process. Harwell says that confidential peer review draws a physician's attention to potential problems without needlessly destroying his reputation on the basis of allegations. The discreet internal process of peer review, he argues, produces the desired result—improved medical practice.

He may be right, but one can imagine that his enthusiasm for that process might not be shared by the patients who suffered infections and who remain wholly unaware that their experience fit into what the hospital itself regarded as a problematic pattern, or that their surgeon was the subject of a formal hospital inquiry. The judge, the lawyer, the good doctor, and the California legislature may all call it confidentiality. My guess is, those patients would call it secrecy.

•   •   •

Secrecy and the sealing of cases reach deep into federal, state, county, and municipal governments, particularly where those entities are themselves either actual or potential parties to litigation. Such secrecy excludes not only observers of the courts but local citizens, who may have to pick up the tab for shadowy litigation and settlements, suffer the consequences of government scandal, or simply feel disenfranchised from their own government. On December 20, 2004, the Riverside County Board of Supervisors, after solemnly pledging allegiance to the flag, met in closed session to discuss, among other topics, litigation involving a case known simply as *Under Seal v. Under Seal*—both the plaintiff's and the defendant's names had been removed from the case.

In this the Riverside Board was hardly alone. Two months earlier, on October 18, 2004, Pasadena's city council met for an hour in closed session. Among the items on the agenda, the case of *Under Seal v. Under Seal*, then before the Los Angeles County Superior Court. Five months before that, Oakland's board of supervisors met in closed session to discuss, among other items, the case of *Under Seal v. Under Seal.*

Those closed sessions each invoked for legal authority California Government Code Section 54956.9. There is a certain irony that this chapter of the state's law, known as the Ralph M. Brown Act, should be a ringing endorsement of open government. It begins with these stirring words: "In enacting this chapter, the Legislature finds and declares that the public commissions, boards and councils and the other public agencies in this State exist to aid in the conduct of the people's business. It is the intent of the law that their actions be taken openly and that their deliberations be conducted openly.

"The people of this State do not yield their sovereignty to the agencies which serve them. The people, in delegating authority, do not give their public servants the right to decide what is good for the people to know and what is not good for them to know. The people insist on remaining informed so that they may retain control over the instruments they have created."

But that same law also gives municipalities and counties great leeway for going into closed session when discussing matters of litigation. In each of these cases, the citizenry was clueless as to what was being discussed behind closed doors. About the only thing they might surmise was that their elected representatives were discussing matters that somehow must relate to the business of governance. There was no reason to suspect that anything sinister is going on in such cases, but if there were, citizens would have no way of finding out.

Across the country it is little different.

Lawrence, Massachusetts (population 70,000), is an aging mill town on the Merrimack River, 25 miles north of Boston. Here, too, secrecy has taken hold. One need look no further than the handling of a rape allegation in the school system. An unnamed 14-year-old student came forward in 2002 and told school officials she had been sexually assaulted. Her assailant, she said, was no stranger. He was Edwin Colon, a school security guard.

Unbeknownst to the city council, in December 2002, the city attorney had entered into negotiations with the student to settle a potential lawsuit and had agreed to pay $250,000 to make the case go away. But it was the taxpayers who would be paying for the settlement; as Bill Ketter, editor of the *Lawrence Eagle-Tribune*, wrote in an editorial, "City officials hid the settlement from residents as long as they could. The first hint came when the City Council was asked to transfer $250,000 from the general budget to pay for the lawsuit. A council subcommittee reviewed the case documents in secret and spoke of it in a public meeting only in whispers." The settlement money was, according to the paper, "hidden in a proposal to set the tax rate." It was even reportedly assigned a bogus agenda number.

Several council members later bristled to learn that the city—severely strapped for cash—had agreed to pay so sizable a sum of money to a 14-year-old even before the criminal case against the security guard went to trial.

But even more unsettling were allegations that emerged when the rape case did finally go to trial five months later—and these were not against the security guard, Edwin Colon, but rather his youthful accuser.

At trial, another security guard, Robert Kenyon, testified that the girl had been suspended for biting a teacher and that she had vowed to retaliate against Colon for his role in getting her suspended. Kenyon said the eighth-grader even said she was going to tell her mother that Colon had raped her.

The jury acquitted Colon, but the girl retained her now not-so-secret payment of $250,000. Meanwhile, some Lawrence City Council members couldn't help but wonder aloud how many other secret settlements the city had paid out. Those who negotiated the settlement on behalf of the city still aren't talking.

•   •   •

The Lawrence case pales beside the Byzantine secrecy that enveloped a New Jersey courtroom in August 2003. Even before then, the case had become so entangled in secrecy that it was nearly impenetrable, not only for the public but also for some of the litigants. New Jersey's Essex County Superior Court Judge Theodore Winard had decided that the complex case of *Lederman v. Prudential* was none of the public's business, that there was no overriding public interest involved in the case that would warrant setting aside confidentiality agreements now being challenged.

Lawrence Lederman, his fellow plaintiffs, and his attorney disagreed. Lederman, a former sales manager for the insurance behemoth Prudential Insurance Company alleged that he and some 358 other current or former employees had been defrauded by the insurer. There were allegations that Prudential had retaliated against him and others for attempting to blow the whistle on Prudential's alleged practice of avoiding business in minority neighborhoods, so-called red-lining. They accused Prudential of avoiding writing auto insurance policies in the inner city and, by extension, for minorities.

There were also allegations of a secret agreement between Prudential and the law firm that Lederman and others had retained to represent them against Prudential in an effort to seek a settlement. Leeds, Morelli & Brown, according to the suit, had accepted a secret $5 million payment from Prudential even as it represented Lederman and the other clients. The whole affair had been sealed from public view at the request of

Prudential and its attorneys, reflecting the terms of confidentiality under which claims had been settled. Prudential steadfastly denied any discriminatory practice, saying it was merely engaged in consolidating its business, and Leeds, Morelli & Brown said they did nothing unethical. (Subsequently, the Grievance Committee of the State Supreme Court of New York, where the law firm was located, found "there was no breach of the Code of Professional Responsibility" on the part of Leeds, Morelli & Brown.)

Now the press entered this cauldron of secrecy, eager to have the matter unsealed. There were, after all, powerful public policy arguments to be made and potentially discriminatory business practices by one of the nation's most visible and influential insurance companies to be exposed. The case, the press said, ought not to be sealed from public view.

But such arguments did not sway Judge Winard. Not content to have the case sealed, he went one step further in what some court watchers said was a bizarre turn even by today's standards of obsessive secrecy. He denied three news organizations—ABC, Bloomberg News, and the *Bergen Record*—access to court records and documents in the civil case and then went on to seal his own opinion denying them access.

Not only were the public and press forbidden from peering into the case, they were even forbidden from catching a glimpse into the judge's reasoning. This he followed with a gag order forbidding the attorneys representing the news organizations from sharing his opinion even with their own clients. All they were permitted to tell their respective news organizations was enough to decide whether they wished to appeal the ruling.

For that, the judge did not have long to wait. An appeal was filed. An attorney representing ABC was asked by a local reporter about the appeal. He said he was forbidden even from discussing his own pleadings.

Some of the former Prudential employees said they had lost all faith in the judicial system and had come to regard the court as a kind of star chamber or captive of big business. In March 2006, their principal attorney, Angela Roper, said she was "shattered" by the experience. "If something doesn't happen to cause this charade to be exposed I don't think I could continue to use 'esquire' after my name," she said. "I will burn my law license out on the street and call it a day. That's how disgusted I am."

Roper was barred by a gag order from fully explaining herself, but she could perhaps be forgiven for her intemperate remarks. Something else she was barred from disclosing was that she had recently been arraigned on criminal charges for violating the gag order. That criminal proceeding was itself secret.

It was not until May 2006 that a three-judge panel of the New Jersey Appellate Court finally weighed in and unanimously ruled that the trial court had no right to seal the case. It said that concerns over whether disclosures in the case might embarrass Prudential or the law firm of Leeds, Morelli & Brown were no justification for sealing the case, especially given the serious public interest issues implicit in it.

"The presumption of openness to court proceedings requires more than a passing nod," Appellate Judge Michael Winkelstein wrote. "Open access is the lens through which the public views our government institutions. It is essential to foster public confidence in the judiciary." But for some involved in the case, long years of suffocating secrecy had already irreparably shaken their confidence in the judiciary. Writ large, the Lederman case raises disturbing questions about the integrity of the judicial system and its vulnerability to capricious and heavy-handed secrecy. Absent the high-profile intervention of the media in that case, it is not at all clear that the secrecy that descended upon the entire case—one arguably suffused with issues of grave societal significance—would ever have been lifted.

•   •   •

If secrecy is often a hallmark of civil litigation, it is also a frequent feature of criminal cases, in many instances determining which cases move forward for prosecution and which are simply allowed to disappear behind a closed door.

It was 6:10 P.M., November 17, 2005, and 22-year-old Krista Raymond was driving south on Route 28 in Andover, Massachusetts (population 31,000), on her way to a baby shower—her own. She was nine months pregnant with Elle Marie and just three days from a scheduled C-section. But that was as far as she would get. At that moment, a 39-year-old woman, apparently oblivious to Raymond's approaching car, pulled her SUV out into traffic and struck Raymond's vehicle head-on. Krista would later die at a Boston hospital. A desperate attempt to rescue her fetus would fail.

In an instant, two lives were snuffed out and Krista Raymond went from being the subject of a baby shower to being the object of a case file for the Andover Police Department to investigate. That task fell to Officer Bob Cronin, a 25-year veteran of the force who has investigated dozens of fatal accidents and whose job it is to reconstruct the causes and set in motion the engines of the criminal justice system.

For Cronin, this case was as easy to reconstruct as it was painful to think about. The night had been clear, the road dry, and visibility excellent. The line of vision by day was some 1,320 feet. At 6:10 P.M., says Cronin, it was dark, headlights were on, and Krista Raymond's car would have been visible well beyond a quarter mile. Cronin took no pleasure in advancing the case. The woman who had pulled out in front of Raymond had just picked up her three children from a day-care center, and whatever the cause of her distraction, there was no suggestion of any involvement of drugs, alcohol, or excessive speed. Still, it seemed clear to Cronin that the law had been broken. Compassion could show itself in the sentencing phase if it got that far, but for now, he believed, justice required that the woman be held accountable. He cited her for failing to use care when entering a state highway and for two counts of vehicular homicide—one for the death of Krista, one for Elle.

From there, the case went to Assistant Clerk-Magistrate Bruce Brown. Officer Cronin imagined that despite the tragic nature of the case, it would not be difficult to meet the minimum evidentiary threshold to move forward with prosecution. All that was needed was a bare preponderance of the evidence, or, as Cronin is fond of saying, a "fifty-one percent" likelihood that the accused had committed a crime. For Cronin, the case was self-evident. Later, there would be time to temper justice with mercy.

Even he did not favor sending the woman to jail, but there were other less draconian alternatives, including probation and suspension of her license. But first things first. The magistrate would have to green-light the case and then it would go to the judge for charges. The January 19, 2006, hearing was held in the Lawrence District Courthouse in a small office-sized room. The press, despite protestations, was barred. The hearing was closed. In attendance were the accused, her two attorneys, Officer Cronin, and Assistant Clerk-Magistrate Bruce Brown. There was no transcript kept, no reasoned opinion issued. And when it was over, the only thing that emerged from the hearing room was the decision it-self. It was a decision that set Officer Cronin and others in the commu-nity back on their heels. Magistrate Brown had decided that there was insufficient evidence to warrant prosecution.

William B. Ketter, editor of the *Lawrence Eagle-Tribune*, later wrote: "Nothing is more intrinsic to freedom than a criminal justice system con-ducted openly. . . . The scary thing is no record is kept of the proceeding and if the clerk-magistrate turns down the complaint, the case becomes a dead letter. No explanation is required or given. No transcript is kept. . . . We protested the closed hearing to no avail. Now we will never know what details or circumstances were described at the hearing. Nor will we know why the clerk refused to issue the complaint. The hearing was strictly hush-hush. . . . It seems strange this could happen in an age when court trials are often seen on television."

Assistant Clerk-Magistrate Brown, like many of his peers in the mag-istrate's office, is not a lawyer. All that is required of his job is an under-graduate degree. None of this is unusual in the state of Massachusetts (or, for that matter, elsewhere in the nation). Magistrate hearings are rou-tinely closed; now, so, too, is the case against the other driver.

She may have been—almost certainly was—racked with remorse, but from a legal point of view, she was now free to drive home and put the accident behind her.

As for Assistant Clerk-Magistrate Brown, whatever his reasons for not issuing a complaint, he's not willing to share them with the public. "I don't know anything about secrecy or secrecy in the courts," Brown told me in a phone interview. "The media continues to refer to this as a secret thing as if something is going on that is illegal. It's merely a prob-able cause determination—the public doesn't have any right to judge anyone until it's determined that a crime has been committed. There is nothing going on in there except a probable cause determination. People make accusations and judgments that are unfair. Until we get it to the point where it's determined that a crime has been committed, the public has no right to know.

"Go into the law books," said Brown, "and you'll find what the sys-tem is. It's not my system. I'm going to end the conversation here now." And with that, the line went dead.

Brown is right. Magistrates throughout the Commonwealth of

Massachusetts do not let the press into hearings, are not obligated to keep notes or transcripts, and do not issue reasons for their decisions. But as for the family of Krista Raymond, I'm not so sure they are not entitled to know why no one is to be held answerable, be it the driver or, for that matter, the magistrate.

8

Case Study: The Chambers Effect

As a young girl, Teresa Chambers fondly remembers moving to Washington, D.C., and, each Fourth of July, being taken to the Mall by her father, being dazzled by the fireworks over the capital, and being stirred by the strains of patriotic music from military bands. So it had special meaning for her all those years later when in 2002 she was named chief of the U.S. park police, the entity charged with protecting our national monuments. She was the first woman to hold that office in its 213-year history.

Her résumé was perfect for the job: she was a 27-year police veteran, she had been the police chief in Durham, North Carolina, had earned a bachelor's degree in criminology from the University of Maryland and a master's in applied behavioral science from Johns Hopkins University. She was a longtime teacher of leadership courses, an unabashed patriot, and a card-carrying Republican as well.

In November 2003, when her press secretary received a request from *Washington Post* reporter David A. Fahrenthold for an interview, she saw no reason not to speak with him. "I knew my obligation was to represent the larger agency, but I also knew my obligation was to be candid, to tell the truth," she recalls. The *Post* reporter had already interviewed others in the Park Service and was focusing on the impact of resource and budgetary shortages. Not one to shrink from a tough question, Chief Chambers acknowledged what was known to many within the ranks of the 620-member Park Police, namely, that 9/11 had put severe strains on the service, and that guarding the national monuments and protecting them from potential terrorists meant drawing resources from other no less critical responsibilities, such as watching the parks and parkways. Chambers suggested that her department was struggling to fulfill both its traditional responsibilities and those that devolved upon it post-9/11.

"The choice at that time was to lie, which wasn't a choice, or to verify and put it in a proper perspective," she says.

The resultant story ran about a week later, on December 2, 2003, on the front of the *Post*'s metro section. It was hardly a bombshell. But that evening, when Chambers returned to her office, there was a message from her boss, Donald Murphy, deputy director of the National Park Service, saying that she was to give no other interviews and suggesting they needed to talk.

Until that moment, it had never occurred to her that she might have done anything wrong. In fact, she imagined her superiors would be delighted and looked forward to hearing from them. "Maybe I was naive," she says. She knew from Murphy's tone of voice that he was perturbed. " 'You know, you just can't talk about the president's budget,' " she was chastised. " 'The president's budget?' " she repeated to herself. It was a term she said she had not even heard before.

Three days later she was instructed to go home and await further word. She was under a gag order, not allowed to speak with anyone from the press. And she was to be isolated. "No one was to communicate with me," she recalls. "It was like I had instant leprosy."

Still, she held on to hope.

"I foolishly believed that once the secretary [of the interior] heard of this or, my God, if the White House hears about this, everybody would be in trouble," Chambers says. It was only a matter of time before this foolishness would be corrected and those who were silencing her would themselves be subject to discipline. But over time it began to dawn on her that the efforts to silence her had support from very high quarters. Seventeen days after the *Post* story appeared, she was told that she was to be fired.

Her alleged transgressions? Lobbying Congress and disclosing secret budget details. After that, her detractors went looking for anything they could find against her.

"I was really in a bubble, a pie-eyed optimist," she says.

"It was the biggest wake-up call that's ever occurred in my life," she says. "Up until that point I'd have to say I was an American citizen who trusted implicitly what my government said and what they suggested we do and what they do for us. I believed that anything they did was in the best interests of all of us."

Her experience at the Park Service shattered all that. " 'Cynical' is probably a good descriptor and perhaps even stronger than that, I am distrustful," she now says. "When I stop to think that the things that were said innocently—if that is somehow privileged information in the eyes of our country's leaders, then it frightens me as an American to think what else we are not being told. When I hear newscasts now and I hear the government said such and such I question its accuracy now, not because of the reporter but because of the official source that gave them the information."

It also changed the way she saw whistle-blowers, something she never until then imagined herself to be. "Most of us don't wake up with a chip on our shoulder," she says. "Most just go to work feeling red, white, and blue all the way through and that it is our job, to do what is right and to speak the truth, and, in so doing, we are doing what our bosses want. If telling the truth is not acceptable, what does that tell us about accepted behavior?"

Besides, it wasn't as if Chambers had not raised the issue of resources internally. In a November 28, 2003, memo she wrote: "We are at a staffing and resource crisis in the United States Park Police—a crisis that, if allowed to continue, will almost surely result in the loss of life or the destruction of one of our nation's most valued symbols of freedom and democracy."

At 49, "Chief" Chambers, as many still call her, is challenging her firing before the U.S. Merit Systems Protection Board, even as she teaches part-time and responds to a wave of e-mails expressing support for her. But she is still somewhat shell-shocked by her experience, trying to make sense of it. In September 2006, in a 2–1 decision, the MSPB ruled against Chambers and upheld her dismissal. Chambers is now taking her fight to federal court.

"I believed that this was the president who wanted me to do everything I could to make sure that the Statue of Liberty would be there for the next generation, and the icons in Washington, D.C." She remembered, when she took the job, being told, "We don't want those icons to fall on our watch."

"The one thing that I didn't want to have happen," she says, "is to have pretended that everything was fine and that we had all the resources that we needed and then suddenly to have my bosses, the secretary of the interior and the National Park Service director and others, standing among the ruins of one of America's icons and [being] told to explain why they didn't speak up."

If silencing those within the Park Service was the message Chambers's firing was intended to send, that message has been received. Today within the ranks of the Park Service there is considerable trepidation about anyone speaking with reporters. "No one," Chambers says, "will speak out and say, 'It's not as safe' or 'It's in disarray.'" Among some Park Service retirees, this chill even has a name. They call it "the Chambers effect."

Sounding the Tocsin

For nothing is secret, that shall not be made manifest; neither any thing hid, that shall not be known and come
abroad.

—Luke 8:17

The same excessive secrecy that grips government now holds corporations in its sway. Years of systemic deregulation, privatization of once-
public services and functions, and the perception that government is as
much the partner of business as its monitor have emboldened many corporations to limit what the public knows of its internal affairs, business
performance, and even product safety. Emblematic of the new era of
laissez-faire and government-business cooperation (some might say
"collusion") was the revelation in November 2005 that the Department
of Labor's Wage and Hour Division had agreed to give the retail giant
Wal-Mart a full 15 days' notice before department investigators conducted site visits looking for child-labor-law violations. The government
even permitted Wal-Mart lawyers to help draft a settlement involving
some 85 child labor violations in three states.

As companies face the threat of new technologies that can instantly
transmit adverse business information to a universal audience, they
have learned to harness those same technologies to furtively gather intelligence on others as well as to help secure their own secrets. Ferreting

out those who have spoken to reporters or communicated clandestinely with the outside world is now a thriving business for private investigators. The elaborate ends to which the corporate giant Hewlett-Packard went to find a leak in the boardroom, including hiring investigators to perform so-called pretexting, or impersonation, to gather personal phone records or financial information, profoundly damaged the company and gave the nation a rare glimpse into the highly secretive and lucrative business of spying that takes place in some major corporations. Other industries implicated in pretexting and covert information gathering include major banks, insurance companies, and car rental firms.

Today the corporate culture of secrecy manifests itself in myriad ways. Day after day, headlines speak to corporate information withheld, denied, or delayed, sometimes with grave public consequences. The impact of corporate secrecy on investors and the marketplace was made painfully clear by the sagas of WorldCom, Enron, Adelphia, Tyco, and a host of other corporate scandals in which corporate bloat, executive extravagances, hidden liabilities, or chicanery were concealed from the public. A recent business-page headline asks an all-too-familiar question: "Mystery at Refco: How Could Such a Huge Debt Stay Hidden?" The October 24, 2005, *New York Times* article referred to some $430 million in debt that had been concealed. Other secrets put consumers at personal risk. Two major data brokers, ChoicePoint Inc and LexisNexis, failed to tell consumers about security breaches that made them vulnerable to identity theft.

And then there are the cases questioning the adequacy of information relating directly to the health and lives of consumers. "FDA Official Alleges Pressure to Suppress Vioxx Findings." In June 2005, Guidant Corporation recalled some 29,000 heart devices, but for the three preceding years the company had neglected to tell doctors that one of those device models was prone to electrical failure.

In both government and industry, individuals who place conscience before career and who are willing to risk all to bring vital information to public light continue to fight the good fight. In some instances they go to the press. Some go to congressional investigators or inspectors general. Still others attempt to sound the tocsin from within their agencies or corporations, taking their concerns to superiors or auditors. All of them risk retribution. In theory, these whistle-blowers are protected by laws that recognize society's profound dependence upon those who make the truth known. But increasingly, they too find themselves victims of secrecy. The information they bring forward, no matter how urgent, is often suppressed, buried, or waylaid, with tragic consequences. Time and again, their courage is rewarded with termination, intimidation, and litigation. Instead of inspiring others to come forward, they are made examples of, their private ordeals turned into cautionary tales that only serve to reinforce the regimes of silence they sought to challenge.

In 2002, *Time* magazine took the unusual step of selecting for its celebrated Person of the Year cover not one but three people: Colleen Rowley, Cynthia Cooper, and Sherron Watkins. What all three women had in common was that they were whistle-blowers. Rowley had tried to sound the alarm within the FBI regarding a French Arab who was taking flight-training lessons. This was before the deadly attacks of 9/11. Cynthia Cooper had tried to alert WorldCom executives of the company's precarious financial state. Sherron Watkins had made desperate attempts within Enron to sound the tocsin. What they also had in common was that, like the ancient seer Cassandra, they were largely ignored and the perils that they foresaw came to pass, despite their best efforts to draw attention to potentially catastrophic problems.

It is a testament to the spread of secrecy and information suppression that these three women should be selected for such a high-profile cover. Only in a society in which information is severely restricted, in which individuals risk their standing and status in an attempt to inform the public, would such figures rise to prominence, even to the point of becoming folk heroes. Noble as these figures may be, their common defeat is a reminder that most of the risks faced as citizens, as investors, as patients, are due not to the truly unknowable but rather to the failure of the few to share vital information already in their possession. It is the difference between a mystery, that which is not known, and a secret, that which is known but withheld.

A year later, in 2003, *Time*'s Man of the Year was "the American soldier," a timely recognition of the military's sacrifice, but also a choice emblematic of an America steeped in the concerns for security and grown comfortable with the soldierly virtues of duty, loyalty, and obedience—all of which tend to reinforce rather than challenge regimes of secrecy. The two *Time* covers evoke American values that are often in conflict: a citizen's right to information and accountability versus respect and deference shown to authority.

At no time is the need for whistle-blowers greater than when government is consumed by secrecy or when it views itself as a partner of business and so lets down its regulatory guard. Where secrecy is pervasive, where information control is paramount, the whistle-blower is often the only conduit by which a vulnerable public may learn of matters of grave importance to its health, safety, and security. But it is in precisely such times that whistle-blowers are most targeted for suppression and retribution.

In theory, government and industry alike provide an abundance of protections for the whistle-blower designed to insulate him or her from a vindictive employer or superior. These protections, embodied in numerous federal and state laws, appear in statutes related to the environment, worker safety, labor relations, and a host of other public interest sectors, all of them a testament to the critical role whistle-blowers play in keeping a democracy informed and safe. But these laws are full of loopholes and in practice may be interpreted narrowly with presumptions favoring the authority of government or employer, leaving the whistle-blower largely unprotected.

In government, the favored tools of intimidation have become the threat of the polygraph, of prosecution, and of ostracism and exile from power. In industry, the same is accomplished with the threat of demotion, termination, protracted and costly litigation, or the simple stroke of a pen on a confidentiality agreement. Secrecy is like a pair of hands around the throat of democracy, cutting off the flow of oxygen to the brain. When all other internal safeguards fail, it is the whistle-blowers who may yet save the day. Silencing them is the last thing a democracy or a corporation may remember before passing out.

Aaron Westrick's story is typical. It begins not with him but with a rookie cop named Tony Zepetella.

On June 13, 2003, Zepetella pulled a car over in the parking lot of the Navy Federal Credit Union in Oceanside, California. Zepetella was 27 and just two months out of training. A model of physical fitness, he had good reason to take care of himself—his wife, Jamie, and a six-month-old son, Jakob. When the department issued him a bulletproof vest, he chose to spend an additional $313 of his own money for an upgrade to the vaunted Ultima model, made by a Michigan company aptly named Second Chance. The vest gave him an added sense of protection, not that his beat was considered that dangerous. No one had been killed in the line of duty in 87 years.

But Zepetella's routine traffic stop instantly turned nightmarish as the driver, a gang member, fired a hail of bullets at him. Two of the 9mm rounds penetrated his vest. One severed his carotid artery. He bled to death after being pistol-whipped.

Ten days later, on the other side of the country, Police Officer Ed Limbacher of Forest Hills, Pennsylvania, was shot with a .40-caliber bullet that penetrated his vest and lodged against his spine, leaving him permanently disabled. That vest, too, was made by Second Chance.

What neither Zepetella nor Limbacher—nor any of the other more than 100,000 police officers nationwide who trusted their lives to the Second Chance vests—could have known was that deeply troubling questions about the reliability of those vests had surfaced more than a year before the officers ever put them on. Those questions were raised by the company's own head of research, Aaron Westrick. He had become alarmed by reports from Toyobo, the Japanese manufacturer of the synthetic fabric Zylon used in the vests, that Zylon degraded when exposed to light, heat, and moisture.

Westrick understood better than most what that might mean. In 1982, while working as a deputy sheriff, Westrick was shot in the chest while chasing a suspect. The bullet went through his hand and struck him just below the badge, headed squarely for his heart. But a Second Chance vest (not made of Zylon) stopped the bullet and saved his life. It was why he had joined the company. Now it was also why he felt he could not be silent in the face of such disturbing data. He felt compelled to sound a warning.

In December 2001, 18 months before Zepetella and Limbacher were shot, Westrick wrote a memo to his bosses to alert them to potentially fundamental defects in the fabric and urging them to forgo a salary bonus to help pay for a recall or whatever other measure might be needed to sound the alarm.

Westrick's memo noted: "Second Chance should make the right, difficult decisions regarding this issue. Lives and credibility are at stake. . . .

This issue should not be hidden for obvious safety issues and because of future litigation." His warning went unheeded and the company continued to promote and sell its Zylon-based vests.

Silence prevailed and sales flourished. The full extent of those put at risk is chilling. After Westrick's internal memo was written, the U.S. Secret Service spent some $53,000 on Second Chance body armor. The day before President-elect George W. Bush's 2001 inaugural, the departure of a Northwest flight out of Traverse City, Michigan, was delayed so that Second Chance vests could be delivered to Washington and worn by the president and First Lady Laura Bush at the Inaugural. Others who would wear the vests included elite members of the military who guard generals, and special units in Iraq and Afghanistan.

By July 2002, Second Chance's president, Richard Davis, found it impossible to simply ignore the problem. On July 29 of that year, he wrote his executive board a memo referring to "unsuspecting law enforcement officers without telling them about these problems." Davis asks, perhaps rhetorically, whether the board wants to continue "operating as though nothing is wrong until one of our customers is killed or wounded" or someone else "exposes the Zylon problem."

But Davis would not step down as president until a week after Zepetella was killed, and it would be another month before Second Chance stopped selling its vests. On September 8, 2003, the company first alerted customers, suggesting that the problems encountered were unexpected.

Not long after, Second Chance found itself in a world of trouble. Attorney generals around the nation queued up to sue them, as did the U.S. Department of Justice, which alleged that Second Chance and Toyobo had conspired to suppress evidence that Zylon degraded when exposed to the elements. Class-action suits followed.

In October 2004, whistle-blower Aaron Westrick was fired and the company slipped into bankruptcy. Today, Westrick sees the human and financial devastation wrought by secrecy and deception. He says he was literally "just waiting for the next body to come in."

"When I think back, it just makes me sick," says Westrick. These days, he teaches criminology, works as a part-time deputy sheriff, and has good reason to keep an eye not only on the streets but on the companies that produce the vests upon which the lives of law enforcement officers depend. His 22-year-old son is about to enter the police academy.

Officer Zepetella's widow, Jamie, spent the three years following her husband's brutal murder seeking justice. Her husband's assailant, Adrian Camacho, is now on San Quentin State Prison's death row. On September 7, 2006, a Vista Superior Court jury in California returned a $2.5 million verdict against Second Chance and Toyobo, the firm that manufactured the vest material.

• • •

There was a certain irony that the claims about the Zylon vest, like the vest itself, ultimately could not withstand prolonged exposure to light. Other secrets lay fathoms deep, well beneath the surface, where light can scarcely penetrate.

On April 18, 2002, 41-year-old Robert Raimo, a seasoned diver with more than 2,000 dives to his credit, entered the warm waters off the Caribbean island of Bonaire. A man of superior fitness, he cherished nothing so much as time in the water. Yet time to a diver can be both a friend and a foe. Too much time below and not enough time taken to surface can cause dreaded decompression sickness, commonly known as the bends. An often-complex computation of blood gases is required of anyone who ventures into the depths, and a miscalculation can prove disastrous, even fatal.

Raimo knew this better than most. He had managed retail stores that sold diving gear and distributed, among other products, a tiny wrist-worn computer that did the unwieldy math for divers, determining, once certain parameters were set, how long and how deep they could go. It was said to be a revolutionary device without peer. The maker of that computer was Uwatec, a Swiss company that by 1996 dominated this niche market. The name of the model Raimo wore on his wrist that day invoked a mix of computer science and magic—the 1995 Aladin Air X Nitrox.

Later, in some ways, Raimo would say that he never fully surfaced from that day's dive. Instead he showed symptoms of serious decompression sickness, including dizziness and loss of memory. Here was a man who had made vastly more demanding dives. This dive he had contemptuously dismissed as a "baby dive" for its lack of challenge. He couldn't figure out what had happened to him. But what he faced was no mystery of the deep. Instead, he would slowly and painfully learn of a string of similar seemingly inexplicable cases of decompression sickness allegedly suffered by veteran divers wearing the same model Uwatec computer. And he would learn that the manufacturer had known more than it was telling divers.

The story unwinds like a skein of yarn, going back a full six years before Raimo fell prey to the bends. The model Raimo wore sold for about $1,000 and was marketed by Uwatec between July 1995 and March 1996. In 1997 the company was purchased by Johnson Worldwide Associates (later, Johnson Outdoors). The first whiff of trouble with the device is believed to have surfaced in January 1996 when a software engineer allegedly wrote an internal memo referring to a "question about the faulty Aladin Nitrox." The memo concluded, "Please keep the information confidential."

Uwatec employees Frank H. Marshall and Patricia Dougherty, the office manager and bookkeeper, were made well aware of a potential problem with the device, in particular with a logarithm that could, under certain circumstances, miscalculate the amount of nitrogen in the body, especially in the context of repeat dives. They were troubled by the notion that something could be wrong with a device to which people entrusted their health. Dougherty says she and Marshall asked Uwatec to issue a product recall, but were told not to pursue it.

Instead, says Dougherty, she and others within the company decided to take matters into their own hands and do what they could to get the product off the market—a kind of secret recall. Each time a customer sent one of the units in for a fresh battery, says Dougherty, they would keep the device and send out a newer model, one they believed to be free of defects. Sometimes, she said, they would pretend that in changing the battery they had inadvertently damaged the screen, requiring the entire unit to be replaced. But addressing the matter one unit at a time still left others at risk.

On April 22, 1996, Marshall and another Uwatec employee, Sean Griffin, wrote Uwatec president Heinz Ruchti, "As mentioned in my letter of April 9, 1996, we need to know when the surface interval calculation changes were made to the software of the Air X Nitrox computers. We still recommend that it would be a good idea to replace these first generation units immediately as we feel an obligation to our customers' safety."

Later that same month, Dougherty and Marshall took the extraordinary step of drafting a recall notice for the product. "In America," says Dougherty, "we are used to being honest about things. We just felt full disclosure was necessary. The degree of danger may have been slim but nonetheless, it should have been disclosed." The draft recall notice read: "Uwatec USA, Inc. announces the mandatory recall of all Aladin Air X Nitrox dive computers made on or before December 1995. All owners of these units are hereby advised to return these units immediately to their dive retailer or directly to Uwatec USA, Inc. . . . The unit will be replaced at no charge and returned within one week. Thank you for your kind cooperation."

They had the notice copied at a Kinko's, but the notice was not distributed. Soon after, they were fired. Dougherty and Marshall were convinced that they had been let go because they wanted to recall the device and issue a public warning. Instead, the bill for the unsent notices was presented to Uwatec USA's new CEO, Bret Gilliam, a legendary diver. Gilliam was persuaded that the recall notices were nothing more than an attempt to embarrass the company by employees facing their own imminent dismissal. (Marshall and Dougherty would go on to cast themselves as whistle-blowers and win a million-dollar verdict against the company for wrongful termination.)

Meanwhile, divers continued to rely upon the Uwatec computer. In November 1997, Maurice Coutts, an experienced diver and an eminent engineer at Princeton Materials Institute, died after diving in Bonaire. On his wrist he wore the Uwatec computer. At the time the device was not implicated, though his son, Lewis Coutts, now wonders whether it could have been at least partially responsible for his father's death.

On June 1, 1998, the body of 45-year-old Dr. Wesley C. Gradin, an Oregon physician, was found in 67 feet of water at the edge of a kelp bed near Friday Harbor, Washington. An autopsy ruled out preexisting medical conditions. An experienced underwater photographer and diver, he too wore the Uwatec computer. It was speculated that Gradin's accident was related to his rebreather apparatus. The conclusion was "diver error"—he had not properly maintained the rebreather. At the time, the Uwatec computer's alleged defect was not publicly known, and once again, it was not implicated in the fatality.

But other divers say their reliance on the device was responsible for their suffering the bends. In late 1998, former Uwatec employee Frank Marshall alerted the Consumer Product Safety Commission, which conducted an examination of the computer but did not order a recall.

On March 19, 1999, Mitch Skaggs and Rezvan Iazdi were diving off the wreck of the *Deep Freeze* near Miami. The next day, the two were flying over the United States when, they say, the bends struck. They became nauseated. At a layover in North Carolina they were rushed to Durham, where they were placed inside recompression chambers. Both men had been relying on their Uwatec computer—in fact, Skaggs was a former Uwatec employee.

Bret Gilliam had left the company in 1998. Still, no warning had been issued regarding the Uwatec device. Sometime after leaving the company, Gilliam apparently remained concerned about the safety of the computer. By chance, he met a diver who was preparing to board a boat for a dive and noticed that he was wearing the 1995 Uwatec device. In an effort to protect the diver from the potentially defective unit, Gilliam repeatedly offered to purchase the device or trade it for his own newer model, but the diver resisted.

Gilliam apparently felt unable to come right out and voice his concerns. Ultimately, he boarded the boat himself and pretended to stumble and knock over a tank that crushed the face of the man's device, rendering it useless. He then gave the diver his own computer and some $500 with an apology. He was walking a fine line, attempting to protect a stranger without publicly acknowledging the existence of a defect.

But divers elsewhere continued to use the device, unaware of the potential risk. In September 2000, David Sipperly was hit with the bends while diving off Rhode Island. He too used the Uwatec device.

On October 12, 2001, Stewart Esposito suffered the bends while diving off the Cayman Islands. The Uwatec was on his wrist.

On January 27, 2003—six years after the recall notices were copied at a South Carolina Kinko's—Robert Raimo's attorney, David G. Concannon, says he urged attorneys for Johnson Outdoors to seek an immediate recall. On February 5, Raimo sued the company, adding his name to the list of injured and disabled divers. One of the attorneys for Johnson Outdoors' insurance company threatened to sue Concannon for slander and mocked his spelling, grammar, and lack of understanding of the litigation process.

But that same day, February 5, 2003, the Consumer Product Safety

Commission issued an immediate recall of the device. The problem? Johnson Outdoors called it a "software glitch," the very problem that had led Marshall and Dougherty six years earlier to seek a recall. In a press release, the company pointed out that it was a voluntary recall and a company spokeswoman, Cynthia Georgeson, said the timing, on the very eve of the filing of the Raimo case, was "a pure coincidence." The company had indeed notified the CPSC months earlier of suspected problems with the device.

Johnson Outdoors' recall announcement stated that "software in the dive computers may inaccurately calculate desaturation times, resulting in possible decompression sickness under aggressive dive conditions. . . . Consumers should stop using these dive computers immediately and contact Uwatec for a free replacement." The recall eerily echoed the word of the notice printed by the two former Uwatec employees years earlier.

Cynthia Georgeson says the company acted promptly to recall the product as soon as solid evidence surfaced of its defect and that any suggestion that the firm attempted to conceal a dangerous flaw in the device is utterly unfounded.

Today, Raimo remains a shadow of his former self. The after-effects of his decompression sickness have ended his diving, affected his memory, altered his personality, and put a burden on his marriage. A friend says damage to his central nervous system is so severe that Raimo can barely wield a hammer.

In time, the company settled with divers Skaggs, Iazdi, Sipperly, Esposito, and Raimo. Former employees Marshall and Dougherty believe the injuries could have been averted if only their recall notice had been sent out. Several of those who say they were hurt by the device, as well as some former Uwatec and Johnson employees, say confidentiality agreements still limit what can be said about the matter. Even today, while admitting there was a defect in the device, Johnson Outdoors will not acknowledge that anyone was injured by it and will not discuss any details of its settlements with the divers beyond saying that all parties agreed to its confidentiality provisions.

Johnson Outdoors never actually sold the defective devices and says that when it acquired Uwatec in 1997 it was completely unaware of any defect. According to Georgeson, Uwatec signed warranties assuring the acquiring company that its product was defect-free. Even though the two fired employees, Dougherty and Marshall, sued Uwatec, alleging that they were whistle-blowers, Johnson Outdoors says Uwatec told them there were no problems with the computer and that it was simply "disgruntled employees" trying to make trouble for the company.

"People kept the facts from us by both omission and commission and that prevented us from doing what we would have done and what we did when we had all those facts—which was doing the right thing [the recall]," says Georgeson. "We are a victim of secrecy." And there is yet another secret surrounding the matter. Georgeson says she is forbidden from discussing what, if any, settlement Uwatec may have made with Johnson Outdoors over the matter of the former's nondisclosure.

•   •   •

The District of Columbia Water and Sewer Authority is hardly a place that conjures up images of heroism, which is why, perhaps, some of those who run WASA, as it is called, felt emboldened to treat James J. Bobreski as they did. In 1999, Bobreski, who worked for a WASA contractor, became concerned about conditions at the Blue Plains Wastewater Treatment Plant in southwest Washington, D.C., specifically the sensors and alarms designed to alert employees of a leak of potentially deadly chlorine. Bobreski discovered that sensors designed to pick up even trace amounts of leaking chlorine were not functioning. Nor were the alarms. To Bobreski it appeared they had been deliberately disabled. He recognized the potential for disaster. Chlorine gas was used as a weapon by the Germans in World War I. In the worst case, the chemical chlorine used at Blue Plains could leak as a gas that could spread at ground level across many miles, reaching even the U.S. Capitol and bringing with it death to thousands.

Bobreski brought the matter to his superiors, but to no avail. Finally, he contacted the *Washington Post*. The resulting front-page story brought swift attention to the problem. The story's third paragraph got much of the city's attention: "At least 180 tons of chlorine is stored at Blue Plains—some days there is as much as 630 tons—in a liquid form so toxic that even if only a portion of it were accidentally released, it could kill plant workers in seconds and create a poisonous plume more than 30 miles long."

Bobreski's reward was that he was fired, allegedly for incompetence. Unemployed for months, Bobreski finally found work as an electrician. Eventually he sued WASA as a whistle-blower. His legal action was based upon whistle-blower provisions in a half dozen different statutes—the Clean Air Act, the Clean Water Act, the Toxic Substances Control Act, the Solid Waste Disposal Act, and the Comprehensive Environmental Response, Compensation and Liability Act of 1980.

Bobreski could be forgiven for concluding that the government was closing ranks against him. When his attorney subpoenaed Mikal Shabazz, the EPA's regional coordinator of the Chemical Accident Prevention Programs, the agency resisted, saying it would not be in the EPA's "best interests" to have him testify, and it successfully challenged the authority of the administrative law judge to compel that testimony. Ultimately, Bobreski would have to be counted among the lucky few, as whistle-blowers go. He won his case, though the judgment was appealed. Vindication was not his until July 2005, five long and litigious years after he first lost his job for doing the right thing. Alice M. Craft, an administrative law judge for the U.S. Department of Labor, in a stinging rebuke to WASA, ruled that Bobreski had indeed been fired for blowing the whistle on the inoperative gas sensors and said that he would be eligible for back pay and benefits as well as compensatory and punitive damages, to be decided later.

Such episodes are often part of a pattern in agencies that are captive to a culture of secrecy and preoccupied with their own image. WASA's disregard for public safety did not end with its treatment of Bobreski. Nor did its efforts to suppress other information vital to the public's wellbeing.

No one understands this better than Seema Bhat, who was WASA's water quality manager. A chemist by training, she became alarmed by tests that in 2002 showed high levels of lead in the drinking water of the capital. She said that she repeatedly brought her concerns to her supervisor's attention but that nothing was done. WASA, she concluded, had a culture of secrecy, that public image and customer relations mattered more than public safety. She and her peers, she said, knew that whatever problems they might observe were not to be made public. But the lead levels were deeply worrisome. Lead is an insidious public health threat that attacks the brain and nervous system and puts at particular peril young children and pregnant women. "They told me, 'You deal with it case by case. You don't have to make a big deal of it.' They told me in those words, 'You take it slowly, don't talk about it much.' "

Finally she decided she could no longer wait for her agency to take action. She sent a memo directly to the EPA and sent a copy to her superior. To her surprise, the EPA did little, and in March 2003 she was summarily fired, in no small part for alerting the EPA of the lead problem. That danger did not become public for nearly a year, notwithstanding that later tests showed lead levels in some D.C. homes were more than 20 times the levels set by the EPA. On February 25, 2004, the District of Columbia Department of Health issued a warning advising pregnant women and children under the age of six living in homes with lead service lines not to drink unfiltered water from the tap. They also were advised to get blood tests and have their lead levels examined.

In June 2004, the EPA signed a consent agreement with WASA in which federal regulators ruled that WASA had violated the Safe Drinking Water Act and illegally withheld test results that could have alerted the public a year earlier. Numerous irregularities in testing were cited as was a pattern of invalidating unfavorable test results.

A month later, an independent inquiry was commissioned by WASA's board of directors, headed by former deputy U.S. attorney general Eric Holder. It revealed that WASA withheld information that showed the drinking water of thousands of District residents was contaminated with lead. The conclusion: WASA had failed to inform its own board, city officials, and residents of the dangers.

The investigation was particularly disturbing for what it had to say about government at large and its penchant for secrecy. Neither the EPA nor the District of Columbia's Department of Health nor the Army Corps of Engineers would permit its employees to be interviewed for the investigation. The denial of access to "key witnesses" and critical documents blocked the investigation's ability to get the full picture, but could not obscure the taint of wider complicity.

Since being fired, Seema Bhat says, she has received thousands of letters of support, but none of these are of much comfort. In 2005, two years after she was fired, her whistle-blower claim was still unresolved, awaiting a decision from an administrative judge with the Department of Labor. She had been unemployed since losing her $73,000-a-year job, and feared she was unemployable. Then 59, she had interviewed with numerous utilities, the EPA, the Department of Homeland Security, and consulting firms—and always with the same result: they would ask her why she left her last job. When she explained that she was fired because she was a whistle-blower, the interviewers would suddenly lose interest. "Whistle-blowers are not welcomed," she says. In a culture of secrecy, she is a pariah.

In November 2005, Bhat got the vindication she had long sought. Stuart A. Levin, an administrative law judge with the Department of Labor, ruled in her favor, granting her $50,000 compensatory damages, $10,000 in exemplary damages, back pay, benefits, interest, and attorneys' fees. Levin also ordered that Bhat be reinstated in her job with WASA. But Bhat had had enough of the agency. She declined the offer.

•   •   •

When someone like Doug Parker raises a question about the use of pesticides in the national forests, it may be a good idea to listen. A veteran of 39 years with the U.S. Forest Service, he holds bachelor's and master's degrees in forest entomology and has been assistant director for forestry and forest health in the Forest Service's Southwest Region and the service's national herbicide specialist.

What he observed in late 2002 and early 2003 as the Forest Service prepared to wage war on bark beetles in the forests of Arizona made him worry. He says he went to his supervisors to argue that before powerful insecticides could be used, the service should conduct the routine and required environmental and risk analysis. The response, says Parker, was to strip him of oversight responsibilities and push ahead with the project.

In each of the years 2003, 2004, and 2005, Parker says, the Forest Service used somewhere around 2,700 pounds of the insecticide carbaryl in Arizona's Apache-Sitgreaves National Forests. Parker protested that the services had failed to comply with the provisions of the National Environmental Policy Act (NEPA) and that in so doing it had put a natural treasure in jeopardy.

His warnings, he said, went unheeded, but he did not take his concerns outside the service. Then, in 2004, he said he learned that the top managers of the Southwest Forest were going to apply herbicide aerially in the Cibola National Forest, New Mexico, Texas, and Oklahoma to control the spread of an invasive species commonly known as salt cedar, also known as tamarisk. Parker said he wrote the regional forester noting that NEPA required that an environmental impact statement be done. He called for an investigation and said he believed that he was seeing a pattern of indifference to policies and regulations governing the use of pesticides and herbicides in the Southwest region.

Parker said that instead of focusing on the pesticide issue, the service turned its attention on him and made him the target of retaliation. He filed a complaint with the U.S. Office of Special Counsel, whose job it is to investigate and protect government whistle-blowers. In May 2005, Parker was suspended for ten days, allegedly for failing to file a monthly progress report and for failing to train and certify those who use pesticides. Parker said he was ordered by a supervisor not to speak of these matters.

But Parker was not about to be silenced. He notified the inspector general of the Department of Agriculture. Then the U.S. Office of Special Counsel turned his case down. In September 2005, Parker was fired, ostensibly for failing to follow his supervisor's instructions, filing tardy and improperly formatted progress reports, and falling behind in monthly training goals. Parker was convinced it was for speaking out. Parker said he then encountered still more secrecy as he sought to secure documents from the Forest Service pertaining to the use of pesticide. Ultimately, he says, he had to sue for those documents. Finally he went to the Merit Systems Protection Board seeking reinstatement in his job. His case remains unresolved.

Parker's encounter with secrecy and a gag order has not changed his mind about speaking out. "I thought it was important enough to do it right and I do care about the protection of the environment and I do care about the Forest Service. It was principle. If anybody needs to do it right, it's the federal government."

He continues to run up against secrecy. Upon learning that the Office of the Inspector General of the Department of Agriculture had conducted an investigation of his allegations, he requested a copy of its findings. On September 14, 2006, he got his answer: Deirdre MacNeil, an attorney with the Department of Agriculture, wrote to say that the department was withholding the report because its release could interfere with law enforcement proceedings and jeopardize the investigation.

Parker still wants his job back. That, and his reputation.

•   •   •

Parker is not the only whistle-blower who, in an effort to protect the nation's natural habitat, has run afoul of bureaucrats who would quash dissent and smother unwanted attention to sensitive problems. For 31 years Bob Jackson has been a seasonal Park Service ranger in the most isolated stretch of land in the lower 48 states. Known as "the Thorofare ranger," Jackson has traveled by horseback, stayed in cabins miles from any road, and at times not emerged from the wilderness for months at a stretch. Poachers knew him as a force to be reckoned with and the Park Service regarded him as a kind of poster child for the wild and romanticized life of the ranger. In Yellowstone he is a legend. Like the lonely westerners of old, he is fiercely independent, not one to spoil for a fight but not one to back down either. He was perfectly willing to stand alone if need be and that is exactly what he would be called upon to do.

Beginning in the 1990s, he saw a problem emerging within and around Yellowstone that posed a threat to both people and the endangered grizzly bears and that eroded confidence in the laws of the U.S. Park Service. It began when Jackson observed that the number of elk hunters working with outfitters on the edge of Yellowstone's wild boundary had begun to multiply. To satisfy the ever-increasing numbers of hunters, guides and outfitters were routinely resorting to the practice of placing salt just outside the park's borders to draw out the elk. It wasn't just an issue of unsportsmanlike conduct. There are laws, he says, against using salt to lure the elk, and for good reason. The hunters would often strip the elk's horns and cape—the pelt from the head and neck—and maybe carry off the most accessible cuts of meat, but then leave the rest of the carcass, not even gutting it.

These carcasses would attract the endangered grizzlies from within the park, who would feast upon the fallen elk. Over time, says Jackson, the grizzlies became habituated to feeding on what the hunters had killed. It led to sometimes deadly conflicts. In one season alone, eight endangered grizzles were killed and there were isolated cases of people being mauled by the bears.

Jackson attempted to draw his superiors' attention to the problem, but they showed little concern or interest, he said. When his comments began to appear in area newspapers, the Park Service clamped down and forbade him from speaking to reporters. Finally, Jackson was informed that his services would no longer be needed for the upcoming season, that after three decades in which he had distinguished himself as a champion of Yellowstone's management and a vigorous enforcer of its antipoaching provisions, he was through. Jackson and many others were convinced that his termination was retaliation for his speaking out and also for offending certain politically well-connected outfitters in the area. There was big money involved—individual hunters were paying up to $5,000 per hunt.

Jackson is not one to quietly melt away, and he had some powerful allies of his own. Conservation groups identified him as a whistle-blower, and Sen. Chuck Grassley, an Iowa Republican, demanded an explanation from the Park Service. "I'm intent on stopping this kind of intimidation so other government workers who are willing to speak up about problems are not deterred," Grassley declared.

Ultimately, in July 2003, after considerable pressure and press scrutiny, Jackson got his job back for another year and he and the Park Service negotiated a settlement agreement. The terms were, of course, secret.

Even today Jackson wonders at the energy and effort that was put into silencing him. "All I was doing was my job," he says. He's not a man easily frightened, but what he saw of the system and of secrecy unnerved him. "All at once," he observed, "you can go from a democracy to something else."

•   •   •

Secrecy has many faces, none more inimical to democracy than that of the censor—the very word conjures up an environment toxic to free expression, research, and science. But it was not some metaphorically hostile climate that troubled Dr. James E. Hansen; it was, literally, the climate of Earth itself. Hansen, one of the world's leading authorities on global warming, is director of the Goddard Institute for Space Studies, part of the National Aeronautics and Space Administration (NASA). When Dr. Hansen writes that the effects of human activity on the planet are putting it in dire jeopardy, it draws national and international attention. It also makes politicians who have sought to discredit global warming uncomfortable.

The Bush administration's position with regard to global warming—acknowledging some link between human behavior and global warming but resisting limits on greenhouse emissions and calling for ever more research—has put it at odds with the majority of scientists both within and outside government. In response, it has attempted to keep science itself a secret, to brand findings as opinion, and disparage calls for action as premature and excessively costly.

In January 2006, a decision was apparently made within NASA to rein Hansen in, to limit his access to the press, and to have him walk a line more consistent with that drawn by the White House. One of those who allegedly took on this task was not a scientist and had no background in science (though he did speak up for the doctrine of intelligent design and apparently favored adding "theory" to each mention of "the Big Bang"). He was a 24-year-old political appointee named George C. Deutsch, who had worked on Bush's reelection campaign and inaugural committee and who now reported to NASA's Office of Public Affairs. Those were his only credentials. He also claimed to have a B.A. in journalism from Texas A&M, but that turned out to be a fabrication. According to Hansen, Deutsch attempted to block his access to the media and to edit his findings to bring them more in line with the Bush administration's take on global warming.

What makes Dr. Hansen a whistle-blower is that Hansen went public with his grievance in January 2006. His story resonated throughout a bureaucracy that has increasingly subordinated science to politics and that has attempted to gag any number of experts whose findings met scientific standards but threatened political objectives. Hansen cited similar political pressures on scientists at the National Oceanic and Atmospheric Administration.

"It seems more like Nazi Germany or the Soviet Union than the United States," Hansen told an audience at the New School in February 2006. His prominence in the field and within NASA gives him a certain immunity to retribution and intimidation that other government scientists do not enjoy.

The censorship that Hansen endured was also faced by Rick Piltz, senior associate with the U.S. Climate Change Science Policy Office. Piltz recalls that the White House Office of Science and Technology Policy deleted or diluted phrases that expressed an active stance on global warming.

"When science tried to come forward in the public arena," says Piltz, "there were a multiplicity of mechanisms. This was when the political gatekeepers would step in. They would edit, they would suppress, they would deny, they would misrepresent, they would censor. It was death by a thousand cuts. There were so many mechanisms by which the administration would impede the flow of honest communication about climate research and its implications in order to conform the science to a predetermined political position—we were not going to have a regulatory policy on greenhouse emissions. The politics was to spin out a sense of scientific uncertainty."

In March 2005, Piltz could not take it any longer. He resigned from the Climate Change Science Policy Office in protest.

Among the more memorable instances in which the White House stymied scientific communication was one involving Philip Cooney. As chief of staff for the White House Council on Environmental Quality, he altered language in key government climate reports to cast doubt on the urgency of global warming. Cooney was not a scientist but a lawyer, one who, before helping to define America's environmental priorities, was an oil industry lobbyist.

One of the changes Cooney made in a major climate report was to cross out a section that examined ice- and snowpack melting with a note that suggested it was "straying from research strategy into speculative findings/musings."

Despite the administration's best efforts, however, global warming has proved to be a hard secret to keep, and labeling the accelerated melting of global ice- and snowpacks "speculative" has become something of a fool's errand. In February 2006, researchers at the University of East Anglia in England reported that the increase in temperatures over the course of the twentieth century was the greatest in the past 1,200 years. That same month scientists reported that Greenland's glaciers were melting at an alarming rate—twice as fast as previously predicted. Reports of polar bears drowning because it was not cold enough to support the ice floes they depend upon lent graphic detail to the arguments.

So too did reports that the United States and Canada were discussing shipping rights through the Northwest Passage, linking the Atlantic and Pacific oceans, as ever-greater global warming meant that the passage would be free of ice and open to shipping for longer and longer periods. From around the globe, other scientific studies reached the same disturbing conclusions regarding the perils of ignoring global warming.

But to be successful, one need not silence every senior scientist in government. One need only manage to cloud the argument with enough doubt to stave off passage of legislation limiting domestic engine emissions, which are opposed by the oil industry. This, government's "gatekeepers" have accomplished.

James Gustave Speth, dean of Yale's School of Forestry and Environmental Sciences, says, "The active suppression of information, the active attack on science and the active disinformation campaign" have all contributed to America's inaction and resistance to addressing the situation. "The world we have known is history," lamented Speth in a February 24, 2006, letter to the *New York Times.* "It is easy to feel like a character in a bad science fiction novel running down the street shouting, 'Don't you see it!' while life goes on, business as usual.

"We are going to have enormously serious consequences even if we get real serious about the problem now because we let the problem creep up on us," says Speth. "It's very scary."

•　　•　　•

Today, whistle-blowers face a regime of secrecy, suppression, and retaliation. Often the issues that stir them to come forward are of paramount importance to the nation and cut across party lines.

Sibel Edmonds was a 32-year-old Turkish American who joined the FBI as a translator in the aftermath of 9/11. In March 2002, less than a year later, she was fired. Edmonds says it was because she tried to bring attention to security risks and shoddy performance within the ranks of translators. The vulnerabilities she described were directly related to the security of the nation. Four months later she sued the federal government and challenged her firing. Her case was dismissed as the government invoked state secrecy. The Justice Department inspector general's report investigating Edmonds's allegations and the handling of her case was classified.

But the substance of her allegations did not go unheard. On July 9, 2004, Sen. Patrick Leahy, a Vermont Democrat, and Sen. Charles Grassley, an Iowa Republican, jointly wrote a letter to Attorney General John Ashcroft, making clear their concerns: "Indeed, in recent months questions have been raised by ourselves, by the 9–11 Commission, and by the media about the competency and abilities of the translation program at the FBI—concerns that should reverberate in the highest levels of the Department of Justice and the FBI. The FBI itself has provided alarming information about problems in the translation program during briefings to congressional staff. Yet two years after the allegations made by Ms. Edmonds triggered two investigations, we are no closer to determining the scope of the problem, the pervasiveness and seriousness of FBI problems in this area, or what the FBI intends to do to rectify personnel shortages, security issues, translation inaccuracies and other problems that have plagued the translator program for years."

In April 2005, Edmonds's appeal went to the U.S. Court of Appeals for the District of Columbia Circuit. The courtroom was closed to all but the attorneys. An emergency motion filed by the *Washington Post*, the *New York Times*, and other leading news organizations to open the courtroom was denied. Behind closed doors, the appeals court flatly rejected Edmonds's court challenge, upholding the lower court's ruling that pursuing the case threatened to compromise national security. Once again, Sibel Edmonds had been silenced and secrecy prevailed.

The Edmonds case is one in a long line of cases in which whistleblowers have attempted to draw public attention to critical issues. Bunnatine Greenhouse was a chief contracting officer with the Army Corps of Engineers. Despite resistance from her superiors, in 2003 she tried to sound the alarm on what she believed were troubling irregularities in contracts worth up to $7 billion awarded to Halliburton, the oil services company formerly run by Vice President Dick Cheney. In 2005 Greenhouse was demoted. The Army said it was for poor performance. Greenhouse said it was retaliation.

A 20-year veteran in procurement matters, Greenhouse told a congressional hearing in June 2005 that what she observed was "the most blatant and improper contract abuse I have witnessed during the course of my professional career."

Another voice the government attempted to squelch was that of David J. Graham, associate director for science, Office of Drug Safety, at the Food and Drug Administration. He was among the first to try to alert the public to the risk of heart attacks and death associated with the pain medication Vioxx, made by Merck & Co. At the peak of its sales, in 2003, the drug reportedly represented a $2.5 billion market.

Graham was preparing to disclose at an international conference in France that high doses of Vioxx put patients at risk of heart attacks and sudden death, but his planned disclosure triggered what he would later call an "explosive response" from the FDA's Office of New Drugs, which had approved Vioxx and regulated its use.

On November 18, 2004, Graham told a congressional committee, "The response from senior management in my office, the Office of Drug Safety, was equally stressful. I was pressured to change my conclusions and recommendations, and basically threatened that if I did not change them, I would not be permitted to present the paper at the conference."

Graham dates his concerns over Vioxx to November 2000. On September 30, 2004, Merck voluntarily withdrew Vioxx from the market. By July 2006, the company faced some 16,000 lawsuits in state and federal court, and allegations that the product caused heart attacks, strokes, and deaths.

Graham's reward for coming forward, he says, was that he was censored, that he feared for his job, and that he was the subject of a "smear campaign" he believes came from within the FDA, in concert with Merck. Sen. Charles Grassley (R-Iowa) asked the inspector general of the FDA to investigate Graham's allegations and cited notes taken by a Merck employee referring to an October 13, 2004, conversation with an FDA official about an "opportunity to get [the] message out" about Graham. A month later 22 members of Congress joined in the call for an investigation into allegations of a "smear campaign" intended to discredit Graham. Merck argued that it had every right to represent its views and to challenge those it believed were not fair or balanced in their presentations affecting the company and its products.

Like other whistle-blowers, Graham concluded that all this was the price of challenging those who would suppress the truth and who value secrecy above public safety.

"Vioxx is a terrible tragedy and a profound regulatory failure," Graham testified. "I would argue that the FDA, as currently configured, is incapable of protecting America against another Vioxx. We are virtually defenseless."

•   •   •

Silencing whistle-blowers or failing to rally to their defense is the final step in protecting the machinery of secrecy, the sealant that prevents individuals from going outside the bureaucracy and directly to the public. Secrecy can prevail only if would-be whistle-blowers doubt that they will be protected, only if the threat of termination, demotion, or reassignment appears real and irreversible.

The person in government most responsible for protecting whistle-blowers from retaliation and for insisting upon a review of their allegations is Scott J. Bloch, the head of the Office of Special Counsel (OSC), which enforces the whistle-blower protection laws passed in recognition of whistle-blowers' inestimable value to the nation's security, public health, and well-being. A Bush nominee and loyalist, Bloch came to OSC by a somewhat circuitous route, having spent the preceding two years with the Task Force for Faith-based and Community Initiatives at the U.S. Department of Justice.

During his tenure at OSC, Bloch has been dogged by controversy and allegations that his real mission is not to protect whistle-blowers, but rather to protect the administration from them—a charge he vigorously disputes. Critics say an ever-decreasing number of whistle-blowers are getting support for their allegations and fewer whistle-blower cases are getting OSC's approval for review. Public Employees for Environmental Responsibility (PEER), which represents a number of whistle-blowers, says the OSC's own figures support that claim: in 2002, OSC reported 126 "favorable actions"; in 2003, it was 115; in 2004, 68. Of most concern to attorneys and public interest groups who represent whistle-blowers is the height at which the bar has been set for whistle-blowers' allegations to win OSC support. Less than 1.5 percent of whistle-blowers' disclosures, says PEER, are referred for investigation.

Some of Bloch's former employees at OSC allege that not long after he took office, he opened up field offices across the country in an effort to purge those who disagreed with his agenda by removing them from Washington headquarters and transferring them, another allegation he denies. The staff affected were given only days to accept the reassignments. One of those reassigned to a new Detroit field office was Cary Sklar, the senior executive who oversaw the Investigation and Prosecution Division. He was fired for refusing to move.

The Office of Special Counsel is also charged with investigating allegations of arbitrariness and capriciousness in responding to requests under the Freedom of Information Act, but OSC is itself hardly a model of First Amendment openness. In March 2005, Debra S. Katz, an attorney, filed a formal "complaint of prohibited personnel practices against Special Counsel Scott Bloch" on behalf of "anonymous career employees of the U.S. Office of Special Counsel," and a coalition of four major public interest groups supportive of whistle-blowers' rights. The complaint cites "Mr. Bloch's obsession with secrecy and his aversion to transparency," a description not likely to inspire confidence in would-be whistle-blowers contemplating coming forward with their own allegations.

On October 20, 2005, the U.S. Office of Personnel Management announced that it was investigating "a complaint of prohibited personnel practices against U.S. Special Counsel Scott J. Bloch." The complaint, the announcement noted, was from four public interest organizations and a group of former employees of the Office of Special Counsel.

One of Bloch's early directives was widely interpreted by those who worked for him as a gag order prohibiting them from speaking to the press. This, too, Bloch dismisses, but inquiries with OSC's field offices in the spring of 2006 drew a uniform response. "I am not allowed to speak with you," said someone in the Dallas field office. "I would really like to." From the San Francisco field office: "I apologize for what I am about to say, but I am not going to help you. It's because I am a member of management and feel I owe allegiance to them. I haven't told you anything that is or isn't the case," he said nervously. "I won't speak to the press without getting permission from my superiors."

The spokesman for OSC's Washington headquarters is Loren Smith; he promised to respond to my questions and arrange interviews. But Smith never called back, and without Smith's clearance, those in the field refused to speak.

Bloch also stirred up a storm when he cleared—some have said "whipped through"—a backlog of hundreds of pending whistle-blower cases, processing them in ways that won praise from some for his efficiency, and criticism from others, who saw the action as a wholesale trashing of allegations. Rep. Henry Waxman (D-Calif.) fretted that they had been "dismissed arbitrarily."

Under Bloch, the Office of Special Counsel, charged as it is with protecting whistle-blowers and safeguarding federal workers, has shown what some believe is a remarkable disregard for its own employees. In September 2006, the office's employee newsletter set forth an exacting dress code of dos and don'ts that some within the agency saw as an in-

sult. Women were advised not to wear tight skirts or pants and instructed, "Before choosing a skirt to wear, sit down in it facing the mirror." Employees were to wear "a conservative watch," and advised that
"a tailored purse . . . that hangs on your shoulder is often advantageous
as it frees your hands for greetings (hand shakes) or holding a bever-
age." Such effort, some employees pointed out, would have been better
spent in vigorously enforcing the whistle-blower provisions of the law.

If Bloch has been portrayed as insensitive to the needs of whistle-
blowers, the same may not be said of his sensitivities with regard to
politicians, particularly those of his own party and the Bush administration. In September 2006, only days after the dress code surfaced, the
Office of Special Counsel was slated to host a special tribute to Leroy
Smith, a prison safety manager whom the office had proclaimed "Public
Servant of the Year" for bringing to public attention life-threatening conditions in a prison-operated factory.

Only hours before the ceremony was to commence, and after Smith
had flown in to Washington from Arizona, the event was abruptly can-
celed. Bloch said a senior official in the office who had played an integral
part in handling Smith's whistle-blower case had suffered an unexpected death in the family and could not attend the event. But another
explanation for the cancellation was advanced by some at PEER, a group
long critical of Bloch's handling of whistle-blower cases. They pointed
out that the relative had not died suddenly, not even on the day of the
ceremony, and that the cancellation had more to do with the honoree's
intention to use the public forum to criticize the agency's handling of his
and other whistle-blowers' cases.

In a May 2005 letter to Congress, the directors of two public interest
groups that represent whistle-blowers concluded, "Filing a whistleblow-
ing disclosure at the OSC has become akin to spitting in the wind."

Epilogue

Perhaps it is a universal truth that the loss of liberty at home is to be charged to provisions against danger real or pretended from abroad.

—James Madison, in a letter to Thomas Jefferson
dated May 13, 1798

In the weeks and months following the attacks of 9/11, I took to wearing a small blue and gold lapel pin featuring a profile of Thomas Jefferson that I had purchased on a long-ago trip to Jefferson's home, Monticello. I wore it as a reminder to myself and to others that when the nation is at war, not only lives and property are at risk, but civil liberties and democratic values as well. Jefferson understood that well. "Information is the currency of democracy," he observed. He and his peers knew firsthand the suffocating reach of excessive secrecy and foresaw that even in some distant, indeterminate future there would be the need to guard against the instincts of those in power to close the doors of government. Jefferson repeatedly spoke of the need for each successive generation to be on its guard. "Lethargy [is] the forerunner of death to the public liberty," he wrote in 1787. In a letter penned 34 years later, he wrote, "Let the eyes of vigilance never be closed."

It may be that the citizenry have now finally awakened and are willing to exercise the vigilance of which Jefferson spoke so eloquently.

In November 2006, some 79 million Americans took to the polls and voted for change. In handing over both houses of Congress to the Democrats, they empowered a long-disenfranchised party to press for answers and, perhaps, to break down some of the barriers of secrecy.

In the months leading up to the election the rhetoric of transparency was a mantra of hopeful Democrats. California representative Nancy Pelosi, the future Speaker of the House, had repeatedly spoken of "increasing the transparency and openness of government." On January 18, 2006, 11 months before the midterm election, she vowed that her party "will create the most open and honest government in history." On the eve of the election, in the flush of victory, she again spoke reverently of open government.

It was not a new theme for her. One month to the day after the attacks of 9/11—on October 11, 2001—she wrote to Gen. Michael V. Hayden, then director of the National Security Agency, expressing her concerns over expanded domestic surveillance. That letter, itself once classified, was declassified (in part) and released on January 3, 2006. To what degree the Democrats' publicly stated misgivings about excessive secrecy will translate into a reversal of direction, or at least a period of serious self-examination, remains to be seen.

Still, a change in power means that the instruments for penetrating secrecy—congressional hearings, the full authority of the subpoena, the investigative resources of the Government Accountability Office, the bully pulpit that goes with majority status—are all now in fresh hands.

Outspoken Democratic critics of expanded secrecy, veteran legislators like Rep. Henry Waxman (D-Calif.), Barney Frank (D-Mass.), and Charles Rangel (D-N.Y.), long relegated to the back bench of minority status, are now poised to wield the chairman's gavel in congressional committee hearings. Perhaps that power will be used to pry open the windows of government and let the light in, to reinvigorate government regulation and reporting requirements, and to begin to rein in the culture of secrecy.

But even if this group of legislators should decide to promote greater transparency, it is likely they will meet stiff resistance from a White House accustomed to getting its own way, from a Justice Department enthralled with the theory of the "unitary executive," from a constellation of agencies and departments run by industry insiders and party loyalists, and from a Supreme Court whose recent appointees have, by and large, demonstrated considerable deference to the White House and its invocations of secrecy and privilege.

Even the staunchest advocates of transparency find it hard to resist the institutional sway of secrecy and the political advantages it can afford. Pelosi, for all her talk of transparency, offered a motion on September 26, 2006, to have the entire House of Representatives go into a rare secret session to discuss intelligence regarding world terrorism and Iraq. Her motion failed. And one of the first moves the emboldened Democrats took after regaining control of Congress was to vote themselves a majority leader—by secret ballot. And no sooner had the Democrats gained control of the Senate than they held a closed-door meeting of that body. Democratic presidential hopeful Joseph R. Biden, an ardent proponent of transparency, closed the door to the public and the press as he chaired 2007's first meeting of the Senate Foreign Relations Committee, a briefing on intelligence in Iraq.

Still, as of this writing, it appears that some sort of battle is about to be joined, and that is cause for hope. If so, then perhaps this moment in history may be better suited for a prologue than an epilogue.

If 9/11 represented the failure of American intelligence to detect and thwart the plotters of that attack, then the nation's precipitous slide into compulsive secrecy represents failure of a different sort. Representative government does not obviate the need for citizens to be ever watchful. Vigilance cannot be delegated. Once again, Jefferson: "If once the people become inattentive to the public affairs, you and I, and Congress and Assemblies, Judges and Governors, shall all become wolves. It seems to be the law of our general nature, in spite of individual exceptions."

In the years since 9/11, there has been much discussion about what should rise in the place where the two towers of the World Trade Center once stood and what sort of memorial might adequately pay homage to those whose lives were lost that day. On 9/11, when the towers fell, down came crashing some 572,000 square feet of glass, the towers' 43,600 windows from which those inside had gained an extraordinary view of the world, the best vista being that from the restaurant Windows on the World, atop the 107th floor of the North Tower. These were buildings not designed to be a fortress or a bunker, but a soaring testament to America's vitality, vision, and confidence. Like democracy itself, they represented a rare balance of steel and glass, of strength and vulnerability, security and transparency. Nothing the architects and masons can conceive of could be a more fitting tribute to the victims of 9/11 than restoring that balance and defending the values of openness and transparency that are the hallmark of a healthy democracy.

Acknowledgments

Acknowledgments are the place where writers recognize their debts to others. Here I must confess that the privileged view I enjoy was gained only by standing on the shoulders of others whose work has, at times, I fear, been all that has stood between those of us who believe in representative government and methods we find loathsome. This book would not have been possible but for the efforts of scores of journalists and writers who have in recent years challenged those who would keep information vital to the public from the public. While I have attempted to bring some fresh reporting to this effort, I readily admit my profound debt to legions of stalwart reporters at papers and magazines large and small, and only hope that my attempt to contextualize their work and mine will provoke others to debate the place of secrecy in a democracy.

Among the publications I have come to rely on as guides through the labyrinth of secrecy are the *Washington Post,* the *New York Times,* the *Wall Street Journal, The New Yorker,* the *Los Angeles Times, Time* magazine, *Newsweek,* the Associated Press, Knight Ridder, and an array of regional newspapers that includes the *Detroit Free Press,* the *Seattle Times,* the *Boston Globe,* the *Chicago Tribune,* the *Atlanta Journal-Constitution,* the *Miami Herald,* and the *San Francisco Chronicle.* I have also found the work of the major networks, as well as CNN and NPR, to be invaluable. Cumulatively and individually, their work has been indispensable to this project, and I would be remiss if I were not to give them all the credit they are due for pursuing difficult stories under trying circumstances. I have liberally drawn upon their work and used them as divining rods to find other stories.

Some few reporters are in a class by themselves and my debt to them, direct and indirect, cannot go unmentioned. Among these are Seymour Hersh, James Bamford, Bob Woodward, Walter Pincus, Steve Coll, Scott Shane, Dana Priest, Kate Boo, Sari Horwitz, and Anthony Lewis. Without them, the landscape in which all of us live and work would be even more inhospitable. Together, they keep the door of democracy ajar just enough that the rest of us may find our way in. I am also forever indebted to Ben Bradlee.

In addition to newspapers, magazines, radio, and television, I find myself beholden to an array of public interest groups whose tenacity and persistence in pursuit of stories, whose service in defense of transparency, has provided me an endless fount of stories and encouragement. Among these are the National Security Archives, Public Employees for Environmental Responsibility, the Project on Government Oversight, the National Whistleblower Center, Reporters Committee for Freedom of the Press, Investigative Reporters and Editors, the Government Accountability Project, the Center for Public Integrity, Public Citizen, the First Amendment Center, openthegovernment.org, and a variety of coalitions. Steven Aftergood, head of the Project on Government Secrecy at the Federation of American Scientists, is, in my view, our leading authority on secrecy and as close to a Minuteman as we have, having taken the field long before others and holding it long after others have left.

There are also many individuals in federal, state, and local government and in industry who showed courage in speaking with me about matters that were forbidden or considered sensitive by their superiors. In an age of secrecy it would be a cruel form of reward to recognize them by name, but they know who they are and they have my abiding appreciation. So too does J. William Leonard of the Information Security Oversight Office, who has shown by example that security and transparency are not rivals but allies.

Then there are the ghosts of those who fought the good fight before, individuals who bravely resisted the shadow of obsessive secrecy whenever it fell across the land. Among these I count Sen. Daniel Patrick Moynihan, the *Washington Post* editorial writer Alan Barth, newsman Edward R. Murrow, political cartoonist Herb Block, writer E. B. White, the fiercely independent I. F. Stone, Walter Lippmann, and Edward A. Shils, author of *Torment of Secrecy*, a seminal work published in 1956 that as much as any single book inspired the book you now hold in your hand. A half century later, his fears are mine.

I also thank my agent, David Black, who entreated and then cajoled me to undertake this work, convincing me that because I knew something about secrecy and fretted so about its impact on democracy, I was suited for the task. As you can see, he can be very persuasive.

I am also deeply indebted to the Guggenheim Foundation for its financial support and to Harvard University's Joan Shorenstein Center on the Press, Politics, and Public Policy, where I was a fellow in the fall of 2003. My gratitude also goes to Case Western Reserve University, which granted me an extraordinary two-year leave of absence to work on this book.

And to personal friends who endured my ramblings as I tried to make sense of the scene, I say "thank you." Among them are Mike Riley, Alex Jones, Susan Tifft, Regina Brett, Thrity Umrigar, Howard Landau, Forrest and Karen Wardwell, and a constellation of others too numerous to name.

My editor at Doubleday was Kristine Puopolo. Her faith in me and her substantive aspirations for the book made all the difference, especially when my own confidence flagged. She is a formidable editor.

Finally, I acknowledge my wife, Peggy, to whom this book is dedicated, and my sons, Matthew and David. Peggy helped me grapple with an often contradictory and always complex subject. She was my eyes and ears, my clipping service and my confidante. (Yes, even someone writing about obsessive secrecy needs someone who can be trusted with a secret or two.) As for my sons, Matthew and David, now 16 and 17, they were my constant reminders of why it matters.

Notes

Note on Sourcing: In researching this book, I interviewed hundreds of government officials from dozens of agencies and departments, members of Congress and their staffs, political scientists, journalists and authors, city and state officials, university faculty and administrators, lawyers, judges, litigants, corporate officials, lobbyists, executives and staffers of public interest groups. A fraction of those people are listed below in reference to specific observations or statements of fact. But it was the cumulative influence of all those interviews that in large measure determined the shape and direction of this book. In addition, there were numerous books, studies, and lectures, some of which are cited after the list of sources, both as source references and as suggested reading for those interested in pursuing the subject of secrecy and its impact on democracy. I have starred those I found to be particularly influential to my own work.

Silent Encroachments

1 **Today the Justice Department resisted calls** *New York Times*, 2/2/06, p. A1.

2 **This day a blistering report** *Washington Post*, 2/2/06, p. A5.

2 **"I'm stunned to the quick"** Testimony of Porter Goss before the Senate Intelligence Committee, 2/2/06.

2 **Negroponte, has already failed his "first test"** *Washington Post,* 2/2/06, p. A9.

2 **the Patriot Act has been extended** Associated Press, *Washington Post,* 2/2/06, p. A4.

2 **Also reported this day is the existence of a secret team** *New York Times,* 2/2/06, p. A15.

3 **"This vote," NPR reports** *All Things Considered,* National Public Radio, www.npr.org, 2/2/06.

3 **"This bill is Exhibit A for special interests"** *Washington Post,* 2/2/06, p. A1.

3 **news is reference to a closed-door session in which House Republicans** *Washington Post,* 2/2/06, p. A1.

3 **Another story involves** David Espo (reporter). Associated Press, 2/2/06.

3 **On this day, it is reported** Cox News Service, *Cleveland Plain Dealer,* 2/2/06, p. A8.

3 **San Diegans are given the records** *San Diego Union-Tribune,* 2/2/06, p. B3.

4 **On this day, February 2, 2006** *Carbondale Southern Illinoisan,* 2/2/06.

4 **a bill that would deny citizens** *Richmond Times-Dispatch,* 2/2/06.

4 **the Fort Wayne newspaper takes up a loophole** FortWayne.com, *Journal Gazette News,* 2/6/06.

4 **And in the nation's capital** *Washington Post,* 2/2/06, p. B4.

4 **This same day, Enron's former head of investor relations** *New York Times,* 2/2/06.

5 **"Sunshine Week," a national observance** Reporter Bob Dart, Cox News Service, *Cleveland Plain Dealer,* 2/2/06, p. A8.

5 **in 2003, as American Airlines struggled** MSNBC report of 4/16/03 by Jon Bonne; Associated Press report of 4/18/03, by David Koenig; *New York Times* editorial, 4/23/03.

5 **"FDA Official Alleges Pressure to Suppress Vioxx Findings"** *Washington Post,* 10/8/04, p. A23.

5 **"U.S. Not Told of 2 Deaths During Study of Heart Drug"** *New York Times,* 1/4/06.

6 **"Antidepressant Makers Withhold Data: Info from Clinical Trials on Children Kept Secret"** *Washington Post,* 1/29/04.

6 **In Los Angeles, the police commission** *Los Angeles Times* editorial, 2/9/06.

7 **Those investigating the failure of the intelligence community** Executive Summary, *The 9/11 Commission Report: Final Report of the National Commission on Terrorist Attacks Upon the United States.*

7 **Behind closed doors, federal lawmakers** *Washington Post,* 1/24/06, p. A1.

7 **Environmentalists are barred from seeing routine dam** For example, see Federal Energy Regulatory Commission rules on Critical Energy Infrastructure Information at www.ferc.gov/legal/ceii-foia/ceii.asp.

7 **The search for hundreds of children** *Washington Post,* 12/23/05, p. A6.

7 **In 2006, the Reporters Committee for Freedom of the Press** "Hidden Docketing System Keeps Hundreds of Cases Shrouded in Nation's Capital," RCFP news release, 3/4/06.

8 **In recent years, the number of government secrets has exploded** Information Security Oversight Office Annual Report, 2005.

8 **The direct cost to government** "Hidden Docketing System."

10 **A few years ago, Porter Goss** Interview with author.

11 **The United States Department of Agriculture** Interview with Department of Agriculture spokesperson, Amanda Eamich, 7/14/06; "State Can't Say Who Sold Beef; Rules Bar Telling Which Stores, Restaurants Had Tainted Meat," *San Francisco Chronicle,* 1/23/04; also, "USDA Keeps Tainted Meat's Destination Secret," *Spokesman-Review* (Wash.), 6/27/04.

11 **A 2004 study found that only half of the contaminated meat** Interview on 11/1/06 with Neal Hooker, Ohio State University researcher whose study was published in the journal *Food Control,* vol. 15, no. 5, pp. 359–67.

12 **But in July 2003, early-warning data** See lawsuit, *U.S. District Court for District of Columbia, Public Citizen, Inc. v. Norman Mineta, Secretary, U.S. Department of Transportation.*

12 **The National Practitioner Data Bank** See National Practitioner Data Bank regulations at www.npdb-hipdb.hrsa.gov/npdb.html, Section 60.13.

12 **In Florida, a state with one of the nation's highest populations of retirees** Senate Bill 1202, signed into law by Gov. Jeb Bush on 5/15/01.

13 **"They held their consultations always under the veil of secrecy"** From *The Federalist,* no. 55, "The Total Number of the House of Representatives," *Independent Journal,* February 13, 1788: "To the People of the State of New York . . ."

13 **"Give us at least a plausible apology"** Virginia Ratifying Convention, June 9, 1788, www.constitution.org/rc/rat_va_07.htm

14 **The U.S. House of Representatives frequently held secret sessions** Mildred Amer, "Secret Sessions of Congress: A Brief Historical Overview"; Report of the Congressional Research Service, 10/21/04.

15 **The speaker? Then secretary of defense Donald Rumsfeld** Remarks to the American Society of Newspaper Editors, 4/22/04.

16 **In part, the decline reflected the bulk declassifications of older documents** Interview with J. William Leonard, Director, U.S. Information Security Oversight Office.

19 **On March 19, 2003, in one of the more ironic displays of contempt for openness** Letter of protest from the Radio-Television News Directors Association and Foundation (RTNDA), sent to James Foster, President, City Club of Cleveland, from Barbara Cochran, president of RTNDA.

19 **A year later, on April 7, 2004, while giving a speech** See Denise Grones, "Two Reporters Told to Erase Scalia Tapes," Associated Press, 4/8/04.

20 **When the *Newark Star-Ledger* reported** *Newark Star-Ledger,* 10/31/06.

20 **When the Office of the Special Inspector General** *New York Times,* 11/3/06.

21 **The report cited Parliament's condemnation of James II** "Declaration of the Lords Spiritual and Temporal, and Commons," February 13, 1689; David Lewis Jones, *A Parliamentary History of the Glorious Revolution* (London: Her Majesty's Stationery Office, 1988), pp. 42–45.

22 **It was also a familiar strain** Interview with author.

22 **In 2004 the number of court-authorized secret wiretaps** Report of the Director of the Administrative Office of the United States Courts on Applications for Orders Authorizing or Approving the Interception of Wire, Oral, or Electronic Communications, April 2005.

23 **Dale Moore, a former lobbyist** Judy Sarasohn, "Under Bush, the Revolving Door Gains Speed," *Washington Post,* 10/27/05, p. A25; Christopher Drew and Richard A. Oppel Jr., "Mines to Mountaintops," *New York Times,* 8/9/04.

24 **In 1971, Daniel Ellsberg reportedly spent six weeks** See Alasdair Roberts, *Blacked Out: Government Secrecy in the Information Age* (New York: Cambridge University Press, 2006), p. 73.

Case Study: Inescapable Secrecy

Based on author's multiple interviews with Melissa Boyle Mahle, 12/8/04, etc. For further readings on Mahle, see her book *Denial and Deception: An Insider's View of the CIA from Iran-Contra to 9/11* (New York: Thunder's Mouth Press/Nation Books, February 2005).

National Insecurity, Part I: A Secrecy Born of Fear, Not Reason

32 **On a clear April morning in 1971** Author's multiple interviews with Peggy Thomson, John Seabury Thomson's widow, and writings of John Seabury Thomson, provided by his widow. See also John Seabury Thomson, "The Top Secret Slurry Caper," Swarthmore College Alumni Bulletin, October 1973.

33 **Few have a better vantage point** Author's multiple interviews with J. William Leonard.

33 **In June 2003 he wrote** J. William Leonard's introductory essay "A Look to the Future of the Security Classification System in a Post 9/11 Environment," published in the 2002 Annual Report of the Information Security Oversight Office, online at www.archives.gov/isoo/reports/2002-annual-report.html.

34 **Today, some 99 percent of government secrets** Annual Reports of the U.S. Information Security Oversight Office, 2003, 2004, 2005.

35 **In 2004, the vast Department of Homeland Security** *Washington Post,* 11/16/04, p. A23.

36 **By May 2004, the queue of government workers** Interviews with Derek B. Stewart, Director, Defense Capabilities and Management, Government Accountability Office.

37 **"These guys are using Eisenhower-era processes"** Author's interview with David Wagoner, 7/4/06.

37 **"The signal boys—NSA—don't trust HUMINT"** Author's interview with Harold Relyea, Congressional Research Service, 10/14/04.

38 **"They had no money to pay for it," says the OPM's associate director** Author's interview with Kathy Dillaman, Associate Director, OPM, 7/13/06.

39 **Take 24-year-old Spc. Joseph Fabozzi** *Asbury Park Press,* 11/12/03.

40 **The Pentagon asked the JASON Group** Report number JSR–04–132, "Horizontal Integration: Broader Access Models for Realizing

Information Dominance" from the JASON Program Office, December 2004.

41 **In one agency, "R" means "releasable"** GAO Report number GAO–06–706, "Managing Sensitive Information: DOD Can More Effectively Reduce the Risk of Classification Errors," released 6/30/06.

42 **One caveat: At a press conference announcing the appointment** "Official to Check Screening Complaints," *Washington Post,* 2/15/02; letter from Rep. Henry Waxman, then ranking minority member, Committee on Government Reform, to then Committee Chairman, Christopher Shays, 3/1/05.

42 **In 2003, the Pentagon, in an act imbued with supreme irony** Martha Mendoza (reporter), Associated Press, 2/13/03.

43 **On October 31, 2005, Mary Margaret Graham** "Official Reveals Budget for U.S. Intelligence," *New York Times,* 11/8/05.

48 **"The people who leak information are not the mid-level people"** Author's multiple interviews with William McNair, 11/12/04, etc.; *Washington Post Magazine,* 5/31/92.

50 **Former secretary of state Colin Powell's senior advisor** Lawrence B. Wilkerson interviewed by Steve Inskeep, National Public Radio, 11/3/05.

52 **In March 2006 the GAO reported** GAO Report number GAO–06–385, "Information Sharing," March 2006.

53 **In March 2006, the GAO, the official,** Ibid.

53 **For more than 20 years, William McNair was with the Agency** Author's interviews with William McNair, 11/12/04, etc.

57 **Prior to capture she was said to have emptied her M-16** " 'She Was Fighting to the Death'; Details Emerging of W. Va. Soldier's Capture and Rescue," *Washington Post,* 4/3/03, p. A1.

58 **The truth, which emerged much later, was that her gun had jammed** See Christopher Hanson, "The Press Finds The War's True Meaning," *Columbia Journalism Review,* Issue 4, July/August 2003.

58 **Three years into his administration, George Bush** "Bush's Press Problem," a Q & A with Ken Auletta, *The New Yorker,* 1/13/04.

62 **But instead of vigorously going after Deutch** "Report of Investigation" by the Inspector General of the Central Intelligence Agency, "Improper Handling of Classified Information by John M. Deutch," 2/18/00, No. 1998–0028–IG.

62 **In March 2006, the federal prosecutor in the case, Richard G.**

Convertino Eric Lichtblau, "Ex-Prosecutor in Terror Inquiry Is Indicted," *New York Times*, 3/30/06. At the time of publication, the trial was still pending.

64 **"Discipline has broken down dramatically"** Author's interview with James Pavitt.

65 **In January 1953, famed Princeton physicist John Wheeler** See Gregg Herken, *Brotherhood of the Bomb: The Tangled Lives and Loyalties of Robert Oppenheimer, Ernest Lawrence and Edward Teller* (2002), p. 259.

65 **At Virginia's Mt. Weather, the once-secret underground mountain retreat** Author's interview with the late Bud Gallagher, who oversaw Mt. Weather. He died on 8/22/00.

66 **That information came in response to an e-mail** E-mail exchange with Kristy Kalo, Vice President, Washington Speakers Bureau, 7/10/06.

Case Study: A Secret Hell

Based on at least half a dozen telephone interviews with David Day (10/4/97, 10/15/97, 11/26/97, 12/1/97, etc.); his widow Ann Adams-Day (3/19/04), and William Israel, former Worker's Compensation Claims Examiner, Special Claims Unit, Department of Labor (11/26/97, etc.), who worked on the Day case within the Department of Labor; and Employees' Compensation Appeals Board decision, Docket No. 97–2437, a "Classified Case."

71 **With the support of those records and Day's psychiatrist** Based on the decision of the three-person Employees' Compensation Appeals Board.

National Insecurity, Part II:
Secrecy Means Not Having to Say You're Sorry

73 **Left to its own, the system will likely corrode** Remarks of J. William Leonard, Director, Information Security Oversight Office, to the National Classification Management Society's Annual Training Seminar in Reno, Nevada, 6/15/04.

73 **"If this were a graduating class of CIA case officers"** *Washington Post*, 5/13/06, p. C1.

74 **Thirteen days later, on August 20, the U.S. retaliated** See Oriana Zill's PBS *Frontline* piece, "The Controversial U.S. Retaliatory Missile Strikes." Also see debates in U.K. Parliament for 3/24/99, regarding doubts about the legitimacy of the Al Shifa Factory bombing.

74 **A veteran senior CIA officer** Author's interviews with former senior-ranking CIA officer involved in the Al Shifa targeting decision; the former Agency official would speak only on the condition that he not be identified by name or precise position.

79 **Forty years ago, the CIA sought to poison the Congo's Patrice Lumumba** Author's interview with former CIA operative Lawrence Devlin; see also Ted Gup, "Bad Chemistry," a profile of the late Sidney Gottlieb, former CIA scientist in the technical branch of the Agency, *Washington Post Magazine*, 12/16/01.

79 **In 1962, the Joint Chiefs of Staff** See the discussion of "Operation Northwoods" in James Bamford's *Body of Secrets: Anatomy of the Ultra-Secret National Security Agency* (New York: Doubleday, 2001), pp. 82–91. Also see declassified documents of 3/13/62 from Joint Chiefs of Staff, and cover letter from L. L. Lemnitzer, Chairman, Joint Chiefs of Staff.

80 **Anyone who imagines that today's government is not so bold** Richard Norton-Taylor, "Blair-Bush Deal Before Iraq War Revealed in Secret Memo," *The Guardian*, 2/3/06. (Norton-Taylor is the paper's security affairs editor.)

80 **Ordinarily it would be difficult to imagine** See Alan Sipress and Karen DeYoung, *Washington Post*, 4/23/01; and Douglas Jehl and David Johnston, *New York Times*, 2/6/05.

81 **What was needed was to let the Agency off the leash** Author's interviews with Porter J. Goss as Chair of the House Permanent Select Committee on Intelligence, prior to becoming director Central Intelligence, 1/12/01 and 10/1/03.

82 **He picked a friendly Georgetown audience** Ted Gup, *Washington Post* Op-Ed Page, 2/7/04, p. A23.

83 **For a true definition of "rendition"** One of the more comprehensive articles on rendition appeared in *The New Yorker*, 2/14/05, by Jane Mayer, titled "Annals of Justice: Outsourcing Torture"; also see DeNeen L. Brown and Dana Priest, "Deported Terror Suspect Details Torture in Syria," 11/5/03, p. A1.

85 **Among the growing list of casualties** Author's interview with James Yee, 5/1/06; also see Larry Hobbs, "Charges Dropped Against Muslim Chaplain," Associated Press, 3/19/04.

86 **J. William Leonard . . . spent 30 years at the Pentagon** Author's interview with William Leonard.

87 **Hatfill would become notorious as the "person of interest"** Ted Gup, *Washington Post* Outlook Section, 8/18/02, p. B1.

87 **Norman M. Covert was the public affairs officer** Author's interview with Norman M. Covert.

88 **Nearly four decades ago, a young second lieutenant** Author's interviews with Patrick Marshall Hughes, former head of the Defense Intelligence Agency, 4/21/05, 8/11/06, etc.

Case Study: Blacked Out: A Secret the CIA Won't Release

Section based on author's 6/23/05 interview with retired CIA officer Walter James McIntosh, who retired from the CIA as Chief of Vietnam Operations; also based on articles appearing in the Indian publication *Blitz,* archived at the Library of Congress.

Secret History

98 **On September 10, 2001, the last "day like any other"** Author's interview with John Steinbeiss, 3/18/05.

100 **In March 2003, members of the Society for History in the Federal Government** Author's interview with Suzanne White Junod, past president of the Society for History in the Federal Government. Also see official 3/14/03 Conference Program held in Shepherdstown, West Virginia.

101 **Among the documents withdrawn was a 1948 CIA memo** Scott Shane (reporter), *New York Times,* 2/21/06.

103 **To quash the study and keep it out of the hands** Scott Shane, "Doubts Cast on Vietnam Incident, but Study Stays Classified," *New York Times,* 10/31/05.

104 **Anna K. Nelson is no stranger to either history or secrecy** Author's interview with Anna K. Nelson.

105 **Steven Tilley oversees the vast paper holdings** Author's interview with Steven Tilley.

106 **Judith Palya's story goes to the heart of the subject of secrecy** Author's multiple interviews with Judith Palya.

107 **The ruling created a benchmark legal precedent for state secrecy** See article by Timothy Lynch of the Cato Institute, "In '48 Crash, the U.S. Hid Behind National Security," 6/30/03.

109 **In the 19 years between 1954 and 1973** *Washington Post*, 5/13/06, p. A3, citing study of the Reporters Committee for Freedom of the Press.

110 **The oldest classified records at the National Archives** Freedom of Information Act lawsuit filed by the James Madison Project (JMP), case heard in U.S. District Court for the District of Columbia; press release of James Madison Project (contact Mark S. Zaid, JMP Executive Director), 3/30/99.

111 **Suzanne White Junod, the FDA's historian** Author's interview with Suzanne White Junod.

111 **Even by the standards of the Library of Congress's Manuscript Room** Computer printouts of all classified documents in the Library of Congress Document Reading Room are available online; a researcher provided me with printouts of all documents in the Reading Room that were not available to researchers because they were deemed classified; all specific references to materials, extracted from the collection and placed in the vault, are based upon the Library of Congress's individual collection files, organized by name of subject.

113 **Ernest Emrich is the classified-documents archivist** Author interview with Ernest Emrich, Manuscript Reading Room, Library of Congress, 1/9/07.

114 **Roger Heusser doesn't remember the year.** Author's interviews with Roger Heusser, 10/27/04, 10/28/04, etc.

115 **O'Leary's introduction to secrecy** Author's interviews with Hazel O'Leary, former secretary of the Department of Energy, now president of Fisk University, 3/22/05, etc.

119 **In an elegant act of protest** Referred to in Richard Reeves's address at the 2002 National Freedom of Information Day conference.

119 **Among the bureaucrats who wield the stamp of secrecy** Author's interviews with Fletcher Whitworth.

123 **State Department historian Marc Susser** Author's interviews with Marc Susser, *FRUS* general editor Edward Keefer, and other staff members, 3/16/05, etc.

127 **One of the most impassioned defenders of CIA secrecy** Author's interviews with William McNair, 10/14/04, etc.

128 **"The CIA kept changing the personnel"** Author's interview with Warren Kimball, former chair of the State Department's historical advisory committee.

128 **"There are all kinds of rationalizations"** Author's interview with
Robert A. Pastor, 11/11/04.

129 **In the summer of 2003** Reuters story, *Washington Post,* 7/1/03, p. A8.

Case Study: He Who Must Not Be Named

131 **I called the CIA to ask why I should not give Jose's last name**
Author's interview with Michelle Neff, Public Affairs, CIA Media
Branch, 7/19/06.

133 **You will find references to "Jose" in the** *Washington Post* "CIA to
Remain Coordinator of Overseas Spying," *Washington Post,* 10/13/05,
p. A4. Also see "Undercover CIA Official to Oversee New National
Clandestine Service," Associated Press story, 10/14/05.

133 **In March 2004, his full name was reported** Theodora Tongas, "CIA
Anti-Terror Director Meets with Olympic Organizers," Associated
Press, 3/23/04; same article with "Jose's" full name appears on the
New York Times website, www.nytimes.com/aponline/sports/AP-Oly-
Athens-Security.html.

134 **The identity of that author was hardly a secret to many reporters** See
CBS's *60 Minutes* interview with correspondent Steve Kroft, aired
11/14/04.

Secrecy and the Press

In preparation for articles related to secrecy that were to run in
Columbia Journalism Review and elsewhere, the author interviewed Bill
Keller, then managing editor of the *New York Times* and now executive
editor; Jill Abramson, then Washington bureau chief, now managing editor; as well as a score of *Times* reporters. James Risen declined to be interviewed and believed that I had a conflict of interest in writing about
him for the *Columbia Journalism Review* because he had, in his words,
"killed the *Times* review" of my previous book, *The Book of Honor*—a fact
not known to me until he left me a voice mail to that effect.

140 **Byron Calame, the** *Times's* **public editor** Byron Calame, "Behind the
Eavesdropping Story, a Loud Silence," Public Editor Column.

142 **From that time on, Wen Ho Lee** See Lee's account of the ordeal in his
book *My Country Versus Me* (New York: Hyperion, 2002).

145 **Neither reporter expressed remorse** Author's interview with Jeff

Gerth. Risen declined to be interviewed, but through his editors at the time he defended the stories' accuracy and fairness.

149 **Editorial page chief Gail Collins has said that her greatest regret** Collins interview with Joe Strupp of *Editor & Publisher*, 7/15/06.

150 **Those words were written more than 80 years earlier** "A Test of the News," *New Republic*, 8/4/20.

150 **In an ironic twist for one so adept in trafficking in secrets** See Howard Kurtz (reporter), *Washington Post*, 5/26/03, p. C1.

150 **That memo identified one of her principal sources as Ahmad Chalabi** Dexter Filkins, "Where Plan A Left Ahmad Chalabi," *New York Times*, 11/5/06. As Filkins notes, the Jordanians now seem ready to pardon Chalabi of the embezzling charges.

152 **Jack Nelson, a Pulitzer Prize–winning journalist** "Confronting the Seduction of Secrecy: Toward Improved Access to Government Information on the Record," Washington Press Club Conference held 3/17/05.

153 **At the March 2005 conference on secrecy and sources** Ibid.

154 **On April 2, 2006, the *Washington Post* reported** Chris Cillizza, "Harris Campaign Leaking Staff," *Washington Post*, 4/2/06, p. A4.

154 **A quote critical of her chances to win election** Ibid.

156 **Parts of at least 20 stories were entirely made up** *USA Today*, 4/22/04.

158 **Those few willing to take a position against secrecy** "White House Is Pressed by Press Corps over Sourcing," *New York Times*, 5/4/05, p. C3.

159 **In July 2006, the *Wall Street Journal*'s conservative editorial writer** See "Times of War," www.opinionjournal.com, 7/17/06.

159 **"The administration wants journalism stopped"** Congressional Record, 5/09/06, pp. H2302–H2304.

161 **Andrew Jay Schwartzman, president of the Media Access Project** Author's interview with Jay Schwartzman, 8/16/06.

162 **Post-9/11, efforts to control what Americans hear and know** "600 Antiwar Demonstrators Hold Protest at Del. Base," *Washington Post*, Nation in Brief, 3/15/04.

163 **Jeff Fager, the program's executive producer** "Alumnus Dives Right In as New Head of *60 Minutes*," *Colgate University News*, 6/16/04.

164 **Jonathan Dienst, an investigative reporter** Author's interview with Jonathan Dienst, 8/4/06.

165 **At least two senior officials within the Department of Homeland Security** See *Newsday*, 10/19/05, and *New York Daily News*, 10/21/05.

168 **In July 2006, Christine Axsmith** *Washington Post,* 7/21/06.

169 **Less than a month after** *Newsweek* **was humbled** Robert Burns, "U.S. Confirms Urine Touched Quran at Gitmo," Associated Press report, 6/4/05.

170 **Rep. Deborah Pryce (R-Ohio) urged people to cancel their subscriptions** Carlos Sanchez, "Tip of Anonymous Iceberg," *Waco Tribune-Herald* (Texas), 5/22/05.

170 **In the summer of 2005, Clifton wrote a column** Author and *Cleveland Plain Dealer* editor Doug Clifton exchanged e-mails on the subject of anonymous sources and the two stories that were held because of fears of being subpoenaed.

173 **Ben Bagdikian, the** *Washington Post's* **former assistant managing editor** Ben H. Bagdikian (reporter), *American Journalism Review,* August/September 2005 issue.

175 **In January 2006, two senior officials of the Mine Safety and Health Administration** *Washington Post,* 2/21/06, p. A13.

176 **When the Watergate reporters, Bob Woodward and Carl Bernstein** See www.utexas.edu/features/archive.

176 **Some 70 journalists planning to travel to Guantánamo** See Charles Savage (reporter), *Boston Globe,* 8/27/04; and "Military Commission Media Rules Released," Reporters Committee for Freedom of the Press website, www.refp.org/news/2004/0819guant.

177 **Two years after the** *Post* **reporter's fiasco of a trip** Josh White (reporter), *Washington Post,* 11/1/05, 11/5/05, 11/18/05, 3/15/06, etc.

177 **In the summer of 2006, when reports surfaced of three detainee suicides** See Society of Professional Journalists (SPJ) News, 6/16/06.

Case Study: A Crime of Secrecy?

181 **But it was, some now say, precisely those qualities that led to her being indicted** Author's interviews with several former colleagues of former dean Patricia O'Toole. None of these individuals would speak on the record.

181 **That was when the Cuyahoga County prosecutor's office charged her** Cuyahoga County Criminal Case #481615; author's interview with O'Toole's attorney, Edward Heffernan; James F. McCarty, "In Local Sec Cases, Failure to Report Crime Charged," *Cleveland Plain Dealer,* 6/7/06.

182 **Specifically, the student expressed concerns that her father, a detective, would find out** Letter to O'Toole from alleged victim, provided by O'Toole's attorney, Edward Heffernan.

182 **That superior has reportedly said** Author's interview with O'Toole's attorney, Edward Heffernan.

182 **On October 13, 2005, O'Toole wrote the student** Ibid.

182 **Notre Dame's president, Dr. Andrew P. Roth** Author's request for an interview was declined.

183 **And after touting the importance of the case** Author's request for an interview with the prosecutors was declined by office spokesman Ryan Miday.

183 **"From our standpoint, we don't think she did anything wrong"** "Hollins University Supports New Dean Through Indictment," *Roanoke Times,* 9/27/06, p. B4.

Secrets and the University

185 **In 2004, members of a University of Nebraska search committee** *Chronicle of Higher Education,* 7/9/04.

186 **In 2003, Rev. Bernard P. Knoth** *Chronicle of Higher Education,* 5/23/03.

186 **Just miles away, at Tulane University** Author's interview with Dr. Mary Bitner Anderson.

186 **In 2004, the board of trustees of the University of Utah, a public university** *Chronicle of Higher Education,* 9/29/06.

186 **That same year it admitted misrepresenting** Ibid., 1/16/04.

186 **Auburn University's board of trustees was found to have violated that state's sunshine law** Student Press Law Center Report, Winter 2001–02, vol. XXIII, no. 1, p. 14.

186 **In June 2004, an Ohio University graduate student, Thomas A. Matrka** *Chronicle of Higher Education,* 3/10/06; "Panel on Cheating Says Fire Chairman," *Columbus Dispatch,* 6/1/06.

187 **There is true cause for concern** Author's interview with Charles N. Davis, professor at Missouri School of Journalism.

187 **Mark Goodman, executive director of the Student Press Law Center** Author's interview with Mark Goodman.

188 **"The official position [of universities and colleges] has to be"** Author's interview with Daniel Carter, Vice President, Security On Campus.

189 **Just ask Deborah and Jeffrey Shick** Author's interviews with Deborah

and Jeffrey Shick, 11/19/06, etc.; articles from *The Hoya*, Georgetown University's school newspaper, beginning on 2/25/00.

191 **And Colin Campbell, a former Georgetown professor of public policy** Author's interview with Colin Campbell, now at the University of British Columbia.

191 **In August 2001, Kate Dieringer was a freshman** Author's interview with Kate Dieringer, 4/30/05.

192 **Finally, in January, still haunted by that night** Author's interview with Carolyn Hurwitz.

194 **On September 12, 2002, Kate's mother, Janet** Author's interview with Janet Dieringer, 5/09/05.

194 **At the University of Virginia, alleged rape victims** Liesel Nowak, "Suit Ends with $150,000 Award," *Daily Progress*, 9/1/05.

195 **It ordered Georgetown to halt the use of such nondisclosure forms** See *The Hoya*, Georgetown University newspaper, 8/4/04.

196 **Morin was a freshman in 2004** Author's interview with Alphia Morin.

196 **That same year, the University of Central Florida's Victim Services** Author's interview with La'Shawn Ruffin, University of Central Florida (UCF) Victims Services, 5/23/05; author's interview with Troy Williamson, Records, UCF Police.

198 **Morin's rape counselor, La'Shawn Ruffin** Author's interview with Ruffin, 5/23/05.

198 **There, a university vice president, Dr. Maribeth Ehasz** Author's interview with Dr. Maribeth Ehasz, 5/27/05.

202 **In contrast, no one was more interested in having the Hutchinson-Hafer report released** Author's interview with Morris Judd, 5/5/05.

202 **A distinguished chemist and two-time recipient of a Guggenheim** Biographical records and correspondence of Irving Goodman provided by the Guggenheim Foundation.

203 **Half a century later, Judd, his daughter, Nina, and Paul Levitt** Author's interview with Paul Levitt, Professor of English, University of Colorado.

203 **The paper took the regents to court** Author's interviews with *Boulder Daily Camera* reporter Clint Talbott.

203 **One board member, attempting to put the best public face on it** Quotes are from the minutes of the University of Colorado's board meetings; the author's repeated requests for interviews with board members were declined. Those requests were made of Milagros Cortez, secretary to the Board of Regents.

204 **Allegations of sexual assaults, recruiting scandals, and questions of financial irregularities** See "Lawsuit Claims CU Athletes Pressured Police," *Colorado Daily News*, 7/1/04.

206 **That's when Amit Paley, a Harvard sophomore** Author's interviews with Amit Paley, now a reporter with the *Washington Post*.

207 **His request was passed to the desk of the university archivist, Harley P. Holden** Author's interview with Harley P. Holden.

207 **A professor of computer science, Lewis** Author's interviews with Harry Lewis, Harvard professor of computer science.

208 **That was 101-year-old Albert Hamilton Gordon** Author's interviews with Albert Hamilton Gordon.

209 **The mission of the secret court was to root out students** See "The Secret Court of 1920," *Harvard Crimson*, 11/21/02.

210 **Mitchell, a onetime PR man for Nike** Author's interview with Robert P. Mitchell, Harvard's Director of Communications.

Case Study: A Case Unsealed

213 **Until that moment on September 4, 2002** Author's interviews with Kirk Wolden, attorney for Sarah Davis.

213 **But on the afternoon of September 4, 2002** See "Plaintiff Sarah Davis' Motion for Sanctions," filed 9/20/02 in Superior Court of the state of California, County of Placer, Case No. SCV9736; and main case file for *Sarah Davis vs. The City of Auburn . . . American Honda Motor Co., Inc. . . . See Superior Court of the State of California, County of Placer, Sarah Davis, Plaintiff, v. The City of Auburn . . . American Honda Motor Company, Inc; Honda Automobile Division . . . ,* Case No. SCV9736, dated 10/3/02.

214 **As Judge James D. Garbolino later wrote in his opinion** Ibid.; author's interview with retired judge James D. Garbolino, 3/16/06.

214 **Never happened, says Gratzinger's attorney** Author's interview with Mark O'Connor, 9/27/06; Robert Gratzinger declined to be interviewed.

214 **He turned his attention to Honda's attorney, Paul Cereghini** Author left repeated and detailed messages with Cereghini's office, but no calls were returned.

215 **On October 10, 2002, pursuant to the terms of settlement** See Judge Garbolino's order to vacate earlier order of 10/3/02, filed 10/11/02.

215 **One of the attorneys representing the boy's interest** Author's interview with Barbara Bozman-Moss.

216 **Acknowledging that his earlier decision to seal the record had been a violation** "Order Unsealing Record and Striking Portions of Sealing Order," filed by Judge James D. Garbolino on 10/26/05, in Superior Court, State of California, County of Placer, *Sarah Davis v. The City of Auburn.*

Secret Courts

219 **The American Bar Association held a symposium** American Bar Association Section of Litigation Symposium on the Vanishing Trial, San Francisco, 12/12/03–12/14/03.

219 **In 1972 the percentage of federal civil cases disposed of by trial** Stephan Landsman, DePaul University College of Law, in the *Journal of Empirical Legal Studies,* vol. 1, issue 3, November 2004, pp. 973–84.

220 **Two hundred years ago, the English jurist Sir William Blackstone noted** *Ehrlich's Blackstone,* J. W. Ehrlich, ed. (San Carlos, Calif.: Nourse Publishing Co., 1959); Sir William Blackstone, *Commentaries on the Laws of England (1765–1769).*

220 **"The evidence trials generate may be of value not only to litigants"** Stephan Landsman, DePaul University College of Law, in *Journal of Empirical Legal Studies,* vol. 1, issue 3, November 2004, pp. 973–84.

220 **Landsman and other legal scholars who have studied the justice system** Author's interview with Stephan Landsman, Robert A. Clifford Chair in Tort Law and Social Policy, DePaul University College of Law.

221 **These are not mere abstractions, especially not for James Lammey** Author's interviews with James Lammey, now a judge in Tennessee.

222 **His father, then a Memphis prosecutor, sued Ford** *Lammey v. Ford Motor Company, et al.,* filed 2/19/99 in Federal Court in Western District of Tennessee, Case No. 99–2156–D/V.

222 **He hired a local Memphis attorney, Todd Kaplan** Author's interview with attorney Todd Kaplan.

222 **Ford retained a Nashville attorney, John Randolph Bibb Jr.** Author's interview with Attorney Bibb, now with the Nashville law firm of Waller, Lansden, Dortch and Davis, 9/25/06.

222 **But what happened next is not something** Order of Dismissal by U.S. District Judge Bernice B. Donald, 6/11/02.

223 **For her, there was no miracle** Author's interview with Charles

Iantosca and son, Charles Jr., 1/10/06; see *Charles J. Iantosca, Executor of the Estate of Grace Iantosca, and Charles J. Iantosca, Individually, Plaintiffs, v. Ford Motor Company, Defendant,* Commonwealth of Massachusetts, Superior Court, Case No. 95–1363, and Judgment of Dismissal on 7/2/98.

223 **As Tim McGrath recalls** Author's interviews with Timothy McGrath, 1/9/06, etc.

225 **The attorneys in the case refused to discuss it** Author's interview with plaintiff's attorney, R. Bradford Wash, who spoke generically of secrecy and settlements, and would not talk about the particulars of the Farr case. The case, *Farr et al. v. Newell Rubbermaid,* was filed on 4/18/00 in U.S. District Court for the Northern District of Alabama, Docket #5:00–cv–00997–pwg; the presiding judge was Paul W. Greene.

225 **In recent years Graco has been the subject** See U.S. Consumer Product Safety Recalls for Graco products dated 12/19/97, 4/13/00, 6/14/00, 7/31/02, 7/13/04, 3/22/05, 10/31/05, 12/21/05.

226 **In March 2005, Graco agreed** John Files (reporter), *New York Times,* 3/23/05.

227 **But Bradford Wash has never met Judge Joseph F. Anderson** Author's interviews with U.S. Judge Joseph F. Anderson.

228 **Determined to challenge the system, Anderson proposed a radical solution** For extensive discussion of the dangers of secret settlements in court, see David S. Sanson, "The Pervasive Problem of Court-Sanctioned Secrecy and the Exigency of National Reform," 33 *Duke Law Journal* 807; also see *The State* newspaper (Columbia, South Carolina), John Monk, "Medical Mistakes Kept Secret," 6/18/02, and "Medical Errors Kill, Injure S.C. Patients," 6/17/02.

229 **As if to defend this position** Federal Judicial Center's 2004 study "Sealed Settlement Agreements in Federal District Court."

230 **Of the 1,270 sealed settlements cited in a sampling** Ibid.

231 **Fewer than half of the state courts** Davis S. Anson, "The Pervasive Problem of Court-Sanctioned Secrecy and the Exigency of National Reform," 53 *Duke Law Journal* 807; and "Materials on Secrecy Practices in the Courts," 2000 Forum for State Court Judges, Roscoe Pound Institute, 7/29/00.

231 **An internal March 31, 2006, memo that went out to all clerks** "Memorandum to All Clerks, United States District Courts, Subject: Management of Sealed Cases on CM/ECF" by Robert Lowney, Chief,

Administrative Office of the United States Courts, 3/31/06; copies were also sent to all chief judges of the U.S. District Courts.

232 **Gary Bockweg oversees the technical side of the case management system** Author's interview with Gary Bockweg.

233 **Consider Carol Forte** Author's interview with Carol Forte, an attorney with Blume, Goldfaden, Berkowitz, Donnelly, Fried & Forte, 3/31/06.

233 **In the spring of 2002, her website** See www.njatty.com/articles/medmal/cfwn0.

234 **Take, for example, a 2002 case before California's State Court of Appeals** See Cal.App.4th, 113 Cal.Rptr.2d 309, 01 Cal. Daily Op. Serv. 9441, 2001; Case No. F037760

234 **An external reviewer for the hospital concluded** Dr. Raymond Berg cited in the above case. The spokesperson for Saint Agnes Medical Center did not return repeated calls requesting an interview or response.

235 **The presiding justice who wrote the opinion** Author's interviews with Justice James A. Ardaiz.

235 **Only "hospital disciplinary actions that resulted in the termination"** For a list of what physician information is public and what is confidential, see Medical Board of California, "Physician License Lookup," at www.medbd.ca.gov/Lookup.htm.

235 **In this case, the hospital's judicial review committee** Court of Appeals of California, Fifth Appellate District, Case No. F043928, filed 12/21/04.

236 **The "Unnamed Physician" is not talking, but his attorney, John Harwell, is** Author's interviews with attorneys John Harwell and Daniel O. Jamison, both of whom represented the physician.

238 **An unnamed 14-year-old student came forward in 2002** See *Lawrence (MA) Eagle-Tribune* (Lawrence, Massachusetts) stories of December 2002 and 5/16/03.

238 **Unbeknownst to the city council** Author's interview with Gilbert Frechette, Vice President of Lawrence City Council.

238 **But it was the taxpayers who would be paying** Author's interviews with *Eagle-Tribune* editor Bill Ketter.

239 **At trial, another security guard, Robert Kenyon** See *Eagle-Tribune* of 5/16/03.

239 **The jury acquitted Colon** See Ibid., 5/21/03.

239 **New Jersey's Essex County Superior Court Judge Theodore Winard**

Author's repeated requests to interview Judge Theodore Winard were declined.

239 Lawrence Lederman, his fellow plaintiffs, and his attorney disagreed. Author's interview with plaintiff's attorney, Angela Roper, 3/24/06.

239 There were allegations that Prudential had retaliated against him and others See *Lawrence Lederman v. Prudential Life Insurance Company of America, Inc., et al.,* Superior Court of New Jersey, Law Division, Essex County, Civil Action, Dockets Nos. ESX–L–010547 02, ESX–L–11106 02, ESXNL–11329–02, ESSX–L–001706–03, ESSX–L–002466–03, ESX–L–05588–03.

240 He denied three news organizations "Press Is Refused Access to Files in Prudential Fraud Case," *New Jersey Law Journal,* 9/5/03.

241 It was not until May 2006 that a three-judge panel Superior Court of New Jersey, Appellate Division, Docket No. A-1449–04T5, decision written by Judge Michael Winkelstein.

241 It was 6:10 P.M., November 17, 2005, and 22-year-old Krista Raymond Author's interviews with Andover Police Officer Bob Cronin, who investigated the accident involving Krista Raymond.

242 The press, despite protestations, was barred. *Boston Globe,* 1/20/06.

243 William B. Ketter, editor of the *Lawrence Eagle-Tribune* From Ketter's essay, "Democracy Works Best When the Sun Shines on Machinery of Government," in the *Eagle-Tribune,* 3/17/06.

243 As for Assistant Clerk-Magistrate Brown Author's request for an interview with Assistant Clerk-Magistrate Bruce Brown was declined.

Case Study: The Chambers Effect

245 As a young girl, Teresa Chambers Author's interviews with Teresa Chambers.

246 Not one to shrink from a tough question, Chief Chambers acknowledged See *Washington Post,* 12/2/03, p. B1.

246 Seventeen days after the *Post* story appeared See *Washington Post,* 12/19/03, p. A1.

Sounding the Tocsin

249 Emblematic of the new era of laissez-faire and government-business cooperation See Inspector General's Report released 10/31/05, and *Washington Post,* 11/1/05, p. D3; also see Department of Labor news release of 2/14/05, "Wal-Mart Agrees to Pay Fine for Violating Child Labor Laws."

250 **The elaborate ends to which the corporate giant Hewlett-Packard went** "Ex-Chairwoman Among 5 Charged in Hewlett Case," *New York Times,* 10/5/06.

250 **"FDA Official Alleges Pressure to Suppress Vioxx Findings"** *Washington Post,* 10/8/04, p. A23.

250 **In June 2005, Guidant Corporation recalled some 29,000 heart devices** Barry Meier, "Citing Flaws, Maker Recalls Heart Devices," *New York Times,* 6/18/05.

251 **Rowley had tried to sound the alarm within the FBI** Rowley letter to FBI director Robert Mueller, 2/26/03; and Rowley's letter to Mueller, 3/6/03.

252 **On June 13, 2003, Zepetella pulled a car over in the parking lot** *San Diego Union-Tribune,* 1/28/04; *Detroit Free Press,* 11/21/05 and 11/22/05.

253 **Those questions were raised by the company's own head of research** Author's interviews with Aaron Westrick.

255 **On September 7, 2006, a Vista Superior Court jury in California** *San Diego Union-Tribune,* 9/8/06.

255 **On April 18, 2002, 41-year-old Robert Raimo** Author's interviews with Robert Raimo's attorney, David Concannon; court documents: *Robert Raimo, Plaintiff, v. Uwatec, Inc., Undersea Industries, Inc., d/b/a/Scubapro, and Johnson Outdoors, Inc., Defendants,* U.S. District Court, Northern District of California, Case No. C 03–0513 WDB.

256 **Uwatec employees Frank H. Marshall and Patricia Dougherty** Author's interview with Patricia Dougherty, 10/4/06.

257 **Later that same month, Dougherty and Marshall took the extraordinary step** Ibid.

257 **In November 1997, Maurice Coutts, an experienced diver** Author's interview with Coutts's son, Lewis.

257 **On June 1, 1998, the body of 45-year-old Dr. Wesley C. Gradin** Author's interview with San Juan County (Washington) Sheriff William Cumming; *Tacoma News Tribune,* 6/1/98.

258 **On March 19, 1999, Mitch Skaggs and Rezvan Iazdi were diving** See *Skaggs v. Uwatec, Inc., et al.,* Case No. 4:01–cv–03303–wdb, filed 8/29/01, and *Iazdi v. Uwatec, Inc., et al.,* filed 12/10/01, both in U.S. District Court, Northern District of California (Oakland); also see

Milwaukee Journal Sentinel, 9/21/03, and *San Francisco Chronicle,*
5/25/03.

259 **Johnson Outdoors called it a "software glitch"** Author's interviews
with Johnson Outdoors' spokeswoman, Cynthia Georgeson, 10/11/06,
etc.

259 **Johnson Outdoors' recall announcement stated that** Recall from
Consumer Product Safety Commission, 2/5/03.

260 **In 1999, Bobreski, who worked for a WASA contractor** See *James J.*
Bobreski, Complainant, v. District of Columbia Water and Sewer Authority,
Respondent, U.S. Department of Labor, Office of Administrative Law
Judges, Case No. 2001–CAA–6; and *James Bobreski, Plaintiff, v. U.S.*
Environmental Protection Agency, Defendant, U.S. District Court for the
District of Columbia, Civil Action No. 02–0732 (RMU).

260 **The resulting front-page story** Eric Lipton (reporter), *Washington Post,*
11/5/99, p. A1.

261 **No one understands this better than Seema Bhat** Author's interview
with Seema Bhat, 3/12/06.

262 **That danger did not become public for nearly a year** *Washington Post,*
1/31/04, p. A1.

262 **A month later, an independent inquiry** "Summary of Investigation
Reported to the Board of Directors of the District of Columbia Water
and Sewer Authority," conducted under direction of Eric H. Holder,
7/16/04.

263 **In November 2005, Bhat got the vindication** Decision of the U.S.
Department of Labor Administrative Law Judge Stuart A. Levin, *Seema*
Bhat v. District of Columbia Water and Sewer Authority, Case No. 2003
CAA 00017.

263 **When someone like Doug Parker raises a question** Author's interviews with Douglass K. Parker, 10/9/06, etc.

265 **For 31 years Bob Jackson has been a seasonal Park Service ranger**
Author's interviews with Bob Jackson.

265 **When his comments began to appear in area newspapers** An
Associated Press story in which Jackson was critical of salt-baiting appeared in the *Billings (Mont.) Gazette* and elsewhere.

267 **He was a 24-year-old political appointee named George C. Deutsch** "A
Young Bush Appointee Resigns His Post at NASA," *New York Times,*
2/8/06.

267 **"It seems more like Nazi Germany"** "Censorship Is Alleged at NOAA," *Washington Post,* 2/11/06.

267 **The censorship that Hansen endured was also faced by Rick Piltz** Author's interview with Rick Piltz, 3/4/06.

268 **Among the more memorable instances** Author's interview with Piltz, 3/4/06; also see www.ombwatch.org/article/articleview/2869/1/346, article published 6/13/05.

268 **That same month scientists reported that Greenland's glaciers** *Washington Post,* 2/17/06, p. A1.

268 **So too did reports that the United States and Canada** "Tiff over Northwest Passage Heats Up as Ice Melts," *USA Today,* 4/4/06, p. 10A.

269 **James Gustave Speth, dean of Yale's School of Forestry and Environmental Sciences** Author's interview with James Gustave Speth.

269 **On July 9, 2004, Sen. Patrick Leahy, a Vermont Democrat** Letter of July 9, 2004, from Sen. Patrick Leahy (D-Vt.) and Charles Grassley (R-Iowa) to Attorney General John Ashcroft, Robert S. Mueller III, Director, Federal Bureau of Investigation, and Glenn A. Fine, Inspector General, U.S. Department of Justice.

270 **Behind closed doors** "Court of Appeals Abruptly Closes Hearing to the Public," Cox News, 4/21/05.

270 **Despite resistance from her superiors** See Robert Burns, AP military writer, "Democrats Demand Probe of Demotion," *Los Angeles Times,* 8/30/05, Associated Press account of 8/29/05, "Lawmakers Ask Pentagon To Probe Firing."

270 **A 20-year veteran in procurement matters, Greenhouse told** Transcript of the 6/27/05 Senate Democratic Policy Committee Hearing, "An Oversight Hearing on Waste, Fraud, and Abuse in U.S. Government Contracting in Iraq."

270 **Another voice the government attempted to squelch** "Lawmaker Alleges FDA, Merck Collaborated," *USA Today,* 7/19/06.

271 **On November 18, 2004, Graham told a congressional committee** Graham's testimony before the U.S. Senate Committee on Finance, "FDA, Merck and Vioxx: Putting Patient Safety First?"

271 **On September 30, 2004, Merck voluntarily withdrew Vioxx** "FDA Issues Public Health Advisory on Vioxx as Its Manufacturer Voluntarily Withdraws the Product," *FDA News,* 9/30/04.

271 **A month later 22 members of Congress joined in the call for an investigation** *USA Today,* 7/19/06.

272 **A Bush nominee and loyalist, Bloch came to OSC** Profile of Scott J. Bloch, www.osc.gov.

272 **Public Employees for Environmental Responsibility (PEER)** Author's interview with Jeff Ruch, Executive Director, PEER, 4/6/06.

273 **On October 20, 2005, the U.S. Office of Personnel Management announced** Press release from U.S. Office of Personnel Management.

273 **This, too, Bloch dismisses, but inquiries with OSC's field offices** Author's inquiries of Office of Special Counsel field offices in Dallas and San Francisco, 4/6/06.

273 **In September 2006, the office's employee newsletter set forth an exacting dress code** "A Published Dress Code Is Dressed Down in Furor," *Washington Post,* 7/7/06, p. A25.

274 **In September 2006, only days after the dress code surfaced** "Special Counsel Cancels Award Ceremony For Whistle-Blower," *Washington Post,* 9/11/06, p. A15.

Epilogue

276 **In November 2006, some 79 million Americans** Pauline Jelinek, "Election Turnout Rate Tops 40 Percent," Associated Press, 11/8/06.

276 **On January 18, 2006, 11 months before the midterm election** Then House Democratic Leader Nancy Pelosi's remarks issued 1/18/06 in support of the "Honest Leadership and Open Government Act."

276 **That letter, itself once classified, was declassified** Press release from the House Democratic leader Nancy Pelosi on 1/3/03, "Pelosi's Declassified Letter on NSA Activities," available at http:// democraticleader.house.gov.

277 **And no sooner had the Democrats** Zachary A. Goldfarb, "Iraq Strategy Redux," *Washington Post,* 1/1/07.

277 **On 9/11, when the towers fell, down came crashing** "A Brief History of the World Trade Center Towers" by John E. Fernandez, Assistant Professor of Architecture, Building Technology Program, Massachusetts Institute of Technology.

Books and Studies

Starred items are those I have found to be particularly influential to my own work.

*Bamford, James. *Body of Secrets: Anatomy of the Ultra-Secret National Security Agency*. New York: Doubleday, 2001.

———. *The Puzzle Palace: A Report on America's Most Secret Agency*. Boston: Houghton Mifflin, 1982.

*Barth, Alan. *The Rights of Free Men: An Essential Guide to Civil Liberties*. New York: Alfred A. Knopf, 1984.

*Bok, Sissela. *Secrets: On the Ethics of Concealment and Revelation*. New York: Vintage Books, 1989.

Columbia Journalism Review. Columbia University Graduate School of Journalism, New York.

Eroding Freedoms: Secrecy, Truth and Sources. Nieman Reports, 59 (Special issue) (2). Cambridge, Mass.: Harvard University, Nieman Foundation for Journalism, summer 2005.

Gates, Robert M. *From the Shadows: The Ultimate Insider's Story of Five Presidents and How They Won the Cold War*. New York: Touchstone, 1997.

Gup, Ted. *The Book of Honor: Covert Lives and Classified Deaths at the CIA*. New York: Doubleday, 2000.

Karpinski, Janis. *One Woman's Army: The Commanding General of Abu Ghraib Tells Her Story*. New York: Miramax Books, 2005.

Kelly, Michael. *Things Worth Fighting For: Collected Writings.* New York: Penguin, 2004.

Lee, Wen Ho. *My Country Versus Me: The First-Hand Account by the Los Alamos Scientist Who Was Falsely Accused of Being a Spy.* New York: Hyperion, 2001.

Leonard, J. William. "The Importance of Basics." Speech at the National Classification Management Society's Annual Training Seminar, 6/15/04.

Leone, Richard C., and Greg Anrig, Jr., eds. *The War on Our Freedoms: Civil Liberties in an Age of Terrorism.* New York: PublicAffairs, 2003.

Liebling, A. J. *The Press.* New York: Ballantine Books, 1961.

Lippmann, Walter. *Conversations with Walter Lippmann.* Transcribed by the Columbia Broadcasting System. Boston: Little, Brown, 1965.

Mahle, Melissa Boyle. *Denial and Deception: An Insider's View of the CIA from Iran-Contra to 9/11.* New York: Nation Books, 2004.

Mapes, Mary. *Truth and Duty: The Press, the President, and the Privilege of Power.* New York: St. Martin's Press, 2005.

*Moynihan, Daniel Patrick. *Secrecy.* New Haven, Conn.: Yale University Press, 1998.

Olmsted, Kathryn S. *Challenging the Secret Government: The Post-Watergate Investigations of the CIA and FBI.* Chapel Hill: University of North Carolina Press, 1996.

Overholzer, Geneva, and Kathleen Hall Jamieson, eds. *The Press.* New York: Oxford University Press, 2005.

Powers, Thomas. *Intelligence Wars: American Secret History from Hitler to Al-Qaeda.* New York: New York Review of Books, 2002.

Ransom, Harry Howe. *Central Intelligence and National Security.* Cambridge, Mass.: Harvard University Press, 1958.

Richelson, Jeffrey T. *The U.S. Intelligence Community.* Boulder, Colo.: Westview Press, 1995.

Roberts, Alasdair. *Blacked Out: Government Secrecy in the Information Age.* New York: Cambridge University Press, 2006.

Schlesinger, Arthur M., Jr. *The Cycles of American History.* Boston: Houghton Mifflin, 1986.

Secrecy: Report of the Commission on Protecting and Reducing Government Secrecy. Washington, D.C.: Government Printing Office, 1997.

*Shils, Edward A. *The Torment of Secrecy.* Glencoe, Ill.: Free Press, 1956; reprint, Chicago: Elephant Paperbacks, 1996.

Singh, Simon. *The Science of Secrecy: The History of Codes and Codebreaking.* London: Fourth Estate, 2000.

Smith, Jeffrey A. *War and Press Freedom: The Problem of Prerogative Power.* New York: Oxford University Press, 1999.

Stone, I. F. *A Nonconformist History of Our Times: In a Time of Torment, 1961–1967.* Boston: Little, Brown, 1989.

Suskind, Ron. *The One Percent Doctrine: Deep Inside America's Pursuit of Its Enemies Since 9/11.* New York: Simon & Schuster, 2006.

The Theodore H. White Lecture Series, Joan Shorenstein Center on the Press, Politics and Public Policy, Harvard University, John F. Kennedy School of Government. Cambridge, Mass.

Turner, Stansfield. *Secrecy and Democracy: The CIA in Transition.* Boston: Houghton Mifflin, 1985.

Wiggins, James Russell. *Freedom or Secrecy.* New York: Oxford University Press, 1956.

Wise, David, and Thomas B. Ross. *The Invisible Government.* New York: Random House, 1964.

Woodward, Bob. *State of Denial.* New York: Simon & Schuster, 2006.

Yee, James. *For God and Country: Truth and Patriotism Under Fire.* New York: PublicAffairs, 2005.

Index